# ON THEIR OWN POWER
## A HISTORY OF MICHIGAN'S ELECTRIC COOPERATIVES

By Raymond G. Kuhl

Published by Michigan Electric Cooperative Association
Okemos, Michigan

Copyright 1998 by Michigan Electric Cooperative Association

Editor: *Michael Buda*
Editorial Assistant: *Deena Carlson*

International Standard Book Number: 0-9660251-0-5 (hardcover)
0-9660251-1-3 (paperback)

# DEDICATION

*To all of the pioneers of cooperative rural electrification in Michigan whose tireless work has enlightened and enriched the lives of tens of thousands of rural families over seven decades.*

# ACKNOWLEDGMENTS

This is a first. In fact, it is several firsts. It is the first written history of the cooperative rural electrification development in Michigan. It is also the first published collection of photographs depicting the early pioneering days of rural electric cooperatives in the state, their struggles and accomplishments, and their leaders.

Of less importance is the fact that *"On Their Own Power"* is my first work in researching and writing a book. I've written hundreds of articles about electric cooperatives, here in Michigan and in my native state of South Dakota and on the national level. I've also authored many commentaries in Michigan *Country Lines*, the publication of Michigan's electric cooperatives.

It goes without saying that a project of this magnitude is a challenging experience. Indeed. Research was conducted at each of the cooperatives, at the Michigan Electric Cooperative Association and at other locations. I interviewed more than 70 individuals throughout the state. The insight I gained was even more than I expected.

While my 37 years working for the cooperatives gave me a good handle on the subject, the perspectives and actual experiences of so many people who built the electric cooperatives were intriguing and sometimes surprising. They instilled in me a new appreciation for their bold work.

I have innumerable people to thank for making this history project a reality. Before I do that, I want to say that this experience of researching and writing about cooperative rural electrification has also been a remembrance to me. Although not raised on a farm, as a child I often visited cousins who lived on farms in South Dakota. They were in the dark until the late 1940s.

It was puzzling to me why they couldn't have electricity when the nearby towns did. However, after a few visits, I began to simply take it for granted just as my cousins did. It was a far different life with no running water and no lights except the kerosene lamp, which may be a nostalgic thing now but it was always a smelly and dangerous contraption to me.

What I want this book to be, more than anything, is a celebration. I hope that every reader feels a sense of joy and an affinity with the hundreds of men and women who blazed the trail for cooperative rural electrification in Michigan. It is those people of commitment and vision to whom this book is dedicated.

Commitment is the stuff character is made of; it is the power to change the face of things. It is the triumph of belief and integrity over skepticism and indifference. Commitment is what transforms an idea into reality. That's what the rural electrification pioneers did.

I thank each person who took the time to talk with me and provided insight for this history project. Each and every one of them enlightened me and contributed to the book. This includes the general managers of the electric cooperatives, assistants to general managers, many board members, people at the Detroit Edison Company, at the Michigan Public Service Commission and Michigan State University.

I especially thank those who generously spent time sharing memories with me. Their revelations make the book much more than a collection of facts and dates and events.

I wish to express very special thanks to Jim Hough, a dear friend and top-notch writer, for his encouragement and his critique of the manuscript, and to his wife, Darl, too. You may know that Jim, who writes a column in Michigan *Country Lines*, has severe sight impairment. Darl read the entire manuscript to him.

Also deserving my heartfelt gratitude is Michael Buda of the Michigan Electric Cooperative Association who not only provided editorial expertise but helped me out of more than one computer jam. We also worked together on selecting and placing the many photographs you see in the book. Thanks very much, Mike, for your valuable input.

My thanks also to Deena Carlson and Beri Wolford at MECA who helped with many details. Deena's expertise in doing corrections, additions and page layouts was indispensable.

Another member of the team who played a role in making this project a reality is my wife, Jackie. She listened to my occasional gnashing and lashing out, usually at the computer, and helped me stay on track in pursuit of the finished product. I sincerely appreciate her understanding and encouragement.

I want to single out two other individuals who were vitally important to me in getting this story told: Bob Badner, who worked in Michigan 36 years for the Rural Electrification Administration, now the Rural Utilities Service, and Bob Daverman, whose Grand Rapids engineering firm worked side by side with Michigan's electric cooperatives since 1938.

Each of the two Bobs shared a wealth of information with me about the struggles and developments of the cooperatives over the years. They personally experienced the many ups and downs of the cooperatives over the years. Their contributions are most significant in giving continuity and affirmation to the history you read in this book.

If you have more light that you or a family member can shed on the Michigan electric cooperatives' history, I would be most appreciative if you would send the information to my attention at MECA, 2859 W. Jolly Road, Okemos, MI 48864. I also welcome your comments on the book.


*Raymond G. Kuhl*



---

*Information on cover photos can be found on pages 14, 23, 35, 107, and 169.*

# FOREWORD
## by Jim Hough

It was a moment in my life 57 years ago that I never forget. I was eight years old.

Evening darkness had just descended on our little Upper Peninsula home at Strongs.

My dad called our family — Mom, my sister Marlene, my brother Don and me — to the kitchen. He blew out the kerosene lamp we had depended on so many years. Then, with a hush in this room full of mystique and magic, he said: "OK, Jim, you are the oldest child. You get to pull the string for the first time."

I climbed onto a kitchen chair and reached above the table where a string hung from the ceiling. I recall a kind of butterfly feeling in my stomach, maybe even a little fear. Finally, with a courageous and quick jerk, I pulled the string.

The bulb lit. The entire room was brighter than any night before. I stood there on the chair amazed. There was an intake of breath from everyone in our family. We could hardly believe it.

I'm 65, now but I have never had a more magical memory than that night in 1940 when our rural electric cooperative, Cloverland Electric, brought electricity to our evening meal. Mom and dad were so thrilled that they hardly spoke a word through that meal. We all kept glancing up there to stare at the glowing bulb.

Although I wrote a daily newspaper column for the *Lansing State Journal* for more than 30 years, I have also written a column for *Country Lines*, a magazine going into all Michigan homes and businesses served by rural electric cooperatives for the past 12 years. The very special spirit of rural Michigan and my association with the electric cooperatives has vastly enriched my life.

That's why I was so pleased when Ray Kuhl asked me to write a foreword for this book — a history of Michigan's rural electric cooperatives, the only such work in our state. As I write this, I am dead sure that my childhood memory is repeated in the recollections of many other folks in Michigan and across the nation.

"*On Their Own Power*" is more than a book title. It is a statement of rebirth — a whole new life — in rural America.

In one way, 60 years seems like such a short period of history. But in the world of rural electric cooperatives, it has been a long and hard struggle to overcome political obstacles and the many skeptics who said it couldn't be done. That special spirit of rural electric pioneers prevailed.

It's an exciting story and we found just the man to write it. Raymond Kuhl has been in the rural electric forefront for 37 years, the last 17 of which he served as general manager of the Michigan Electric Cooperative Association. Ray retired in January, 1996, but he still had a mission. He wanted our lives and our libraries enriched with an insightful history — never before written — about the arrival of electricity to rural Michigan and what it has meant to tens of thousands of people.

A list of Ray's accomplishments in this field is long. He was born in Sioux Falls, South Dakota, and was a 1955 graduate of South Dakota State University in journalism. He has served in many important roles on state and national levels as a manager, writer, and public relations director for the cause of rural electrification. He also helped organized some of the first rural community water systems in South Dakota, an experience he believes was akin to that of the founders of electric cooperatives.

In March, 1997, Ray was honored before 10,000 persons at the National Rural Electric Cooperative annual convention in Las Vegas. He was presented the Clyde T. Ellis Award, the highest honor given for outstanding work in rural electrification.

That was a great moment for me and my wife, Darl, because we have grown to treasure the friendship of Ray and his wife, Jackie.

With great confidence, I say you are going to love reading this fascinating story.

# Table of Contents

## Section One: The Story of Michigan's Electric Cooperatives

Darkness, drudgery and discontent were commonplace in the rural areas of
Michigan in the 1920s and early 1930s without electricity despite experiments
showing the benefits of electrifying farms. The actions of two Roosevelts ultimately resulted in a new and effective government agency, the rural Electrification
Administration.

Michigan farmers begin to organize electric cooperatives — "do-it-yourself" utilities in 1936, but find opposition from within the state. Co-op leaders begin
partnership with the REA in Washington, where engineering innovations cut cost
and make electrification of rural areas economically feasible.

Electric co-op pioneers and Michigan Governor Frank Murphy fight to put the
cooperatives in business. Early leaders take on challenges of "spite lines" built by
other utilities and of power supply and adequate funding. By the end of 1938, all
14 Michigan electric cooperatives were chartered and under construction, thanks
to their irrepressible founding fathers.

Electricity begins to flow to thousands of farms, homes, country schools and
churches from the cooperatives. Co-op members recall the gleeful day the lights
were turned on, and how they first put electricity to work. Although World War II
temporarily halted construction, the electrified farms produced record amounts
of food and fibre to help win the war.

Congress supports new push for building rural lines to all the unserved, and the
cooperative experience serious power supply problems as use of electricity grows
rapidly. Two "generation and transmission" cooperatives are organized and
interconnections with other utilities are initiated to achieve economical and more
dependable supply.

The cooperatives grow as people mover to the country side and enjoy all the
conveniences that electricity brings to the home. And farmers steadily increase
their use of electric power as rates decline. But problems continue to beset the
co-ops as investor-owned utilities launch propaganda attacks and take co-op
customers. State regulation affords some territorial protection.

**Chapter 7**     **Turning Points**                              **Page    71**
By 1970, the cooperatives were serving power to more than 100,000 member-
owners. Their future was threatened, however, when President Nixon sacked the
REA lending program and the 1973 oil crisis, coupled with tough new environmental standards, doubled generating costs. A nuclear power deal also proves
costly to the co-ops. In 1978, the co-ops organize a new statewide association to
gain strength.

**Chapter 8**     **Moving Forward Together**                    **Page    85**
Through the Michigan Electric Cooperative Association, the co-ops step up their
legislative work, training programs and member communications, including
*Michigan Country Lines*. Legislative successes, regulatory gains, self-insurance
and a political action program called "ACRE" show merits of working together.

**Chapter 9**     **People of Commitment**                       **Page    97**
Hundreds of rural people—men and women with a common vision — worked
selflessly on the early boards of directors to "turn on the lights" and hundreds
more have kept the lights burning. The linemen do their job in all weather conditions, typifying the dedication of co-op employees. "They feel they are working in
a cause or a crusade which many of them can't define," a one leader put it.

**Epilogue**                                                     **Page    183**
Several leaders of today's electric cooperatives give their views on the many
emerging issues and challenges facing the co-ops and the electric utility industry
in the 1990s. Mergers and a diversity of new services are part of the changing
picture. Keeping the cooperative spirit—working together—is vital to their future,
the leaders agree.

## Section Two: Individual Histories of Michigan Electric Cooperatives

**One**

# ROOTS OF REA

You could hear the hum of electricity flowing through the high lines when you drove down the main road to town.

At night, you could see the bright lights of the city miles away.

You could almost feel the electricity when you were in town. The grocery store refrigerators, the lights in the barber shop, the feed grinders at the grain elevator — practically everyplace you went in town, there was electricity.

"We could see towns and a few farms where they had lights, but unless we had a thousand dollars or more to give to the power company, we couldn't get electricity."

That's how Walt Cook remembers it in 1937 when he was growing up on his parents' farm in Huron County. By then, electricity had become common in almost every city and town across the entire United States. Thomas Edison's magic had been transforming the city workplace and improving the life-styles of townspeople for decades.

But while the distant cities glittered like stars on a clear summer night, most of the country's farms were in the dark. Except for farms along the main roads that were able to get electricity off the power line strung from one town to another, it was total darkness. That's the way it was in most of rural Michigan in 1937 — 30 years before Cook was elected to the Thumb Electric Cooperative board of directors.

"The drudgery on the farm was unbelievable by our standards today," Cook remembers. "Everyone in the family had chores to do, and it was hard work without electricity to do the many things it does so easily today on the farm. Back then, the day's work on the farm went into the evening and we had only the kerosene lanterns to see by. Just think of all the farmers who had to milk cows in near darkness all those years before REA."

He remembers nights in the house, too. Vividly. "We had to rely on kerosene and the Aladdin lamp to read and do our homework," Cook recalls. "Unless you had a battery-operated plant to generate your own power, you couldn't listen to the radio. We were usually a couple of days behind in the news of what was going on in the world."

In 1935, rural people were left out. They were powerless. They felt like second class citizens.

Did it have to be this way? Glimmers of hope had appeared now and then for large scale rural electrification, even in the 1920s.

In 1923, the National Electric Light Association organized a Committee on the Relation of Electricity to Agriculture, financed and supported by power industry people, equipment manufacturers, farm organization leaders and government officials. To determine if a profitable rural market for electricity existed, the committee set up a demonstration near Red Wing, Minnesota.

Twenty farms were connected by a six-mile electric distribution line of the local utility company. Under the supervision of the state university, half of the farms were equipped with almost every kind of electric appliance and farm machine known at that time, and they were encouraged to use their new electric servants liberally. The farmers soon saw that their lives were more productive and far less tiring using electricity to do the work they had done solely by human labor for years.

And their copious records of power costs and production results clearly showed that as electric use increased, agricultural production increased even more sharply. More significantly, total operating expenses of the 10 farms actually dropped using electricity!

Word of this experiment spread and soon committees in other states were showing selected farmers how to put electricity to work and increase their production. It seemed, however, that officials of most utility companies were not sufficiently impressed. Six years after the Red Wing, Minnesota, demonstration, only nine percent of the nation's farms — and just three percent in Michigan — had been connected to central station electric service while almost every town and village across the U.S. enjoyed the electric life.

In Michigan, Consumers Power Company launched a rural electrification project in Ingham County between Mason and Dansville in 1927. This "experiment" came four years after the formation of the Michigan Committee on the Relation of Electricity to Agriculture (CREA).

The company called it their "pioneer beginning" of rural electrification — "the first rural electric line built in Michigan for the study of electricity's usefulness in farm life." That's the inscription on a marker the utility placed along Highway 36 west of Dansville.

The Consumers Power endeavor consisted of seven miles of line, and "was accomplished through the cooperation of Michigan State College, farm organizations and 12 farm families who wanted electric service," according to the marker. The college reported that "it became apparent electricity was about the most economical helper available to the farmer."

Farm connections in Michigan jumped from 7,000 in 1929 to 27,000 in 1930, according to a CREA newsletter. One contributing factor was the use of a mobile demonstration unit by Michigan State College, Detroit Edison and Consumers Power that showed farmers how they could use electricity on the farm and in the home. The demonstration reached thousands of farm families in 1928, 1929 and 1930.

By the early 1930s, the Detroit Edison Company had a good start in rural areas. According to an April, 1932, company newsletter: "Bright lights are no longer confined to the city alone. Detroit Edison now furnishes 10,448 farm customers with electric service." Recapping the year of 1932, the company reported that "12,137 'dirt farmers' receive electric service from our lines, being 60 percent of all such farms in our territory."

The report went on to say that the farm customers "are served at exactly the same prices as are the urban customers." However, it added, "in sparsely settled districts, the farm customers have contributed to the cost of building the necessary distribution lines." Left unsaid was the fact that many farm folks could not afford to pay for the line extension and, consequently, were left unserved.

After acquiring the Michigan Electric Power Company in 1935, Detroit Edison connected some 4,700 farms in that area. When the Thumb Electric Cooperative began building lines in 1937, Detroit Edison stated in its annual report that "in view of our progress toward meeting all reasonable demands (for electrifying farms), why the cooperative project should have been proceeded with is beyond our knowledge or understanding."

In Detroit Edison's company history, *"The Force of Energy,"* published in 1971, author Raymond Miller commented on the emergence of the Thumb co-op: "Even the rural cooperative in the Thumb area, so small and yet so irritating to the Company leaders when it was launched, became accepted in time." He noted that the cooperative started purchasing significant amounts of power from Detroit Edison in the 1950s.

In 1938, Detroit Edison said that the Thumb cooperative's first 1,560 lines, energized in 1938, "are scattered among, but rarely duplicate, our farm lines in three counties... At the end of the year (1938), the task of rural electrification approaches completion." In the same report, the company speculated that an additional $1,200,000 investment would be needed to "finish the job" and lamented that "we are lucky if we can earn our out-of-pocket expenses from farm business with only three or four customers per mile of line."

Yet, the Detroit company and the Michigan Public Utility Commission allowed the rural service rates to be the same as the utility's urban rates — a level considerably lower than the Thumb co-op's original electric rates. Today, Thumb's rates for rural residences and farms are lower than Detroit Edison's. It should be noted, too, that there were few nonfarm residences in rural areas in the 1930s; today, they outnumber farms.

At the end of 1934, it was estimated that 42,000 farms were electrified in Michigan — less than 25 percent of the state's farms. Most Michigan farmers were still in the dark in 1935 when REA was established by President Franklin Roosevelt.

A different Roosevelt, however, had sown the seeds of rural electrification earlier in the century. President Theodore Roosevelt boldly advanced the ideals of multiuse development of river systems for flood control, irrigation, recreation and electric power production along with the principle that the power should flow to the people rather than private profiteering interests.

He left little doubt about his philosophy and his administration's policy when he stated in his February 9, 1909, message to Congress, accompanying the Report of the Country Life Commission: "It is the obvious duty of the Government to call the attention of farmers to the growing monopolization of water power. The farmers above all should have that power, on reasonable terms, for cheap transportation, for lighting their homes and for innumerable uses in the daily tasks on the farm."

That Country Life Commission report made continual and critical references to the fact that most of America's farms were without electricity and recommended ways rural people might go about getting power. Federal hydro power and organizing their own cooperatives were mentioned. It was the first expression of concern from a federal body regarding the farmers' need for electricity. Here's what the Commission said:

"The introduction of effective agricultural cooperation throughout the United States is of first importance....Organized associative effort (cooperatives) may take on special forms....It may have for its object the securing of telephone service, the extension of electric lines, the improvement of highways, and other forms of betterment."

The Commission's report gave special attention to the plight of farm women, deprived of the many benefits of electricity: "The burden of the hardships falls most heavily on the farmer's wife....Her life is the more monotonous and the more isolated, no matter what the wealth or poverty of the family may be."

One of the most stark and revealing examples of the farm woman's dreaded work was the weekly chore of washing clothes. The scene: a huge vat of boiling water over a roaring fire and three large zinc washtubs and a dish pan on a bench. The clothes are scrubbed on a washboard in the first tub; after vigorous scrubbing, the woman wrings out each piece, removing as much of the dirty water as possible and puts the clothes in the vat of boiling water. Often, she needs to use a wooden paddle or broomstick to stir the clothes, moving them swiftly up and down like today's agitator in an automatic washer for 10 or 15 minutes.

Next, she transfers the clothes from the boiling water to the second tub — the rinse tub — and she bends over and rinses each piece individually. Then, she wrings out each item to get out as much of the dirty water as possible and places the clothes in a third tub which contains bluing to make clothes whiter and brighter, and then into the dish pan for starching. For each load, the water in each of the washtubs has to be changed. The woman lifts bucket after bucket of water into the tubs, after hauling the water from the well. At the end of the day, the farm wife is exhausted, her back aches, and her hands are raw and swollen.

Each week the farm woman did the wash in this way, while her city cousin did it by pressing a button on her electric washing machine. Then there was the ironing. Suffice it to say that this task was no easier than the washing, for it involved lifting a seven-pound iron repeatedly from a wood-burning stove.

Life on most Michigan farms in 1935 continued in darkness and drudgery, and to make matters much worse the Great Depression brought more hardship.

Ironically, the roots of REA and cooperative rural electrification took firm ground in the early Depression years.

The economic chaos and extreme hardships brought on by the Depression hit farm and city, sweeping across America like a plague. For rural areas, drought and sinking farm prices made life on the farm almost unbearable, and many farmers and businessmen in town went busted. With little money of their own and banks going broke, farmers thought their chances of getting electricity were nil.

The election of 1932 changed that gloomy outlook. The Governor of New York, Franklin Delano Roosevelt, was elected President of the United States and he knew something about electrification and what it would take to extend its benefits across the country to farms, to rural schools and churches and homes. He had created the Power Authority of New York which, among other things, was to develop data about the cost of distributing power to farms and small consumers.

Under Roosevelt's direction, Morris L . Cooke and other experts, who had been studying what they called "giant power," closely examined power plant operations and the cost of building distribution lines, including poles, wire, transformers, labor, and engineering. They determined that a mile of rural power line could be built for $300 to $1,500 cheaper than the utilities claimed.

"Widespread rural electrification is socially and economically desirable, and financially both sound and feasible," Cooke concluded. He would later have the opportunity to demonstrate that in a big way.

Roosevelt was inaugurated as President on March 4, 1933. Pledging a "New Deal for the American people," he moved swiftly to bring relief from the Depression and to put people back to work and help restore their dignity. He signed the Tennessee Valley Authority Act on May 18, 1933, signaling the start of action not only for economic development and thousands of new jobs but for a new and vast source of electric power. The TVA Act provided that "preference" would be given to "states, counties, municipalities and cooperative organizations of citizens or farmers, not organized for profit but primarily for the purpose of supplying electricity to its own citizens or members."

President Roosevelt had not forgotten Morris Cooke's work in the New York State public power and rural electrification projects, and he persuaded him to join his Administration in late 1933. Put in charge of the Mississippi Valley Committee, Cooke continued to advocate a rural electrification program and wrote a special report in early 1935 detailing why and how rural electrification could be accomplished, with the leadership and impetus coming from the federal government.

That report, known as "the 12-minute memo" for the time he said it would take to read it, stated that only 650,000 of the nation's six million farms had high line central station electric service. Much greater progress had been made in several other countries, he noted. He said the "essential elements of a rural electric system are simple and easily manipulated...and even the generating units now obtainable require a minimum of attention." He suggested using diesel engines, hydro and small coal-burning plants in local areas to reduce transmission and distribution costs.

Cooke carefully pointed out that "this proposal does not involve competition with private interests....this plan calls for entering territory not now occupied and not likely to be occupied to any considerable extent by private interests." He predicted that power could be made available in most rural areas at two cents or less per kilowatt hour; however, he added that "real rural electrification implies large average use of current, for without large use, rates cannot be made low enough to effect the coveted social advantages."

With his plan, he believed that the "present average rural rate will certainly be cut in half" if the consumption on farms proved to be as great as he anticipated and costs were in line with his estimates. He envisioned rural power districts to be created by a vote of the rural land owners, although he recognized that most states' laws did not provide for such entities. He also advocated "consumers mutual electric companies" and suggested that there be assistance from federal and/or state governments in the form of advice in accounting, management and engineering just as farmers were being advised by experts in farm crops, animal husbandry, farm accounting, and farm management.

Cooke's historic "12 minute memo" recommended a federal Rural Electrification Section in the Department of Interior. It promptly got the attention of Interior Secretary Harold Ickes and President Roosevelt, who had just taken action to initiate a $100 million appropriation for rural electrification as part of a $5 billion public works bill.

In April, 1935, Morris Cooke had an office for the Rural Electrification Unit in the basement of the Department of Interior. He was ready to do business.

In a matter of days, Cooke advised the President that he would have a draft of the Executive Order setting up the Rural Electrification Administration. Roosevelt signed the order establishing the REA on May 11, 1935.

What the public didn't know then was that Roosevelt had a personal experience years before that convinced him something needed to be done to make electricity affordable in rural areas. In 1924 he noted the cost of electricity for his rural cottage in Georgia was about four times what he paid at Hyde Park, New York. He later said, "That started my long study of public utility charges for electric current and the whole subject of getting electricity in farm homes. So it can be said that a little cottage at Warm Springs, Georgia, was the birthplace of the Rural Electrification Administration."

**Above:** Walter Cook and his wife, Minnie, on their farm in Huron County. Walt has been an active member of the Thumb Electric Co-operative board of directors for 30 years. He remembers the "not so good" old days on his parents' farm before they got electricity; they were among the first to get connected to Thumb's lines in 1938.
**Middle:** One of the thousands of farms in the dark until electric co-operatives were organized in late 1930s was the Centennial farm in the Upper Peninsula owned by Edwin "Bud" Englund. As one of the first employees of the Alger Delta Cooperative Electric Association, he dug pole holes by hand. He later became line superintendent, retiring from the Co-op in 1977.
**Bottom:** This plaque telling of Consumers Power farm electrification experiment in 1927, is displayed at a roadside park along State Highway 36 between Mason and Dansville.

**Above (L):** Commemorative stamp marking the 50th anniversary of REA on May 11, 1985, was first issued at a ceremony in Madison, SD. Speakers praised the program for its fiscal responsibility and service to more than 12 million rural families. **Middle (R):** Farm wives and children were just as interested in the REA as the men. This group looked carefully at plans to make sure their farms were on the map of proposed lines financed through the new government agency created by President Franklin Roosevelt in 1935. **Bottom (R):** Walter Cook's farm relies on electric power to do countless chores. Although farms are now the minority of electric co-operatives' member-customers, they use more electricity than most other customers. Electric power has enabled US farmers to become the most productive in the world.

*AT THE MAY 2, 1997, DEDICATION OF THE NEW MEMORIAL in Washington, D.C. honoring President Franklin D. Roosevelt, President Bill Clinton said of FDR's "New Deal" legacy: "He electrified the farms and hollows, but even more important, he electrified the nation..." After a modest beginning in 1935, REA became one of the most successful programs in U.S. history with the participation of thousands of rural people who organized cooperatives. More than 30 million Americans are now served electric power by 950 cooperatives.*

# COOPERATIVES TEAM UP WITH REA

The mood in rural Michigan in 1935 was a mix of frustration and faint hope. Frustration and despair were on the faces of farmers and their families as they eked out a living with falling incomes and no electricity to relieve the drudgery of daily farm and household chores.

But some farmers hadn't given up on the idea of getting electric service. They saw a real need for power to help them cut costs and increase production. They knew that the Cooperative Extension Service had developed programs on many farm uses of electricity, and they wanted to take advantage of the programs, if they could just get the power.

Hearing about the newly formed REA in Washington, farm leaders met and discussed the prospects of "REA power." But when the Michigan Farm Bureau and State Grange invited representatives of Consumers Power Company and Detroit Edison Company to Lansing to address the group, they ran into opposition.

According to Chester Graham, who was then secretary-treasurer of the Michigan Farmers Union, the power companies brought piles of financial records to show how "they were making sacrifices on their rural power lines for which they charged farmers $1,000 or more per mile."

They talked about how their companies could hook up the farms where it would pay out for them, but the others would have to wait. The meeting concluded with adoption of a resolution stating that no REA funds should come into Michigan other than as loans to private power companies, like Detroit Edison and Consumers Power, with the possible exception of sparsely populated northern counties.

Graham quickly called a meeting of Farmers Union members at Owosso and the group organized the Michigan Rural Electrification Association to seek REA loans. Graham said he set up seven "mass meetings of interested farmers in strategic areas of lower Michigan" over a two-week period in 1936, and committees were formed at the meetings to proceed with loan applications.

In his autobiography, *"The Eighty-Year Experience of a Grass Roots Citizen,"* Graham wrote: "The Monday evening meeting of the second week was scheduled in a new town hall near Big Rapids. Some men came in to break up the meeting, but the local chairman ably carried the meeting through to completion and a continuing committee was elected. We never found out who sent these men to the meeting." But Graham had his suspicions.

Graham went on to describe the seventh meeting scheduled in a school house south of Ithaca in Gratiot County. "Two men came into the meeting early and broke it up before Carl Thompson (of the Public Ownership League) had a chance to speak. A later unofficial report claimed these men were sent to the meeting by the County Agricultural Extension Agent."

Graham said he stopped at a local committee meeting in Diamondale in Eaton

County where farmers were talking about applying to REA for a loan and found a group of men visiting on the steps of the town hall. "They told me that the County Agricultural Agent had visited most of the farms in the area to tell the farmers that REA would not be possible in their county." Graham and some of the farmers went into the hall, opened the meeting, and "entered some items of business in the minutes and set the date for the next meeting," Graham wrote. Soon after, the Tri-County Electric Cooperative was formed and became one of the first cooperatives in the nation to get approval of an REA loan.

County Extension Agents were not directed to oppose REA, but some appeared to be influenced by the large investor-owned utilities and the Michigan Farm Bureau to discourage farmers from forming cooperatives and applying to REA for funds.

Across the nation, County Agents were actively assisting farmers in organizing electric cooperatives. In a northern Michigan county, the County Agriculture Agent became a champion for cooperative rural electrification and many others in Michigan were supportive of the farmers' efforts to organize electric co-ops, and later conducted workshops on farm uses of electricity.

The Michigan Farm Bureau's allegiance to the big private power companies was made known in its *"Michigan Farm News"* in 1936. In a front page article of this publication, the Farm Bureau stated:

*The Michigan Farm Bureau is taking a leading part in this effort to bring electric power to thousands of Michigan farmers on a basis whereby the power companies can afford to construct the lines without cost to the farmer. The immediate problem is what shall be considered a sustaining and paying revenue from the farmer, based on sound figures on operating costs?*

*The larger Michigan power companies have indicated that they can finance power lines if they will produce $150 or more in revenue per mile per year. The Farm Bureau and the Farm News present this analysis to give our readers the best information on rural power line costs and sustaining revenues at this time.*

The same article explains that the Farm Bureau, the Grange, Michigan State College, the Michigan Public Utilities Commission and investor-owned power companies, working jointly as the Rural Electrification Committee for Michigan, had developed strategy to bring power to more farms without tapping REA for construction money.

"Developments have been fast," the *Farm News* reported later in 1936. "The utilities commission said October 5 that it has applications for new power lines totaling 1,700 miles in the Consumers Power Company territory alone." But the fact remained that four out of five farms in the state were still in the dark.

Meanwhile, developments were occurring at a feverish pace in Washington, D.C., where the fledgling Rural Electrification Administration was putting together a group of qualified engineers and accountants to draft policies and procedures for what would be an unequaled lending program in partnership with tens of thousands of rural people in 45 states.

As the staff was being assembled, REA got a boost when President Roosevelt made it an independent agency separate from the public works programs.

In those early days of REA, Cooke was led to believe that the investor-owned utilities were willing to work with his agency and he asked them for proposals on how they would utilize REA loan funds in a national rural electrification plan. Although a handful of companies did borrow from REA, he was disappointed by the timid response of the utilities. The few utilities responding wanted to take the entire $100 million available to connect mostly the "cream" of the unserved rural population, contending that "very few farms requiring electricity for major farm operations are not now served."

Despite Cooke's disillusion with the power companies, he and his staff were not convinced that the farmers could do the job of building and running a utility themselves. But applications came pouring in by the hundreds to REA from farm groups, and by January of 1936 it was clear that the farmer cooperatives were eager to borrow the funds needed to get going and build their own power systems. Farmers were tired of waiting for the investor-owned companies.

One of Michigan's electric co-op pioneers, Clarence Babbitt of Oceana County, recalled that many of the farmers "would do almost anything to get electricity — that is, electricity they could afford." He was one of the founders of the Oceana Electric Cooperative and put in some long days to get sign-ups. "Some farmers were leery and some had a tough time coming up with the $5 co-op membership fee," said Babbitt. "In those days, five dollars was a lot of money."

Babbitt said his father wanted electricity years before REA started, but he couldn't afford the $500 Consumers Power wanted to hook him up. The Babbitts saw the cooperative as the answer "because it was for the common people, just as President Roosevelt and Congress intended," said Clarence.

Jim Clarke, longtime director and former board chairman of Tri-County Electric Cooperative, Portland, can remember how desperately his father, William J. Clarke, wanted electricity so he could use cattle feeders and other labor-saving equipment on his farm. "He talked to a lot of people about getting a co-op started because he did threshing on most farms in our area," said Jim. "He got involved on the committee that put in the loan application to REA in 1936."

Another veteran co-op board member, William Parsons, from the Top O' Michigan Electric Company, Boyne City, describes those early days of organizing as "rough going" — partly because they were told they needed a minimum of 250 firm memberships to get the go-ahead from REA. "We met in schoolhouses, town halls and homes throughout the area to generate interest and convince people it could be a reality," said Parsons. "Some were skeptical that farmers could run an electric co-op, even though they wanted electricity," Parsons recalled. After all, what did farmers know about running a utility?

Skepticism was justified when you look at the situation that many Michigan farmers faced in 1935. According to the *Rural Electrification News* of October, 1935, three-fourths of the farms in Consumers Power Company's general service area were not connected and many of the farmers had been quoted large figures to run lines to their places. Few could afford to pay what the power companies wanted. Getting electricity seemed out of the question.

With the emergence of REA and increasing efforts to organize cooperatives, the Michigan Public Utilities Commission, supported by the Michigan Farm Bureau and Consumers Power Company, issued what the *News* described as "one of the most advanced orders regulating rural extensions yet promulgated by any state."

It was an awakening to the "new conditions arising out of the widespread demand for rural (electric) service," a reference to the initiative being taken by the Federal Government in creating the REA. The new PUC regulations eliminated a construction charge for extending service in cases of five or more farm customers per mile of line, providing that the prospective customer would guarantee an annual payment to the utility of at least $150 per year. The Commission thus asserted its control over rural extensions, but left cooperatives out of the picture.

The Michigan PUC plan was rejected by the Michigan Rural Electrification Association, organized by the Farmers Union and others. Lynd A. Walkling, secretary of the association, publicly stated that the cooperative plan was the best for the farmers and would get the most farms electrified.

Walkling charged the power companies were intentionally trying to confuse the situation and hinder the federal REA program. He also charged that some officials at Michigan State College had shown themselves "antagonistic" to the federal program.

By 1936, rural electrification had become a contentious subject in Michigan with strong differing opinions expressed by many individuals from the private and public sectors. Much of the talk was rooted in politics or an affiliation with the investor-owned utilities. Farmers kept pushing to get co-ops organized, but they encountered overt opposition as it became evident that Consumers Power Company would put what obstacles it could in the path of the cooperatives.

When the Rural Electrification Act was passed by Congress and signed into law by President Roosevelt May 21, 1936, the future of electric cooperatives in Michigan was muddled. Not only were aspersions being cast by opponents, some farmers had their doubts about risking $5 on something they knew little or nothing about. And there were nay sayers contending the co-op venture would fail and the members could lose their land to the government, which was not true.

So, what kind of partnership would this be between rural people and their Federal Government? Not unexpectedly, opinions ran the gamut. "We had a bushel and a half of opinions," said Bill Parsons, former Top O' Michigan co-op board chairman.

"A good many folks seriously questioned that it would really happen," recalled another longtime co-op director, Carlo Heikkinen, from the Ontonagon County Rural Electric Association in the western Upper Peninsula.

But there were enough believers to push forward: people like Edward Doll, the first board chairman of the Cloverland Electric Cooperative, Dafter, and Rolfe "Doc" Wells, key organizer of the Fruit Belt Electric Cooperative, Cassopolis, and Charles Kokx, chairman of the Oceana Electric Cooperative's original board.

Bernard Doll, who succeeded his father on the Cloverland board, said of his father, Edward, "He was one of the optimists who said it could be done and he worked diligently to get the co-op incorporated and off the ground. He was a happy man when we got the electricity and plugged in our milkers."

Rolfe Wells, Jr., who has served on the Fruit Belt board for the past 26 years, said that his father, "Doc" and others like him, "had to have a heck of a lot of determination as well as faith in fellow man to put in the long days and countless miles for sign-ups." Rolfe, Jr. knows because as a young boy he was with his father on many of those days. "Doc" went on to be the co-op's first board president.

Ray Kokx, son of Charles Kokx from Oceana County, said his father asked him if he could take care of the farming operation for a year while the elder Kokx dedicated his time to getting memberships for the co-op. Ray did, and Charles got the memberships, leading the way to Oceana's start-up in 1938.

Another firm believer was Elmer R. Rautio of Ontonagon County, where the sparsity of rural people didn't deter efforts to put together a feasible project. "We had to do a lot of legwork to get enough signers, but most folks wanted electricity so we moved right along and got incorporated in the fall of 1937," said the pioneer.

While these men worked night and day to see a dream come true on their farms, a growing staff of government employees at REA in Washington became enamored and enthused with their job: developing a way to make electric co-op dreams reality.

Administrator Cooke recruited some of the top graduates from engineering schools and accounting programs across the United States and gave them a full year's training. They were prepped to tackle a heretofore un-met challenge: make national rural electrification economically feasible and in an expeditious manner. Sound management principles were learned from recognized experts in industry, and the REA crew soon developed what one employee described as "the REA feeling." In his words, "there was not only a high degree of skill, but a certain enthusiasm, a missionary spirit" with which staff members approached their jobs.

John Carmody took the helm as REA Administrator in early 1937, and the pace of processing loan applications increased. The time between loan approvals and awarding of contracts was cut from 36 weeks to 12 weeks. Armed and anxious to work with the cooperatives and get projects built, many REA staffers worked into the night and, at one point, Carmody called a meeting to ask the employees not to work such long hours. (Yes, this was in Washington, D.C.)

Carmody recalled: "Things really got rolling in 1937. The program was alive. Enthusiasm ran high in REA and through rural areas. Buried projects were dug out....the status of every project from application to construction was put on the table in view of the entire staff for examination. We had weekly production meetings."

By the summer of 1938, there were 400 REA-financed projects underway in 40 states, including Michigan. President Roosevelt himself went to a gathering of 40,000 rural people in Georgia on August 11, 1938, to energize the power lines of Lamar Electric Membership Corporation. He said that electricity is a modern necessity of life and "ought to be in every village, every home and every farm in every part of the United States."

The president said the Georgia electric co-op's event was "a symbol of the progress being made by REA — and we are not going to stop."

REA engineers and management specialists came up with new, unique designs and construction methods to reduce the cost of constructing power lines. These revolutionary techniques accelerated the cooperative rural electrification program in 1938 and 1939.

The REA people used a combination of innovations to achieve their goal:

■ use of new high-strength conductors, which permitted longer spans and, thus, fewer poles;

■ development of a single-phase line with strong poles, without the crossarms;

■ system-wide planning, using "assembly line" construction.

Manufacturers followed the REA designs and so did the contractors who used the REA specs. Otherwise, they were dropped from the approved lists. The standardization and the "assembly line" technique worked and, by 1939, the average cost of a mile of rural electric line had been slashed from more than $1,500 to $538.

The partnership of rural people with their federal government was not only effective, it also saved money. Millions of dollars in construction costs were saved in a matter of a few years, thanks to the expertise, the innovation and the cooperative spirit of the REA employees — those in Washington and in the field.

REA placed field engineers in every state where there were loan applicants. They worked closely with the cooperatives on loan applications, helping to select the best routes for right-of-way, clarifying financial requirements and advising on a host of other elements vital to a project that would merit REA's approval.

REA officials would sometimes insist that two or more embryo groups get together and form one larger, more viable cooperative. That happened in several areas of Michigan, resulting in larger co-ops than in most Midwestern states. Average size of Michigan electric co-ops is 15,000 to 20,000 members, twice the average in neighboring states.

When a project was provided its first funding, a great deal of direction from REA came with it: precisely how the money was to be used, how contracts were to be awarded and, of course, the "specs" to be followed in line design. REA would give constant oversight to the projects, and the infant co-ops needed REA's approval on every proposed expenditure.

How did this go over with the co-op boards? "Well, we didn't really have a choice," said Oceana Electric Cooperative founding director Clarence Babbitt, "and besides, we didn't have any experience to go by as a board."

The farmers in Michigan and the government workers in Washington found themselves in an alliance almost by themselves, until the success of their cooperative venture appeared imminent. Detractors continued to spread skepticism. Later, when the lights came on and farmers started purchasing appliances and electric equipment, Main Street became a friend and politicians took note of the "new kind of electric utility"— one that grew from the grass roots and from the roots of years of discontent and distrust.

One of the top REA engineers in Washington, Clarence Winder, came to Michigan on several occasions to work with the cooperatives and, more importantly, to assist them in getting legal standing in the state. In 1938, Winder was asked to serve on the staff of the Michigan Public Utilities Commission to help resolve problems and coordinate work with the co-ops. His insight and leadership proved invaluable to the Michigan cooperatives as he became the bridge between the PUC and the cooperatives. Winder's role was above the norm of REA's assistance, necessitated by Michigan's acrimonious situation between the PUC and the co-ops.

The state Public Utilities Commission had been allied with Consumers Power Company in the early 1930s. PUC Chairman William Smith said private utilities were doing a good job of rural electrification and REA wasn't needed. When a new governor was elected in 1936, new Commissioners were appointed and the PUC became supportive of the co-ops, with Winder's help. Then, in the 1938 election, the tables were turned and the five Commissioners resigned and five new members were appointed in February, 1939.

In a history of the Commission published by the MPSC in 1995, the frequent turnover of Commissioners in the 1930s is noted with the following statement: "Political pressure again began to mount to abolish the Commission (appointed in 1937) because of a new alliance the Commission had formed with the New Deal's Rural Electrification Administration, which was interpreted by Consumers Power Company as adverse to their interests."

The "new alliance" apparently refers to the position of the 1937-38 Commission in support of the electric co-ops.

The Legislature, witnessing the volatile politics of the PUC and lobbied by Consumers Power, passed a law in 1939 abolishing the Public Utilities Commission and established the Public Service Commission. However, the new law did not remove politics from the appointments of Commissioners.

Despite the changing political climate in Lansing, the cooperatives forged ahead with the guiding hands of REA. As the banker/lender, REA kept close tabs on the co-ops where it had loan funds invested.

An example of REA's role in the early years was the almost daily guidance given to Alger Delta Cooperative Electric Association in the Upper Peninsula when a large area, known as the Menominee project, petitioned to be added to the co-op project. REA carefully evaluated the feasibility of the project and, at one point, expressed "doubts about the advisability of moving forward with the Menominee project," but confided that it would likely be approved.

REA representatives also urged the Alger Delta organizers to get more members. They suggested the co-op's maintenance man "go house to house and find out why some members are not wired."

Usually, REA's recommendations were followed but, at times, there were disagreements. That is revealed in minutes of some of the early co-op board meetings.

Alger Delta's first Project Superintendent, Julius Sivula, at a board meeting in 1939, "strenuously objected to REA representative MacClinchie's interference in the matter of territories to be served by the cooperative and by the M & M Power & Traction Company" — a dispute triggered by M&M's activities. However, such discord between a co-op and REA was the exception, not the rule.

Still another example of REA's close watch over the co-ops in the early years is this excerpt from Alger Delta's November 16, 1938, board meeting: "Mr. R.J. Ballard (REA's field engineer in Michigan) instructed us to get a good new truck and when writing to Washington about same, we should mention the amount of snow and mud that we have here, which was one reason that we chose the International truck, and we should also state that Mr. Ballard recommended said type of truck."

While REA practiced micro-management — some might say autocracy — over its debtors, the larger picture seen by co-op rural electrification leaders was one of the federal government enabling farmers and other rural people to get affordable and reliable electric service to join with the rest of the country in the benefits of electricity.

This vision became blurred, however, when the co-op organizers ran into obstacles, some anticipated and some unforeseen.

**Top row (L):** Longtime Tri-County Co-op director Jim Clarke and his wife, Dorothy, reminisce about electricity coming to their farm in Eaton County in 1938. **Top row (center):** Bill Parsons, Charlevoix, farmer, served on Top O' Michigan board for 24 years. **Top row (R):** Rolfe Wells, Dowagiac, followed his father, Rolfe Sr., on Fruit Belt Electric Co-op board. Both have had leadership roles in rural electrification. **2nd row (L):** Chester Graham, Muskegon, shown here with his wife, Margaret, were involved in early struggles to get electric co-ops organized in Michigan. **2nd row (R):** A 1948 Tri-County Electric membership certificate signed by co-op member Ernest Hatinger. (Thanks to Mary Hatinger of Edmore for providing the original certificate.) **3rd row (L):** Edward Doll, Cloverland Electric Cooperative pioneer. **3rd row (R):** Bernard Doll, son of Edward, has served on the boards of Cloverland, Michigan Electric Co-op Association and the National Rural Electric Co-op Association. **4th row (L):** Carlo Heikkinen, L' Anse, member of the Ontonagon Electric Co-op. **4th row (R):** Clarence Babbitt and Ray Kokx reflect on the early years of Oceana Electric Co-op.

**Top:** Getting right-of-way easements without payment was one key to making "area coverage" rural electrification feasible, and often it was the farm wife who said "yes" as in this 1937 photo in Presque Isle County. **Middle:** Workers put in long days digging holes for the first power lines at Presque Isle Electric Cooperative. The pay wasn't as much the incentive as getting "the electric." Local farmers pitched in and many were temporarily employed by contractors building the lines. **Bottom:** Driving the first stake on power line right-of-way in Oceana County in the fall of 1938 is Charles Kokx, the first board president of Oceana Electric Cooperatives. Others, from the left: Ed Daverman, engineer; unidentified man; Jim Fagley; Dick Ridell; Loyal Churchill, first Oceana manager; Jesse Davis, board member; Lyle Tompkins; Keith Glaza, and Bob Daverman, engineer, whose firm did extensive work for the cooperatives.

# TRIALS AND TRIBULATIONS

"For anyone to believe that the farmers were capable of such an undertaking was considered to be foolhardy in 1936, but our charter members had the courage to face all criticism, opposition, ridicule and misunderstanding, and also had the ability to overcome all obstacles placed in their way to prevent an electric cooperative from being established."

This description of the electric co-op pioneers' work was part of a front page article in the *Presque Isle County Advance*, published at Rogers City July 28, 1955, on the occasion of the dedication of Presque Isle Electric Cooperative's new headquarters building at Onaway.

Otto Grambau and the other six founders of the Presque Isle co-op would likely agree with the newspaper's appraisal if they were living today. Grambau was the first board chairman and led the small but determined band of pioneers through difficult times. Not on the board, but a driving force in organizing the co-op, was Presque Isle County Extension Agent Jack Brown. Another leader was Bernard Kline, who worked tirelessly to get the co-op going and came on the board of directors the year after its incorporation in 1937.

Kline and others called on farmers to get right-of-way so the lines could be staked and built. But, as he recalled, "there were lots of complications and many times I'd spend most of a day figuring out how to convince someone to sign the easement. REA wouldn't allow a co-op to pay for easements, and some people thought their land could be taken by the government if the project failed, so it was rough going."

Brown, widely recognized for his work with Presque Isle and other cooperatives, had initiated the first meeting of the organizing committee in the fall of 1936. He helped steer the group to incorporate the following February and apply for an REA loan in March of 1937. Brown reportedly used his own money to pay for the incorporation seal. Construction contracts were awarded by the co-op in July and the first pole erected in September. The partnership of REA and rural people was at work in Michigan.

In a matter of a few months, Presque Isle became the first electric cooperative to energize REA-financed lines in Michigan. It was Christmas Eve, 1937, a day never to be forgotten by the 82 families who turned on their newly-wired lights for the first time. REA power was a reality in Michigan.

While some surely saw the "new electric" as a Christmas present, the group of gritty men who sacrificed untold days and nights in meetings and driving hundreds of miles on dirt roads would readily agree with what an REA employee in Washington had said: "The best project in the United States is no bed of roses."

A myriad of problems and obstacles confronted the electric co-op pioneers, starting with skeptics who wouldn't sign a membership and those who didn't want to grant right-of-way for fear of losing their property to the government. The doubts put feasibility of many co-op projects in Michigan in jeopardy.

In the words of Presque Isle Electric Co-op Board Treasurer Edgar Rambadt, who served in that position for 28 years, "we knew very little about setting up an electric cooperative and even less about how to run one, but we were determined. REA wanted us to get four members per mile of line and that seemed impossible, but we continued to work and we built our first 75 miles of line in 1937 to serve about 300 members." In his farewell message in 1965, Rambadt said, "From that humble beginning, we now have over 2,700 miles of line in six counties serving 13,000 members. I guess we did some things right."

REA was firmly in the driver's seat through those early years. "Washington has every intention of keeping a hand on the wheel and a foot on the brakes," is how Jack Brown described the influence of REA through the first years of an electric cooperative. He was critical of what he felt was a lack of attention to the management of co-ops and, specifically, that REA was "willing to accept men of unknown quality who have no experience in the utility field."

He believed, as did many others, that the manager is the most important part of a cooperative undertaking, demonstrated by several other types of farmer co-ops. Brown felt that the Extension Service could have been more helpful to the co-ops in getting qualified management. But there weren't many qualified people available who wanted to "take a gamble" with this new breed of utility.

Some came from contractors and other utilities – lineworkers and electricians – and a few from within the original group of organizers. A consulting engineer who worked more than 40 years with the co-ops described these men as "rugged, hands-on kinds of people, relentless in their mission."

An exception was Cyril Clark, who became Ontonagon County Rural Electrification Association's project superintendent and then manager in 1938. He was a graduate of Michigan Tech and "young and daring" in his words. "It was an education for all of us — the board and myself — as we strived to get the memberships and start construction of a system that eventually turned out to be 13 separate service areas."

The co-op manager or project superintendent, as they were first called, was expected to run the office and handle the finances, see that right-of-way and staking was being accomplished, supervise construction, prepare reports to REA and the board, resolve member-customer problems, work with REA and the engineers on rates and technical matters, and be willing to stay up all night to coordinate repair work when storms knocked out power.

It was a formidable challenge that faced the first electric co-op managers and they had to rely heavily upon REA and on-the-job training. Some of the farmer-organizers didn't fear the job.

Among those who took on dual roles was Julius Sivula of Rapid River in the Alger Delta Cooperative. He was one of the five charter board members and was appointed coordinator of the project in 1939 while still on the board. He was an aggressive, optimistic person who spoke at every opportunity about REA and getting electricity for his area.

"He was the guy who really got the Alger Delta Co-op started," said Ray Berger, the co-op's longest-serving board member (45 years) and its former president. Berger's father, Arthur, helped get sign-ups after finding that a power company out of Wisconsin was only interested in serving farms along the main roads in his area.

Sivula later resigned from the board following REA policy — and a provision put into electric cooperatives' bylaws — stating that a member of the board of directors cannot also be a paid employee. However, in the organizational days, it was common for many board members to be paid a fee — usually $3 or $4 a day and four cents per mile — to get right-of-way easements and to do staking.

One cooperative adopted a resolution stating that elected directors could not receive a salary for board services but "it does not preclude any director from serving the cooperative in any other capacity and receiving compensation therefor." The co-ops' founders were true volunteers, not only because they took on the organizational work voluntarily but that they did it without compensation for their time.

When co-op members approved the first bylaws, there usually was a provision for the board members to set a reasonable fee for attending official board meetings. Typically, in 1937 and 1938, the fee was $2 or $3 per meeting and often the payment of these modest amounts had to be deferred because funds were short or nonexistent while the co-op waited for revenue to come in from the first members' monthly bills or REA loan funds.

A troublesome matter to almost every electric cooperative in the state as each approached the construction stage was locating an available, economical source for power supply. "This proved to be a dilemma for some cooperatives," said Bob Daverman, whose Grand Rapids engineering firm did system design work and power supply planning for almost every cooperative in Michigan, starting in the late 1930s. Daverman, who with two cousins and later his brother, Ed, formed an engineering and architectural consulting company, began his work with the fledgling cooperatives even before the company was started in 1939. "I had heard about the REA and talked with the REA field engineer who suggested I contact a co-op starting up in northern Illinois. I did design work for that co-op and then came back to Michigan and helped design the distribution system for Cloverland Electric Cooperative in the Upper Peninsula," Daverman recalled.

Cloverland contracted for its first bulk power supply from the Edison Sault Company and still purchases power generated by the company at hydro facilities on the St. Mary's River. Other cooperatives in the state were not so fortunate.

For the most part, co-op leaders had little choice but to turn to the same power companies who had earlier refused to connect them or had insisted they pay substantial amounts for line extensions. In some cases, the cooperatives were quoted as much as five and six cents per kilowatt hour for bulk "wholesale" power, plus the cost of connection facilities. The retail price of electricity in Michigan in those days ranged from three to five cents per kilowatt hour. The cooperatives — and REA — could hardly agree to pay more than the going retail rate for power if they were to deliver it to co-op members at affordable rates, said Childs.

Marquis Childs, in his book, *The Farmer Takes a Hand*, told of how the power companies wanted to keep control of the sources of power for cooperatives. They bitterly attacked loans made to co-ops for generation — a stance they held for years to come. They were consistently at loggerheads with REA.

REA's own report, issued in January of 1939, stated that "for many months, progress of rural electrification in Michigan was delayed owing to the unwillingness or inability of private companies to provide acceptable sources of power.....Finally, through the good offices of the Michigan Public Utilities Commission and the efforts of REA representatives on the ground, acceptable rates were obtained from two companies. It is anticipated that those other companies which can serve rural projects in Michigan will follow their lead."

Without REA's willingness to finance small diesel and gas-fired plants, some of the cooperatives would have had difficulty getting a supply of power. Working with REA in 1938 and 1939, consulting engineers designed generating projects for several co-ops where satisfactory supply agreements could not be reached or there simply wasn't any alternative source.

In the case of O & A Electric Cooperative, which filed incorporation papers in Ottowa County in December of 1937, the board negotiated with the city of Zeeland for several months to no avail, and found little prospect of purchasing power from Consumers Power Company. In June of 1938, the O & A board applied to REA for funds to build a generating plant in Allegan County. The loan was approved and two diesel generators were installed at Burnips later that summer. The first power flowed through O & A lines October 8,1938, to the charter members.

At Southeastern Michigan Electric Cooperative, Adrian, first known as Lenawee County Electric Membership Association, the board of directors discussed with REA as early as May, 1937, the prospect of installing a generating plant at Adrian. In August, an option for a plant site was approved. The co-op had been among the first to file for a charter and received approval in April, 1937.

The Southeastern plant was built with two 300 KW Fairbanks-Morse diesel generators. The co-op generated all of its power until 1946, when it entered into a contract with Consumers Power.

Fruit Belt Electric Cooperative and the Van Buren Electric Cooperative in the southwestern part of the state also had problems finding a power source. The co-ops, soon to merge under Fruit Belt's name, negotiated a contract with Michigan Gas and Electric Company in March, 1938. Lines were energized July 30.

Soon, more power was needed as more members were connected and negotiations with the power company failed to result in a satisfactory agreement — principally because the company refused to alter the rate regardless of the larger amounts of power needed by the co-op. It was determined that the best alternative would be for Fruit Belt to have its own diesel power plant. REA gave the go-ahead and three Cooper-Bessemer 475 KW diesel generators were installed at Cassopolis in 1940. Two additional units were installed in 1941 after the membership more than doubled. These units would serve the co-op's needs until 1951.

Sometimes the cooperative took initiative by applying for REA funds to build a plant before a power company in the area would come up with a reasonable supply proposal. Such was the case at Alger Delta when the co-op got REA approval for an $8 million plant at Escanaba which would have also provided power for the city of Escanaba. "The city was persuaded otherwise and the proposal was dropped," said the cooperative's longtime board chairman Ray Berger.

At Tri-County Electric Cooperative, an interesting story of its development and first power supply is told by Bryce Thomson of Eaton Rapids, who writes a newsletter for the National Ice Cream and Yogurt Retailers Association. He was employed by the Miller Dairy Farms, famous for its ice cream over five decades in Michigan. Miller's operation used a fair amount of electricity making their ice cream and refrigerating it.

The company bought a site along the Grand River at Eaton Rapids and repaired a century-old dam, installed a hydro generator and served their own electric power needs. Two farmers from the area, William Clegg and James Houston, took note of Miller's installation because they had been trying to get the utility (Consumers Power) to extend service to them.

"Why not sell current to us?" they asked Dennis Miller. "A lot of it is going over the dam every day." Miller replied that he was in the ice cream business. "I don't know a thing about the power business."

The three men agreed the idea was worth pursuing and checked with the newly-established REA in Washington. When several other farmers in the area showed interest and elected Clegg to head the group, REA gave the nod, and in early 1938, Tri-County Electric Cooperative was in business with power from Miller's hydro, augmented by two diesel units. The co-op also bought power from a small dam on the Muskegon River near Altona.

As the cooperative grew rapidly in memberships, additional generating capacity was needed. Diesel power plants were built at Vestaburg and at Portland where the co-op's office was located. Again, REA financing made the projects possible.

The Presque Isle Electric Cooperative in northern Michigan also got its first power supply from a hydro installation. The co-op worked with Alpena Power Company and reached an agreement whereby Alpena would sell a block of power from its Norway dam. Electricity from this dam flowed to 82 farm families when the co-op's first lines were energized December 24, 1937.

In comments delivered at the dedication of Presque Isle's first pole, set September 22, 1937, at Posen, Joseph Donnelly, a member of the Michigan Public Utilities Commission, said that "you people owe a debt of gratitude to Alpena Power Company and its president, Philip Fletcher — their cooperation is of a type not seen in southern Michigan. If we could secure the same cooperation from the Consumers Power Company as you have from Alpena Power Company, you may be sure that Michigan would be far out in front in rural electrification."

Consumers Power Company gained notoriety quickly not only for its position of resistance in reaching wholesale power agreements with the cooperatives, but for its brash moves to "skim the cream" — taking the best prospective farm customers — when the cooperatives got started. In some instances, the company built "spite lines," grabbing territory that the company had previously ignored or rejected.

"Spite lines" were so-called because they were built in locations where a cooperative had staked lines or had actually started construction. The power company lines — sometimes erected overnight — would often mean a significant loss of customers to the cooperative and, thus, put the cooperative's feasibility in jeopardy.

"It was unbelievable," said Bob Lambert, first a lineman and later the manager of Cherryland Electric Cooperative of Grand Traverse County. "It got to be a dog-eat-dog battle, even in the 1950s and 1960s in our area."

Morgan McDermott, one of Cherryland's original directors, used to tell of the experience of George McManus, Sr. in the Leelanau Peninsula. Every year at Thanksgiving time, George would go to the Michigan Public Service Company (predecessor to Consumers Power in that area) and apply for electric service, and every year the company said no. In 1938, his friend, Frank Burkhart, suggested he tell Michigan Public Service that the Cherryland Co-op would be out there to get sign-ups and right-of-way. He did that, and the next day the company was out putting up poles to bring electricity to the peninsula.

"I can still see some of the power company poles going up alongside REA co-op poles, trying to get the better customers," said Ed Daverman, Grand Rapids engineer who designed co-op systems. It became an all too common sight.

The interference of Consumers Power, a utility growing rapidly with the acquisition of smaller utilities in the state, was felt by several cooperatives in the Lower Peninsula. Some feared that the huge utility would take over the co-ops, too, once they got into operation. But that didn't deter the co-op boards from their work.

The minutes of a November, 1937, board of directors meeting of the Fruit Belt Electric Cooperative reveal the consternation felt by the co-op organizers. A resolution was unanimously passed stating: "Whereas the project is ready for construction, in order to protect the project against the constant attempts of private utility companies to extend their lines into the choicest sections (of the co-op's planned service area), we urge allotment of funds (from REA) for completion of the project and, therefore, we ask for prompt consideration."

The Fruit Belt board met with officials of the Indiana & Michigan Power Company and reached agreement on service areas and set territorial boundaries. MPUC Commissioner Joseph Donnelly was instrumental in getting the parties together. He understood the cooperatives' needs as well as the power companies.

However, co-op records state that "some of the power companies decided, after the co-op began distributing power, to extend their own lines...in many of these instances, farmers refused to hook up to the power company line because of all the work and effort they already had put forth in organizing the Fruit Belt Electric Cooperative. The co-op then built lines to these farmers and, in some cases, the power company had to pull a section of line out as all of the proposed customers had signed with the co-op first and refused service from the company."

The O & A Electric Cooperative ran into problems early in 1938 when line construction was getting underway. Minutes of the co-op's April 29, 1938, board meeting tell the story:

"A thorough discussion was held on the activity of Consumers Power Company in this territory in building extensions and 'spite lines' after our engineer had staked out the lines of the cooperative." The board pledged to speed the construction to try to prevent the company "from gaining more ground."

Across the Straits of Mackinac, the Alger Delta Cooperative's plans to extend lines into a large unserved area of Menominee County were stymied for a year or more by the M & M Power and Traction Company's sudden decision to build lines into rural areas. It wasn't until 1941 that electricity flowed through the co-op's lines in that area, long awaited by 500 families.

And at the Ontonagon County Cooperative in the western U.P., where Wisconsin-Michigan Electric Power Company had some rural lines, the co-op's system was starting to look like a jigsaw puzzle. When it was drawn on the map, the cooperative had 13 noncontiguous service areas sprawling into Houghton and Baraga counties, with an equal number of power supply points.

In some states, the spite lines spelled doom for little co-ops trying to get started. A survey by REA in 1940 showed that eight co-ops were wiped out entirely and scores of others weakened. Some 200 cases in 38 states were reported, most of them where companies carved out the larger potential users, such as dairy farms.

None of the cooperatives in Michigan were mortally wounded by the spite line tactics. REA's own report on conditions at the end of 1938 said: "To date, the attempts of Consumers Power Company and other utilities to disrupt cooperative projects have not succeeded, in spite of resorting to some of the most flagrant tactics in the history of rural electrification."

The conclusion of the REA report proclaimed that "the farmers of the state set up such a clamor for cooperative electricity that as the fiscal year closed, Michigan appeared ready to take the lead in the amount of money borrowed, and promised to be among the leaders in REA-financed construction for some time to come."

But more obstacles kept the Michigan co-ops from fulfilling that prediction. One was politics.

The tenacity of the people leading electric cooperatives had been tested in 1936 when a political barrier had been put in their path by the administration of Governor Frank Fitzgerald. Simply put, the State of Michigan would not recognize the cooperatives as legal bodies. But the farmers did not relent.

Otis Klett, head of the Fruit Belt cooperative and president of the Michigan Association of REA Cooperatives, charged in the *Michigan Farm Electric News* of October 18, 1938, that Governor Fitzgerald declined to work with the farmers in getting their electric co-ops incorporated as legal entities and that the state Public Utilities Commission refused to regard the cooperatives as utilities.

Klett told how the farmers in his area had held meetings throughout the area and were ready to form the cooperative only to run into what he and other electric co-op leaders regarded as a political wall. "We had a meeting scheduled at Michigan State College in East Lansing with committee men from each township in the eight counties and Governor Fitzgerald promised to be there at 10 a.m., but he notified us at 8:00 that morning that he couldn't be there."

Consequently, the farmers turned to others for advice and assistance. They included Indiana Governor Paul McNutt, who flew to Lansing the same day and encouraged the group to press on. He said Indiana had several electric co-ops ready to start construction as soon as REA loan funds were advanced. This gave Michigan organizers new hope.

REA had allocated $6,000,000 for loans in Michigan in 1936, but did not process any Michigan applications because of the state government's refusal to act. The co-op leaders were frustrated and distraught with Fitzgerald and his Public Utilities Commissioners. They were angry with the private power companies because they were convinced that the power companies' propaganda and influence were behind the state's denial.

Lloyd Walkling, secretary of the Michigan Association of REA Cooperatives, said the companies spread misinformation in the areas where cooperatives were organizing to confuse the situation and hinder progress of the REA program. Others joined in the outcry that the farmers were doing the right thing and that their newborn cooperatives deserved fair treatment.

The election in November, 1936, changed the outlook for the cooperatives. Frank Murphy, a protégé of President Franklin Roosevelt and a believer in giving people the opportunity to improve their lot, was elected Governor and he gave immediate attention to the stalled electric co-ops. He had been mayor of Detroit, but his home ground was Harbor Beach in the Thumb. He knew the plight of farmers in the 1930s.

When Murphy and his Attorney General, Raymond W. Starr, took office on January 1, 1937, the dilemma of the electric cooperatives was examined by Starr. On March 25, 1937, Starr rendered his opinion to the Michigan Corporation and Securities Commission that rural electric cooperatives were not "public utilities" within the provisions of Public Act 144 of 1909 and that the Securities Commission should accept their articles of incorporation for filing without requiring an order of the Public Utilities Commission.

The opinion was not challenged in court, and paved the way for the cooperatives to move forward. They wasted no time. One co-op after another held organizational meetings and submitted their articles to the Corporation and Securities Commission. Approvals came swiftly and, by the end of 1937, eight electric cooperatives were legal corporations applying for REA funds.

REA annually earmarked funds for each state, but not always in adequate amounts, which was partly due to limited appropriations by Congress and partly unforeseen developments in a given state. Bob Daverman, consulting engineer from Grand Rapids who worked on many of the projects in the late 1930s and into the '40s, said getting the loan applications "to the top of the pile" often required trips to

REA in Washington.

He said he couldn't count the number of times that he accompanied groups of co-op directors to REA's headquarters to personally explain the dire need for advancement of funds. Work would be going on — system design, right-of-way procurement, staking for lines — and the money wasn't in the co-op's bank account to pay the workers.

"Sometimes I'd have to persuade a restaurant owner to continue to feed a survey crew and promise him that we would pay as soon as the co-op received the advance of funds from REA," Daverman recalled. "Contractors and suppliers, like us, would sometimes wait four or five months for pay. But we all knew what it was like to have nothing in the Depression days. We just depended on one another and waited for the money to come through."

The effort to get REA's attention and loan funds advanced could be a trying experience. Undoubtedly one of the most interesting and memorable was the visit of Oceana Electric Cooperative's first manager, Loyal Churchill, to REA in Washington.

"John Carmody was the REA Administrator, so I went to his office right away. There was a big bald-headed guy there who told me there was nothing I could do about the loan." 'Nothing you can do about it,' he said. 'Your application won't be processed for quite some time.'"

"So I said, 'Mind if I stay here? I want to talk to Carmody.' He said, 'He's away and won't be back for a few days.' And I said, 'If I get a couple of magazines and sit here and wait for him, is that all right with you?' 'No,' he said, 'you can't just stay here for any length of time.'"

"I said, 'This is a public office and I'll stay here if I want to.' Pretty soon I heard some laughing in the back room and the door opened and Carmody came out. 'Well, Loyal, the wheel that squeaks the most gets the grease, don't it. What do you want?'

"I told him I wanted that loan application of Oceana Electric approved now — 'or let's forget about it.' He said, 'Okay, where is it?' And the guy reached down and pulled it from the bottom of the stack. 'What's wrong with it?' asked Carmody. 'Nothing really,' the guy said. 'Well then, why aren't you doing something about it?' 'We haven't gotten to it yet,' the employee said."

"Carmody said he could see that and then asked me to tell him more about our cooperative, which I did. He called up the treasurer and they agreed that everything was okay. The engineering department had approved it and the financial department had approved it. The treasurer said he would write a check 'right now' with Carmody's okay. So old John scribbled his signature on the application and said, 'Okay, where's your suitcase and coat?' And I said, 'Right there on the chair.'"

"He took me downstairs and outside, whistled for a taxi and then told the driver, 'Take this man over to the treasurer's office and then wait for him. After he's through there, you take him to the airport for his plane.' Then Carmody pulled five bucks out of his pocket, paid for the taxi and said, 'Good luck.'"

"The Treasurer gave me a check for $161,000 so I was very happy. I came home and we started working on the right-of-way and staking."

Churchill was one of the founding fathers of the cooperative and served as manager until 1946. Oceana's first office employee, Louise Snyder, recalled their first "office" was a desk in the dining room of Churchill's home. "We didn't have money to rent an office."

The infant cooperative gave new meaning to frugality.

When they did move into an abandoned store on Hart's main street — with a monthly rental of $5 — they didn't have money for a desk or chairs, so Churchill had a piece of plywood on two sawhorses for a desk. For paper, he would go to the local printer and get scraps from overruns that the printer would give him free.

Such were the meager beginnings of most of the electric cooperatives. As Bob Daverman said, "We were just coming out of the Depression and everything was tight. It was tough going, but the dedication of those who started the cooperatives was phenomenal. They began with nothing and, through sheer determination and the help of REA, they found a way to succeed."

Obtaining the funds wasn't the only hurdle the cooperatives encountered. Decisions were needed almost daily once they were assured of construction money: bids to let, manpower to help on staking and construction, how to convince member-consumers to get their houses wired — and barns, too — power supply arrangements, accounting and billing systems, and all that goes with a utility's operation.

Newspapers in the Oceana area told how hundreds of local farmers helped construction crews by hauling poles and, in some cases, digging the holes, all done by manual labor. But, even without the equipment and tools the co-ops have today, progress was steady. The REA "assembly line" approach was working.

Although many of the electric cooperative projects were built "piece by piece" as feasibility and funding materialized, one Michigan cooperative developed plans in 1937 that would prove to be "the largest REA project in the nation" in 1938.

The Thumb Electric Cooperative was incorporated in the spring of 1937 and had already submitted a loan application to REA for $2 million, far above the amount of any previous REA loan. The co-op, led by Frank Wilson of Ubly and E.C. Steig of Bad Axe, had the numbers to back up the application: 5,500 signers for electricity, the most of any Michigan cooperative at that point.

Wilson, Steig and a dozen or so other farmers had started the drive for memberships in early 1936. One meeting in Bad Axe had drawn more than 600 farmers. When Governor Murphy and Attorney General Starr cleared the way in 1937 for electric cooperatives to do business, the Thumb group worked fast.

The project would require some 1,400 miles of line, three substations and a good-sized generating plant. With REA's approval of the loan in April, 1937, work got underway for right-of-way and the first pole was set September 10, 1937, by the site of the power plant soon to be constructed just north of Ubly.

"This is the nation's largest REA project," proclaimed REA Administrator John Carmody, who was one of the dignitaries to speak at the dedication ceremonies June 18, 1938, when the lines were energized with power from Thumb's own diesel generators. Governor Murphy threw the switch for current to travel to the first 2,000 families connected, calling it "a milestone in the progress of rural electrification in our great state.

"The development of the rural electric cooperatives during the past year and a half is to my mind one of the most progressive and helpful achievements in behalf of the farming people of Michigan within a generation," said Murphy. "The development of these cooperatives was met by active opposition from some of the utility companies and by a refusal to cooperate from others. Only some of the smaller utilities were actually helpful to the cooperatives."

Murphy credited the Public Utilities Commission for taking action in 1937 to enable the cooperatives to move forward. "Today, after more than a year of trials and problems, and in some cases skilled opposition, the REA development in Michigan is an undeniable success," he said. In 1938, more miles of line will be constructed and ready for service by the co-ops than by all of the utility companies during the past year, the governor declared.

In a speech October 20, 1938, at the energizing of Top O' Michigan Electric Company's first lines, Governor Murphy advocated that every community "large and small" should look at entering the utility field to some degree "for self-protection." He had words of praise and criticism for private utilities: "I do not claim that all private utilities are evil — far from it. A good example of a great utility is Detroit Edison, which does not maintain a staff in Lansing aggressively engaged in the work of blocking legislation that is in the public interest."

Five more electric cooperatives officially organized in 1938 and put in loan requests to REA. They would learn from some of the trials and successes of the other Michigan co-ops. The need to share experiences and to work together to achieve common goals was beginning to be recognized. The feeling of a "cooperative family" was growing.

It was clear that Governor Murphy staunchly supported the advancement of electric cooperatives, believing that they could make a big difference in the lives of rural people. As he put it, "Untold happiness and enjoyment will be the lot of those to whom this blessing is being brought."

Indeed, this prophecy was already becoming reality in parts of the state.

**Above (L):** "Modest" would almost be an overstatement in describing some of the electric co-op offices in the late 1930s. Pictured is Top O' Michigan's first office in Boyne City. **Above (R):** Cy Clark, left, first manager of Ontonagon County Electric Co-op, with Dick Store and Wilfred Bremu at new radio tower near Winona in 1952. **2nd row (R):** Bob Daverman, second from right, was system design engineer for several Michigan cooperatives and worked with construction crews checking new lines. On the right is Clayton Weinschenk, who worked for a contractor and later Cloverland Electric Co-op. **3rd row (R):** Loyal Churchill, organizer and first manager of Oceana Electric Cooperative, shown here visiting with Bob Fredericksen, Hart, who managed the co-op from 1978 to 1991. **Bottom (L to R):** Barney Kline, leader of Presque Isle Electric and Northern Michigan cooperatives in the 1940s and 50s; Raymond Berger, longest serving board member from Alger Delta Co-op (45 years); Bob Lambert, who started as a lineman with Cherryland Electric in 1941 and later managed the co-op for 15 years.

**Above:** Frank Wilson, founding father of Thumb Electric Cooperative, Ubly, was proud of the co-op's generating plants—one at Ubly and one at Caro, pictured above. Wilson is on the left, Don Decker on the right. Thumb buys bulk power from Detroit Edison but continues to keep generators on standby to meet peak load demands. **Middle:** The original Presque Isle office (late 1930s).

## CO-OP HERO, FRANK MURPHY, MOVED TO HIGHER LEVEL

Governor Frank Murphy, a native of the Thumb area who cleared the way for electric co-ops to legally incorporate in 1937, served just one term in the governor's chair.  President Franklin Roosevelt appointed him U.S. Attorney General in 1939 and then elevated him to Justice of the United States Supreme Court a year later.  He's the only Michigan person to serve on the U.S. Supreme Court.

The house where Frank Murphy was born in Harbor Beach is now a museum operated by the Huron County Historical Society.

**Above:** Familiar scenes in the late 1930s and 40s. Truck-mounted "A frame" was the standard method of setting poles in the ground for many years. **Middle, (L):** "Pike poles" and plenty of muscle were required to get poles in correct position. Here, workers build some of the first line in Allegan County. **Middle (R):** For adequate power supply, some co-ops had to build their own generating plants. Western Michigan Electric Co-op installed 3,000 kilowatts of capacity in their original plant in 1941 at Scottville, and added 2,000 more in 1961 before joining the Wolverine group. **Bottom right:** Former Tri-County Electric Co-op director Jim Clarke looks at the Eaton Rapids hydro site where the cooperative got its first power supply in 1938.

# A NEW LIGHT IS SHINING

By Christmas of 1938, an estimated 15,000 families in rural Michigan were enjoying the benefits of electricity, connected to the co-op power lines that they and their partner, REA, made possible.

As tough as it was to get their cooperatives organized and then recognized as legal businesses in Michigan, now they could see their life starting to change. They rushed to get electric irons and washing machines and radios and plug them in, but most important were the lights. At last, electric lights.

Now, thanks to cooperation, they could say, "Here in this place, a new light is shining!"

The new light was soon to illuminate thousands of other Michigan farms and dwellings — approximately half of all farms in the state. But, in 1938, the co-ops still had a long way to go to reach their goals in Michigan and other states.

The official report of the Rural Electrification Administration at the end of 1938 stated that 70,000 miles of line were built in 44 states and that another 80,000 would likely be constructed in 1939. "The record is a tribute to the foresight of Congress. The social soundness of the program has been amply demonstrated. The economic wisdom of bringing farm families out of the dark into the light, out of stark drudgery and out of a past of unnecessary denial into a present of reasonable convenience is beyond question."

The REA report, on its cover, offered the following perspective: "Electric central-station service has been made available to almost as many farm people in three years of the national rural electrification program as in the three decades since rural electrification had its beginnings in the U.S. early in the century."

A neutral but studied observer of the rural electrification scene, professional photographer Arthur Rothstein had this to say: "I had spent a great deal of time traveling across the country photographing the conditions (in the 1930s). I saw the tremendous hardships farmers and their wives and families had to face. I saw that because they were too distant from the lines, they were denied the power and the light.

"And I was so taken with the concept of cooperation as the means by which the government and the people came together to accomplish rural electrification...It was so in keeping with the magnificent trait in the American character, to knit and band together in times of adversity in order to survive.

"Still, the REA people went beyond survival with cooperative rural electrification. They truly brought and built something to and for themselves. Not just the benefits of electricity alone...They built these co-ops to stand as a statement of what they were capable of achieving under cooperative democratic principles."

Rothstein, like many other photographers and writers, was interested in seeing how this revolution in rural living would actually change lives and how it would impact all of America. The impact was a chain reaction as people wired their houses and farm buildings and purchased tens of millions of dollars worth of appliances and equipment.

The REA rural electrification program was creating a boom, the likes of which had never been experienced before in rural America. To help those who didn't have money for wiring, REA offered a special program for wiring and equipment loans through the cooperatives. Rural people started buying electric irons, refrigerators, water heaters and stoves. By 1940, the overall economic impact to the U.S. economy was well over a billion dollars. In Michigan, the total investments and purchases were estimated to approach $100,000,000 in the first three years. Add to that the economic boost of hundreds of new jobs created by the electric cooperatives.

Manufacturers, working with REA, put out "lighting packages" at prices that were considered low even then. A typical package contained nine modern fixtures and sold for about $18. Wiring jobs were being done for $50 to $60.

Still, some were hesitant to get wired and ready for "the electric," because they feared they couldn't afford it. Many of the first co-op rate schedules called for a minimum purchase of $2.50 per month, for which the member would get 30 or 40 kilowatt hours. Records show that the average monthly bill in 1939 was not much more than that.

This conservative tendency, although not surprising for farmers struggling to survive, was cause for grave concern by the co-ops and REA. Revenue was needed to start making payments on loans. Some of the cooperatives, just getting a foothold, were on the verge of financial disaster if members wouldn't make greater use of the electricity.

REA came to the rescue. The agency from the beginning printed brochures and bulletins giving instructions about the use of electric appliances and the average cost per month of operating them. REA employed two full-time home economists to conduct a consumer information program with the cooperatives, and then expanded its efforts and sent six teams of specialists into the field to work directly with co-op members in groups at schoolhouses and co-op offices and in homes, showing them how to best use electricity.

In 1938, REA launched the Demonstration Farm Equipment Tour or, as it soon became known, "The REA Circus" — so-called because most of the demonstrations were conducted under tents and would usually go on for two or three days in one location. REA employees, Extension Service agents and other specialists demonstrated the use of many kinds of farm equipment, emphasizing how to efficiently and safely use their new "hired hand" to milk cows, dry hay, brood chicks, keep baby pigs warm and healthy, and even irrigate crops.

The REA Demonstration Tour reached a million or more farmers in some 30 states. "It was really quite effective," said Edwin "Bud" Englund, longtime employee of the Alger Delta cooperative in the Upper Peninsula.

"Electricity for Profit" meetings for farmers were organized by the Cooperative Extension Service in 1938 and 1939. In the Thumb area alone, the Extension Rural Electrification Specialist, D.L. Ebinger, conducted 24 workshops showing how "lights in the hen house result in more eggs in the winter, feed grinding by electricity cuts costs, electric brooders raise healthier chickens and labor savings result from the use of milking machines and water pumps."

Dairy farmers found electricity an immediate money maker. One Michigan farmer related to REA how he had been paying $45 a month for ice to cool the milk and invested $350 in an electric milk cooler. He happily told how the cooler not only did the job better, but cost only $10 a month for the electricity, meaning he would have the cooler paid for in less than a year.

Fond memories of "when the lights first came on" usually have nothing to do with dollars and cents, but are filled with the sheer joy of dreams come true. "I recall the excitement I had as a child dashing from room to room flipping on lights," Joy Andrews of Lawton related in a letter to Michigan *Country Lines* magazine in 1985, the 50th anniversary of REA.

"My pockets jingled with the nickel-sized slugs I'd begged from the electrician as he removed them from the boxes when he was wiring. The naked bulb in the simple white ceramic fixture in the center of my playroom ceiling was the first light I turned on....Electric lamps saved from earlier city dwelling days were prominently placed on tables by windows for all to see that, at last, our family had electricity."

Another recollection in the 1985 *Country Lines* was that of Mrs. Ellen Pertula of Trout Creek, who said her mother, Sanna Lehto, decided to have "an electric lights party" when electricity to her home was energized in 1940. "That's exactly what we had — a party with Finnish foods — and special guests were John and Fanny Perttula because Mr. Pertula was instrumental in getting electricity to our area. Thanks for the REA...sure beats those Aladdin lamps!"

Cleo Hansen of rural St. Joseph told *Country Lines* readers that those three initials, REA, "still sound magical to me." He recalled a warm April afternoon in 1939 walking home from the country school and being met by his brother exclaiming, "the lights are on."

"As a child of 11 it seemed a miracle in itself that we could have electricity even if it were available. Due to lack of money, my parents were thinking of only having the barn wired because electricity was needed there the most. I could read, my first love, day or night even in the barn! My parents told the story of how they were doing chores in the barn when the electricity was connected. My brother ran to the house, turned on all the lights before removing his muddy, manure boots. I can still see the imprints of those dirty boots on the white counterpane in our bedroom, and I remember thinking 'they aren't even angry with him.'"

Country schools — and there were thousands of them — were beneficiaries, too. Teachers said that electricity made such a difference that many students' grades improved remarkably with better lighting.

Bill Vissers, retired board member of the O & A Electric Cooperative, remembers the changes that electricity brought the day their farmstead was energized in Ottawa County. "Electricity to pump water, run the washing machine and iron, and help us in milking. Electricity meant a new life on the farm."

An unforgettable scene to engineer Bob Daverman while working with the Oceana Electric Cooperative was that of an elderly lady seeing the lights in her house turned on for the first time. "She was so ecstatic that she sobbed. She could hardly believe that she actually had electric lights at last."

"The night the lights came on is still hailed in many rural regions as an occasion ranking with the stature of feasts of Thanksgiving and Christmas," wrote syndicated columnist Bob Considine after visiting the Sioux Valley Electric Cooperative in South Dakota in 1966.

"Electric power changed millions of lives instantaneously, ended lonely isolation, provided leisure time and better education, improved public health, cut deep into farm accidents, provided a tremendous shot in the arm for the American economy, made us the breadbasket of the world, won a war, sealed a peace," Considine concluded.

"Our farm homes are equal to those in the city now, thanks to the REA." That was the essence of hundreds of letters that came into co-op offices with bill payments in the early years.

A member of Tri-County Electric Co-op sent this message in 1953: "Your service is very good...I am amazed at the progress you've made the past three years...Always proud to tell my friends that I have just everything up here at the lake, thanks to you. If you had not come in and heeded our call for help, we would be in darkness. As it is, we are really on the map — a bright spot. Thanks so much."

People in high places, too, have fond memories of getting co-op electricity. Before he became president of the United States, Lyndon B. Johnson pushed hard to get REA funds for Pedernales Electric Cooperative in his home country in Texas because he personally knew the adversities of growing up without electricity. He often made reference in public speeches to the many blessings that electric co-op power meant to him and the people of rural Texas.

Former President Jimmy Carter, speaking to a youth group at the White House in 1978, said that the "best day in my life, the one I remember most vividly — with the possible exception of my wedding day — was the day they turned the lights on in our house in Georgia."

The new light from cooperatives was shining in thousands of rural Michigan homes and barns and schoolhouses by 1941. Across the nation, the number of farms served by cooperatives was approaching one million. More than 800 co-ops were up and running.

The traveling REA farm power demonstrations were having an impact on the co-ops. Together, the educational efforts of REA and the cooperatives spurred increased utilization of electricity and helped make farmers aware of the flexibility and the productivity of the power now at their fingertips.

It was timely that electricity's use on the farm was expanding because it would prove to be an important factor for the nation when World War II broke out and the United States entered the war in December of 1941. While the war was a major obstacle to the cooperatives' progress, it was also an opportunity to prove the value of electricity on the farm.

Work on the rural electric systems came to a virtual halt across the nation soon after the Japanese attack on Pearl Harbor December 7, 1941. Materials needed for line construction were in short supply and manpower became scarce, too, as most able-bodied men went to serve their country in the armed forces or in factories quickly converted to manufacture tanks and other war machines.

Rural electrification was at a near standstill from 1942 to late 1945. REA offices were moved to St. Louis, Mo., and its reduced staff continued to work on loan applications as well as special war-related projects. But the government put the clamps on construction.

During the war years, political skirmishes between REA co-op backers and private utilities took on a new dimension: alleged favoritism in allocating a diminishing supply of materials for utility line extensions and power projects.

In a speech at the national meeting of electric cooperatives in January, 1943, U.S. Secretary of Interior Harold Ickes said: "The farms that we (REA) have electrified are meeting the shock of war and its consequent labor shortage and have continued to increase production of food for our armies, our allies and ourselves. Public power agencies have shouldered their guns as have all of us."

Ickes went on to attack the investor-owned utilities for what he called their "selfish patriotism of money that is without allegiance" and criticized their "piratical practices" and advertisements. Pirating of customers was going on in some areas, including parts of Michigan where co-ops were losing some of their residential customers to Consumers Power.

Charges of less-than-patriotic behavior were exchanged between the two sides. A co-op spokesman said the utilities unduly influenced the War Department and the War Production Board in the interests of "big power trusts."

At REA's urging, the War Production Board did decide to allow some rural line extensions where the distances were not great and it could be shown that electricity would mean a definite increase in food production. That proved to be a wise strategic move because the U.S. Armed Forces and our allies desperately needed food supplies.

"Electric power furnished to REA farms is today helping 1,000,000 American farmers meet their production goals and will prove to be a very effective medium in hastening the victory. Food is as necessary as bullets," said the manager of Top O' Michigan Electric Co-op, Harold Lees, in the cooperative's newsletter.

One farmer wrote to Lees: "We find more use for electricity every day. Electricity on the farm has certainly helped the farmers in helping to win this awful war."

During the war years, U.S. farmers broke one production record after another. Their output of food filled America's own military and civilian requirements, plus part of its allies'. REA instituted its own "REA Production Award" for outstanding farm production using electric power. The pioneering work of REA and the electric co-ops was paying dividends to the nation already.

Rural electrification — although less than halfway to the goal of serving all rural areas when the war hit — also meant that more plants and businesses supplying materials vital to the war effort could be located out in the country. The number of rural businesses on co-op lines tripled during World War II.

While the war veiled problems the young electric cooperatives had encountered earlier, they were still on the minds of many co-op and political leaders. The need for unity and political strength to guard against damaging legislation was prominent in their minds when electric co-op leaders from 10 states — including Michigan — got together in Washington and formed the National Rural Electric Cooperative Association (NRECA).

Dolph H. Wolf, the first manager of the Tri-County Electric Cooperative in Portland, Michigan, was one of 10 leaders who saw the need for a national organization to represent the cooperatives on the legislative front and to develop programs for management training and insurance for the co-ops and their employees.

The group met in early 1942 in Washington, D.C. and formally incorporated NRECA on March 14. By the end of the year, the new association had 266 member cooperatives, including a few from Michigan. Wolf and the other NRECA board members selected a young Congressman from Arkansas, Clyde T. Ellis, to be their first general manager.

Ellis knew the struggles of electric co-ops in his home state as well as many emerging issues in the U.S. Congress directly affecting cooperatives nationally, such as funding for REA, water resource development, preference for consumer-owned electric systems in the marketing of federal power, and a host of others. He had no fear of the large investor-owned utilities who were ever present on the other side of most of these issues.

Ellis soon gained a reputation as a fighter for the electric cooperatives and an inspiring orator. Sometimes his speeches at NRECA membership meetings would consume two hours, but everyone listened attentively and applauded his fighting spirit.

It was the leadership of Clyde Ellis and the enthusiastic participation of people like Dolph Wolf from the grass roots that spelled victory for the cooperatives in some of the legislative battles in the 1940s. There were many, and they would continue on year after year after year.

When Ellis and that first NRECA board looked at all that was at stake legislatively and the political opposition the cooperatives faced, they quickly agreed with a legislator who said "REA was born in politics, and if it dies, it will die in politics." They resolved that NRECA must take an active role in the halls of Congress.

Ellis, who had championed legislation for electric co-ops when he was in the Arkansas Legislature, started to build a small but effective legislative lobbying staff at NRECA. They worked on a multitude of issues, ranging from REA appropriations to federal power projects to taxation of cooperatives. In later years, the *Wall Street Journal* credited NRECA as having "one of the most powerful lobby groups in Washington," citing its success in keeping REA as a viable federal program.

That's an astounding appraisal considering the number of NRECA lobbyists is a fraction of the size of many other associations and utility groups in Washington. It is more of a tribute to the involvement of grass roots leaders from electric co-ops across the nation who make contact with their Representatives and Senators on issues of serious concern.

Through NRECA, the cooperatives have been victorious in Congress more often than not. Credit goes to several individuals who led the way in the early years of legislative fights.

Three key legislative representatives for NRECA in its first 20 years of operation came to the association from REA, the government agency. Richard Dell, Kermit Overby and Robert Partridge were experienced and knowledgeable of the cooperatives' needs and, along with Ellis, had the "missionary spirit" and legislative savvy to be effective with members of Congress.

One big win was passage of the Pace Act in 1944 making REA a permanent agency and enabling "area coverage" to be a reality. This was the covenant between Congress and REA borrowers that electric service would be made available to all who needed service. To help make that feasible, the legislation established the interest rate on REA loans at two percent and stretched the repayment period to 35 years.

NRECA initiated insurance programs for the cooperatives that cut rates for liability and employee medical coverages, and soon developed a series of training courses for managers, key employees and co-op board members. A monthly publication, *Rural Electrification Magazine*, was launched in the late 1940s, bringing vital information to employees and directors.

Most significant in the national organization's success was the fact that NRECA represented unity and strength for the small and still struggling electric cooperatives. Although they didn't agree on every issue or policy matter, they had a forum in which to discuss and ultimately resolve the course of action that would impact their future individually and collectively.

One major issue that brought out sharp differences among board members was the relationship between the electric cooperatives and the American Farm Bureau Federation. Writing about that discussion at an NRECA board meeting in 1951, Marquis Childs said in his book, *Farmer Takes a Hand*, that "all was not sweetness and harmony."

The official positions of local and state Farm Bureaus regarding REA and electric co-ops varied widely. This was reflected at the national level in sometimes heated discussions among NRECA board members.

Bernard Doll, Michigan's representative on the NRECA board in the late 1980s and early '90s, took on the challenge of changing the American Farm Bureau's position on REA loans. He played a key role at one juncture in the NRECA-Farm Bureau relationship. Having served on the Michigan Farm Bureau board for several years and knowing many Farm Bureau officials in other states, he was successful in persuading the American Farm Bureau convention in 1986 to adopt a resolution supporting NRECA's position for maintaining the REA lending program when President Ronald Reagan proposed its termination.

"Some of the American Farm Bureau leaders didn't understand how the REA program works and seemed to be influenced by the private utilities," Doll recalls. But, he said, he was very pleased with the action because it was the first American Farm Bureau resolution he had seen that was "in sync" with the co-ops and NRECA.

Looking back over his 12 years of service on the NRECA board, Doll said partisan politics did not enter into board decisions even though most members were known to be active Democrats or Republicans. As a Republican, Doll said he was 100 percent behind the selection of Bob Bergland, former Agriculture Secretary under President Carter, as NRECA's general manager in 1985.

Bill Parsons, who preceded Doll as Michigan's director on the national board, said he admired the way NRECA General Manager Bob Partridge performed his job in a bipartisan manner when the board grappled with rising electric rates and other tough issues in the tumultuous 1970s.

Since NRECA's start in 1942, Michigan has been represented on the NRECA board of directors by 12 different persons. The board has one representative from each of the 46 states that have electric cooperatives. Records show the following NRECA board members from Michigan, starting in 1942 and going through 1996:

Dolph Wolf, Tri -County Electric Cooperative
Otto Grambau, Presque Isle Electric Cooperative
Dr. Christian Jensen, Top O' Michigan Electric Company
Manning Kingsbury, Fruit Belt Electric Co-op
George Allard, Western Michigan Electric Co-op
Carl C. Johnson, O & A Electric Cooperative
Lyle Wilson, Alger Delta Cooperative Electric Association
Harry Hartzell, Cherryland Electric Cooperative
Elwyn Olmstead, Western Michigan Electric Co-op
William Parsons, Top O' Michigan Electric Company
Bernard Doll, Cloverland Electric Cooperative
Martin Thomson, Presque Isle Electric Cooperative

Longest serving were Doll (12 years) and Parsons (10) years. Doll served on the NRECA Government Relations Committee, and later on the Operations Committee which made recommendations on key policy matters to the full board. Thomson, the current board member, is general manager of Presque Isle Electric & Gas Co-op, Onaway.

Bob Partridge succeeded Ellis as CEO of the national association, followed by Bob Bergland, and the present manager, Glenn English, former Congressman from Oklahoma. Each of these leaders has spoken at statewide and regional meetings in Michigan.

## 40 CENTS PER HOUR —
## AND A PENNY FOR SOCIAL SECURITY

Marion Wolkins of Union, MI, wrote to *Michigan Country Lines* magazine in 1985 telling of his experience in 1938 and 1939 working for a contractor, Laird Construction of Three Rivers, building REA lines:

"We dug holes six feet deep with a spud and a spoon shovel. We dragged the poles from the road to the holes by hand and we set them by hand with pike poles...My brothers, Johnny and Lee, and I worked for 40 cents per hour, and one cent of each dollar was taken out for Social Security."

Their parents, Mr. and Mrs. John Wolkins, lived on a farm near Union in southwest Michigan for 25 years before they got electricity. Thanks in part to their sons, they got electric service over REA-financed lines from Fruit Belt Electric Cooperative in 1939.

**Above:** A memorable moment in rural electrification history for Delta County in the U.P. was the ground breaking for power lines to the Isabella area in the summer of 1945. Local people did the honors. (L to R:) Keith Towns, Emma Goodall, Charles Turan, Grandma Landis, Gertie Granchamp, Mrs. Charles Turan, Elmer Lamberg, Wy Nieuwenkamp (manager of Alger Delta Co-op Electric Association) and Hank Landis. **2nd row:** Ceremony at Posen, Mich, on Sept. 22, 1937 marked the first pole set on the Presque Isle Electric Co-op system. Speakers included State Rep. Frank Buza, Michigan State Ag Extension Chief C.V. Ballard, Joseph Donnelly of the Public Service Commission and Philip Fletcher of Alpena Power Company. The line was the first REA-financed line energized in the state, Dec. 23, 1937. **3rd row (L):** Lyle Wilson, staunch supporter of cooperatives from Menominee County and a leader in organizing the Michigan Rural Electric Co-op Association. **3rd row, (R):** Dolph Wolf, first manager of Tri-County Electric Co-op and Michigan's first representative on the National Rural Electric Co-op Association board. **4th row, (L):** Bill Vissers, O & A Electric board member. **4th row, (R):** Marty Thomson, former board chairman, now manager of Presque Isle Co-op and Michigan's representative on the national board.

**Above top and middle, right:** A gala event at Ubly, Mich., on Sept. 16, 1937, saw the first pole of the first mile of line on the Thumb Electric Cooperative system raised with several dignitaries attending. (L to R, standing:) Mr. Raven from REA; Frank Wilson, Thumb board chairman; Alfred Sauer, project attorney; Rev. Miotke; B. Kowski; Harry Grayson, co-op manager; Rev. Ogle and Mr. Shoemaker. **Above, middle:** Electric brooders to keep baby chicks warm were among the first purchases for many farmers in the 1930s and 1940s, usually after water pumps and the essential appliances for the house. **Bottom, right:** The first bill of Presque Isle Electric Co-op for member Frank Woytaszek, Lachine, in March, 1938, was only $2. With a meter reading of 28 kilowatt hours, lighting and a radio were likely his only electric uses—typical of many rural households when they were first connected to co-op lines. *(Provided by son, Lloyd Woytaskek, Alpena.)*

# Five

# MICHIGAN'S CO-OP FAMILY GROWS

In the early 1940s, the electric cooperatives were not much more than dots on the Michigan map. Material shortages had slowed their progress just as they were getting a good start.

The end of World War II signaled a new push — a new era — for rural electrification. The success of REA and the cooperatives, although limited in scope by the war, was known to many men and women now returning from wartime service to their homes in rural areas. Electricity was part of their daily lives everywhere they were stationed in the Army, Navy, or Coast Guard, excepting for battle zones, and they wanted electricity at their homes and farms when the war was over.

One U.S. army information officer wrote to Top O' Michigan cooperative's newsletter editor: "Keep sending your newsletter to the servicemen...one reason is that it plants hopes of better things to come in the hearts of those who will return to their rural homes after the war is won."

A soldier from Top O' Michigan's area wrote to the co-op: "Am a little surprised at the way our co-op has steadily forged ahead in spite of everything. This surely shows what big things are to come when we are all back home and free again."

The cooperative's newsletter, *Between the Lines*, was mailed monthly to hundreds of men in the military and listed their P.O. addresses so that people could write to them.

Thousands of farm families waited through the war before the local co-op could get the materials and the money to extend lines to them. Most of the unserved were in the more thinly-populated areas. They knew what a difference electricity would mean to them and they were becoming impatient to get service.

The late Vernor Smith, longtime manager of Tri-County Electric Cooperative, Portland, said the toughest part of his job was "facing large groups of people who, after the war was over, came to the office to find out why their extension lines could not be built right away. Some of them had been waiting almost 10 years."

President Roosevelt had said in 1944 that from the standpoint of improving the rural standard of living and more efficient farming "one of the most important projects interrupted by the war is the extension of rural electrification."

Congress knew that the need was pressing and appropriated $550 million for REA in 1946 and 1947, hoping to alleviate the logjam of co-op loan applications. But, as REA later described the postwar situation, "electrifying these farms proved to be a rougher job than anyone had suspected." Manpower and materials, such as poles and transformers, were still scarce and REA was short-handed after the wartime cuts.

In Michigan and many other states, construction of power lines didn't get back into full swing until 1947 and 1948. REA reported that more than 78 percent of the nation's farms were receiving electric service by June of 1949.

When the war ended in 1945, co-op crews were small and the job of a lineman was demanding. Edwin "Bud" Englund, who worked for the Alger Delta cooperative starting in 1939 and returned to the co-op after a stint in the U.S. Army Air Corps, said that he and lineman Oiva Makela usually worked 50 to 60 hours a week just to maintain lines and answer trouble calls.

Harry Pauley, former manager of Presque Isle Electric Co-op who started as a lineman in 1943, said he remembers climbing 26 poles one night after supper fixing storm-caused outages. "We had only three linemen then, so we did many kinds of work and put in long hours."

Pauley said the growth of the cooperative after the war was so fast that they couldn't get enough meters, so they decided to connect some places without installing a meter. He said the demands for electricity exceeded the amount they could get from existing facilities in 1946, "so we started up the new diesel plant at Tower before the roof was even on the plant. I think we hooked up 1,300 new members that year."

Pauley also remembers the postwar boom for appliances. "That's when people really started using electricity in the home and farmers started making more widespread use, too." Typical monthly use then was nearing 150 kilowatt hours per month, but some folks rationed their use to the monthly minimum of 30 or 40 kilowatt hours. Some large farms were using over 500 kwh per month.

The first president of Cherryland Electric Cooperative, Eino Lehto, said it seemed that, as soon as the war was over, all the unserved people wanted electric service at once. But, many of these people had to wait for the co-op to get REA's approval and necessary materials.

Consulting engineer Bob Daverman and his brother, Ed, returned from the Navy and resumed work on co-op projects. When contracts were let, construction crews put lines up as fast as materials became available. One helpful development was the use of aluminum for conductor because copper was still scarce.

REA engineers had told pole producers that they would need some 12 million poles during the first three postwar years and two million per year after that. Suppliers were not able to meet the needs in 1946, but with the use of yellow pine from the South and more efficient processing methods, production increased.

In some cases, labor strikes were holding up production and delivery of line materials, particularly metal products such as transformers and meters. The government's restraint orders on industry to curb inflation didn't help either.

One cooperative manager in Michigan told members in 1946 that "we expect to receive some wire ordered a year ago" and that 3,000 poles, 1,000 meters and 800 transformers were on back order. "Please explain to your neighbors why it is taking so long to give them service," the manager wrote.

With more and more members being added to the distribution system, the problem of power supply — an adequate amount of bulk power — stared the cooperatives in the face again. REA officials were alarmed at what they termed "acute power shortages" for many co-ops across the country. The problem was heightened by the increasing use of electricity on farms. According to U.S. Department of Interior records, kilowatt hour use on farms across the nation leaped 160 percent from 1946 to 1950. One study showed a 25 percent increase in 1950 over 1949.

In Michigan, average farm use of electricity for all farms almost doubled in that span — to about 300 kilowatt hours per month.

Several Michigan cooperatives found themselves pinched for power.

Top O' Michigan, serving parts of six counties, requested that members exercise "practical conservation" at peak use times such as the noon hour and early evening because of a "critical shortage of generating capacity." This was in mid-1946 when the co-op relied upon Michigan Public Service Company for its power supply.

Top O' Michigan's Harold Lees said the shortage "caused us to pull switches, forcing several temporary outages," and explained that was a better alternative than allowing Michigan Public Service Company to shut off power for six hours or more to the entire co-op system.

Wayne Nordbeck, longtime board member of Cherryland Electric Cooperative, can remember his father, Veikko, who served on the Cherryland board in the early 1950s, telling him how the power company (Michigan Public Service, which was later sold to Consumers Power) threatened to stop all power sales to Cherryland in the late 1940s.

Michigan co-op leaders were coming to the realization that they needed to unite in solving the power supply problem. They could see it would be more economical to work together to generate power and interconnect their power sources. An integrated system linked by transmission lines would not only be more efficient, but would mean a more dependable supply of power to their members.

Bernard Kline of the Presque Isle co-op board explained the cooperatives' thinking this way: "By 1948, it became apparent that the growing power requirements of our system would soon exceed the capacity of our existing plants as well as the facilities under construction and the capacity available from Alpena Power and Michigan Public Service. Our studies showed long range advantages in generating with larger units and we joined with two neighboring co-ops in seeking an area-wide solution to the power supply problem."

The three cooperatives, stretching 200 miles across the top of the Lower Peninsula, talked to REA about the idea of forming a generating and transmission co-op (G & T), so they wouldn't have to rely on other utilities for their bulk power supply. The boards of Presque Isle, Top O' Michigan and Cherryland cooperatives took formal action in 1948 creating Northern Michigan Electric Cooperative, with three directors from each co-op serving on the board.

Working with Daverman Engineering and Stanley Engineering Company, the newborn G & T cooperative began ambitious plans for a network of transmission lines and a new coal-fired steam generating plant. The site selected for the 19,000-kilowatt plant was near the small town of Advance on the south shore of Lake Charlevoix. The first contracts were awarded in 1950, with the generators installed in October that year. Work was completed in early 1953.

Work also proceeded on some 300 miles of 69,000-volt transmission line and 20 substations. When the system was energized with power from the Advance steam plant, the three co-ops were serving 15,000 members. That number doubled within the next 10 years.

Use of electricity over the three systems nearly tripled in that time span. Not only did the three cooperatives experience growth in farms and rural residences served, but the trend of seasonal recreation homes, lake cottages, hunting cabins and skiing facilities added thousands of "part time" consumers to the lines.

Generation and transmission facilities have to be able to meet peak demands of all of the loads. Power requirements studies, therefore, had to anticipate and include every type of consumer and their pattern of use of electricity.

Usually, the peak load of the entire Northern Michigan system occurred on a cold winter evening, but for Presque Isle Cooperative the biggest demand for electricity was on the eve of the opening of deer hunting season. Nearly half of Presque

Isle members were seasonal, many of whom owned hunting cabins. This seasonal demand had to be met by Northern Michigan's generating capacity.

By December, 1952, the Northern Michigan G & T represented a $7,273,328 investment, including its new coal-fired power plant. All of the capital was borrowed from REA. Its first office was modest and the staff was small. The headquarters of Northern were in the old Boyne City Railroad building. Twelve years later, the growing staff moved into a new building in Boyne City.

Art E. Steinbrecher, manager of an Ohio co-op for 13 years, was hired as general manager. He saw Northern's generation and transmission system grow from $7 million to $20 million in assets when he retired 22 years later.

The federated power cooperative concept proved effective in producing and delivering the power to each of the three distribution co-ops. Northern Michigan's board president, Bernard Kline, in his 1954 annual report, cautioned the member cooperatives that "we cannot rest on our accomplishments...this is a dynamic growing industry and we must plan ahead to assure that facilities will be expanded when necessary to meet the growing power requirements."

Kline stressed that the co-op needed to improve its financial position and reduce power costs through greater efficiency and growth in sales. For the Northern Michigan G & T co-op to be successful, the three distribution co-ops, he said, must focus on "aggressive development of load potential in their service areas" and strive to improve load factor.

Service continuity on the new transmission system was deemed satisfactory despite a problem with vandalism, chiefly rifle fire damaging insulators. Steinbrecher started the practice of periodic line patrol by airplane over the entire system, resulting in prompt replacement of broken insulators, crossarms and other faulty equipment.

The Northern Michigan G & T financial report for 1954 showed a deficit of $241,226. This wasn't entirely unexpected, officials said, because a new coal plant requires more fuel for tests involving frequent startups and coal was the largest expense in generating power.

When the plant went into full-scale operation in 1953, 28 employees were pulling shifts and burning some 2,600 tons of coal per week to generate most of the power that Northern needed to meet the member cooperatives' growing demands. John Clark was employed as plant superintendent and worked for the co-op 30 years.

In a matter of a few years, Northern Michigan came out of the red and, as the three member co-ops grew in consumers and kwh sales, their G & T cooperative showed operating margins exceeding $100,000. In 1972, Northern recorded a margin of $237,678.

Additional investments had been made in the plant to upgrade its generating capacity to 43,000 kilowatts and to install pollution control devices that cut emissions to meet new Michigan environmental standards. By 1973, Northern Michigan had invested $22 million in generation and transmission facilities.

Little did the Northern Michigan board of directors and management know that an upcoming international event and one of their own decisions in 1975 would bring the G & T to the brink of bankruptcy in the early 1980s.

Even before the three northern cooperatives formed Northern Michigan G & T, two cooperatives to the south of them were discussing the merits of federating their power supply. As Earl Murley, manager of O & A Electric Cooperative at Newaygo explained in 1948, it did not make economic sense for O & A and the neighboring Tri-County Electric Cooperative to keep building separate, independent power plants and transmission lines that would, to some extent, be duplicates.

"Each co-op depends upon the other for a source of power because neither has sufficient generating capacity to provide for uninterrupted service in the event of a breakdown of a major piece of equipment (both have diesel plants). Neither has adequate facilities to meet future increased loads, and both are in need of transmission lines and substations to improve the quality of service," said Murley in support of a new federated cooperative.

"If the two co-ops continue to operate independently of each other, their generating stations would require substantial investments in additional capacity...if their plants could be integrated with one another through one transmission system, each plant would require less capacity — and continuity of service, as well as quality, would improve and the total investment would be less."

Not all of the directors on the two co-op boards initially were in favor of giving up direct control of their generating units, which they had worked hard to get only nine or 10 years earlier. But they could see the prospect of savings and improved dependability, so they voted to create a new generation and transmission cooperative.

A third cooperative, Oceana Electric of Hart, also was interested in the G & T co-op proposal because it had no generating facility and no other assured future power supply. Oceana joined hands with O & A and Tri-County in chartering the Wolverine Electric Cooperative in March of 1948 with Carl Johnson, chairman of the O & A board, as president.

After studies by Daverman Engineering and approval of the REA, the transfer of all of the generating facilities of O & A and Tri-County to the new Wolverine co-op was implemented in 1949 and the debts owed on the generating facilities became obligations of Wolverine.

The Wolverine board, comprised of two directors from each of the three member cooperatives, hired a retired Navy officer, Denis L. Ryan, as general manager. Wolverine was now charged with the responsibility of planning and building a transmission system of more than 300 miles and additional generating capacity necessary to meet all of the needs of the three cooperatives.

In creating a generation and transmission cooperative with all of its capital borrowed from REA — usually several million dollars — the REA stipulated that each of the member co-ops forming the G & T must sign an "all requirements" power contract, meaning that each cooperative agreed to purchase all of the power it would need (through the term of the REA loan) from the G & T.

This "all requirements" provision was very significant and put the future of power supply in the hands of the new federated body — the board of six members in the case of Wolverine and the board of nine members at Northern Michigan G & T.

Generating capacity of the Wolverine facilities in five locations — Hersey, Vestaburg, Burnips, Portland and Eaton Rapids — totaled 19,091 kilowatts in 1951 after adding 7,500 kw to meet the growing needs of the three cooperatives.

Kilowatt-hour sales increased 10 percent from 1949 to 1950, but in Wolverine's 1950 annual report the president's message urged stepped-up action to accelerate consumption: "This increase is heartening, but we must not be lulled into a false sense of security. If we are to meet our financial obligations on completion of the construction program now underway, the rate of increase in sales must be nearly doubled during the next three years."

Wolverine's 1950 report showed a margin of only $1,074 for the year from total revenue of $568,854. The co-op employed 25 in full-time positions, most of those at the generating stations, and four others were hired to procure right-of-way. The cooperative operated at a loss in 1952, 1953 and 1954. In 1955, a margin of $8,391 was reported as sales increased and operating costs stabilized. Total kilowatt hour sales climbed from 38 million in 1950 to almost 100 million in 1960.

In 1951, average kilowatt hour use went up 12 percent and the average selling price dropped three percent. The manager's report encouraged more farmstead uses of electricity such as crop dryers, feed grinders, heated stock tanks and fully automated dairy barns. "The more you use, the lower the cost per kilowatt hour," was the watchword of the utility industry.

In 1952, Wolverine management and staff moved into offices in Big Rapids. The staff included Ryan as manager; John Keen, assistant manager; Don King, line superintendent; and Jim Wood, promoted from plant operator to head of generation.

Keen was named general manager in 1954 and served in that position until retiring in 1982. He was an active proponent of power use and public relations programs, and worked closely with Guy VanderJagt on a weekly television program, sponsored by the cooperatives, before VanderJagt was elected to Congress. As a Congressman for 20 years from the western Michigan district, he and Keen met often to discuss REA and rural development issues. A leading Republican in the House of Representatives, VanderJagt was supportive of rural electric cooperatives and was the headline speaker at NRECA's annual meeting in 1980.

Keen became interested in new, non-conventional power generation technology. He convinced the Wolverine board to sign an agreement with Consumers Power to build a wood-burning 25,000-kilowatt plant in Osceola County in 1980. Opponents of the proposal killed the plant. A similar fate met a proposed storage battery generating project, advocated by Wolverine.

In the 1950s, when the Atomic Energy Commission invited proposals for experimental atomic power plants, Keen talked with the AEC and nuclear engineers. Wolverine applied for grant funds in 1957 to build an aqueous homogeneous type of nuclear plant near Hersey.

Knowing that politics was part of the nuclear picture, Keen worked with members of Congress, including several from Michigan, and was optimistic about the prospect of nuclear power. But a test model at Oak Ridge developed problems and the engineers' revised design costs were three times what the AEC had allowed, so the project was dropped.

The cooperative did not get financially involved in a nuclear power plant until the mid-70s when Detroit Edison launched the Fermi II nuclear plant. Both Wolverine and Northern Michigan G & T co-ops bought into Fermi II.

In 1950, the two Michigan power supply co-ops were among the first in the nation. They were "new ducks in the water," but their generating plants initially operated efficiently thanks to people like Jim Wood, who had experience with diesel generation at Tri-County's Portland plant and in the Navy. Another longtime Wolverine employee who knew the diesel generators well was Dick Arnold, who also worked at the Portland facility and later became superintendent of Wolverine's diesel plants.

Wolverine's diesel generating unit at Hersey received national recognition in 1952 as "the most efficient of all REA-financed internal combustion generating units," an award the plant received four times.

The small diesel units would become obsolete and used only as standby generators for peaking a decade or so later. Some, like those at Vestaburg and Burnips, were converted to gas-fired units.

In 1957, Wolverine began providing power to Western Michigan Electric Cooperative when it outgrew its generating capacity. Six years later, Western Michigan joined Wolverine as its fourth member co-op.

As the demand for electric power kept rising, the cooperatives and several municipally-owned electric utilities in the west central region of the state saw significant economic advantage to be gained by interchange agreements. Tie-lines were built in strategic locations and, from 1958 to 1963, Wolverine made interconnections with the municipal systems of Hart, Grand Haven and Lowell, and also with the Northern Michigan Electric Cooperative.

The interchanges worked well and led to the formation of a larger power pool in 1968 when the two G & T co-ops signed new agreements with the Grand Haven and Traverse City municipal systems.

Across the nation, the generating and transmission cooperatives became important factors in the growth of electric co-ops in the 1950s and 1960s. Although the power generated by the co-ops as a percentage of total power sold was less than 25 percent, the availability of capital from REA for co-ops to build their own generating plants was critical because it gave them leverage in dealing with the power companies for wholesale power at acceptable rates.

**Above:** Step up to new lighter weight electric irons was the theme of this Top O' Michigan Co-op promotion in 1952. Co-op manager Harold Lees holds a pre-electric iron which was usually the first thing to get the heave-ho when electricity came to the farm house. **Middle:** Northern Michigan Electric Cooperative general manager Art Steinbrecher (center) looks over plans for additional transmission lines with Top O' Michigan general manager Harold Lees (left) and John Asher. **Bottom (R):** John Keen manager of Wolverine for 32 years.

**Left, top:** Managers of Michigan's electric cooperatives pictured at a meeting Sept. 1, 1946, in Cheboygan. Front row (L to R): Earl Murley, O & A; Harvey Kapphahn, Cloverland Electric; Dolf Wolf, Tri-County; Gust Kleber, Presque Isle; Robert Thompson, Fruit Belt; and Ed Carlson, assistant manager, Ontonagon. Back row: Loyal Churchill, Oceana Electric; Cy Clark, Ontonagon Electric; Wy Nieuwenkamp, Alger Delta Electric; Harry Hall, Cherryland Electric; Harold Lees, Top O' Michigan; Leo Bradley, Western Michigan, and Orvill Hurford, Thumb Electric. **Middle, left:** Michigan electric co-op pioneers honored at 1985 statewide meeting in Lansing included, seated left to right: William Reutter, Presque Isle; Anna Jenson for Dr. Christian Jensen, Top O' Michigan; Ruth Brandmair, Thumb; Bernard Kline, Presque Isle; and Clarence Haslanger, Fruit Belt. Second row: Clayton Bensinger, Thumb; Raymond Berger, Alger Delta; Mary Butchbaker, Fruit Belt. Third row: Lyle Wilson, Alger Delta; Nicholas Thompson for William Thompson, Southeastern; Francis Hund, Thumb; Harold Ries for Dewey Ries, Southeastern; Bob Daverman, engineer; George Butchbaker, Fruit Belt; John Glaza, Thumb, and Williard Haenke, Tri-County. **Bottom, left:** Wayne Nordbeck, Cherryland Electric Co-op board member and former chairman of Wolverine board. **Bottom, center:** Jim Wood, longtime employee of Wolverine. **Bottom, right:** Vernor Smith, former manager of Tri-County Electric.

# THE GOLDEN YEARS

As the cooperatives were growing, they were handicapped by limited resources. Skeleton staffs worked long hours and in modest quarters. For some, the office was an old house or empty rooms in a store on main street. Monthly rent didn't run more than $40 or $50 for most places.

In 1945, bookkeepers were paid 70 to 80 cents per hour and line workers' wages ranged from 80 cents to $1.10 per hour. One woman worked four months for the co-op before drawing wages.

Some regarded the electric co-ops as "shoestring" operations and doubted their future. While the superintendents and linemen worked diligently to give good service, the cooperatives experienced voltage problems and, with thousands of miles of line in open countryside, they were vulnerable to storms.

Sectionalizing lines to confine outages caused by lightning and fallen tree limbs was badly needed, as were other system improvements. Shortages of material and capital restricted construction.

Critics didn't give the little cooperatives much chance for survival.

A *Detroit News* reporter, William Noble, wrote in 1953 that the "chances of Thumb Electric Cooperative paying off its federal debt of $2.5 million are slim." He cited "worn out" diesel generators, lines in need of repair, higher rates than Detroit Edison, and a dim outlook for new REA loans.

The article quoting Noble said that Thumb Electric "has done a fine job in serving electricity to farmers to date, but the time is not far distant when trouble may start to pop." The writer said it was no secret that many farmers would like to hook up with private utilities.

An article from the *Lapeer County Press* alleged that farmers in the Thumb area were complaining about having to wait to get hooked up to the co-op and that engineers "who have looked at the diesel generators at Ubly remark that their capacity is three times what they'll ever be called on to supply."

In the words of the Lapeer editor, Detroit Edison offered to "take over the lines from the co-op before the extravagant power plant was built and supply juice at D.E. rates. But no, the co-op directors went the New Deal (REA) way, and now the customers are paying."

But to the surprise of critics like the Lapeer editor, growth of the Thumb Electric Cooperative far exceeded the capacity of its diesel plant in less than 10 years. And its rates came down to where, today, they are lower than Detroit Edison's.

The Detroit writer was proven to be just as inaccurate about co-op debt repayments. By 1958, repayments from co-ops to the U.S. Treasury on REA loans exceeded one billion dollars!

Over the years — now 55 to 60 years for most electric co-ops — the REA distribution co-op borrowers have a near perfect record in loan repayments. In fact, more than $200 million in principal has been paid ahead of schedule.

By the end of 1994, the Michigan cooperatives had paid REA almost $318 million, including $152,306,244 in interest. In addition, more than $100 million has been repaid on Generation and Transmission loans to REA/RUS.

The REA program has proven to be one of the most fiscally responsible the U.S. Government has ever experienced, a fact not disputed by the most outspoken critics.

While succeeding financially, the cooperatives began to encounter other problems as they grew and took on the daily tasks and challenges of operating an electric utility.

At Southeastern Michigan Electric Cooperative, and at many other co-ops in the early years, service interruptions became an issue with member-consumers. Some were due to tree problems in storms, some due to power generation problems resulting in brownouts, and some due to the fact that the rural systems, as originally built, did not have the equipment to enable lines to stay in service after a lightning strike or contact by a tree limb.

In 1948, problems came to a head at the Southeastern cooperative and, in March, 1949, a slate of candidates ran for the co-op's board of directors committed to selling the cooperative to Consumers Power Company. Members of the co-op resoundingly defeated the pro-sellout candidates who were backed by the power company.

The challenge of making system improvements while still building lines to connect more farms and rural residences was a real test for the cooperatives. They were able to get loan funds to build tie-lines and more substations that made service more reliable. And, in some areas, they had to build heavier, three-phase lines to replace original single-phase lines.

As the cooperatives extended service to most of the unserved farms by the mid-1950s, three developments were taking shape that would impact the co-ops for several years to come:

1. An explosion of new and increased uses of electricity, both in the home and on the farm.

2. Mechanization of farms and other factors that eliminated some farmers, increasing the size of farms in most states, including Michigan.

3. Migration of people from cities to rural areas to escape congestion and rising taxes and to breathe clean air. More small businesses and industries were also locating in the countryside.

Author Marquis Childs, in his 1952 book, *Farmer Takes a Hand*, said the farmer uses more power to do his work than any other industry except transportation. He saw "the age of electric agriculture" coming because, he said, the farmer has only begun to comprehend what electric power can mean in his work. Childs termed electricity as "cheaper, more efficient to use and more pliable than any of the other forms of energy" and correctly predicted widespread major future uses such as electric-powered irrigation systems and crop processing equipment.

To help farmers and other rural households utilize electricity in new ways, efficiently and safely, the two major Michigan electric utilities and the 13 electric cooperatives joined with Michigan State College in East Lansing to form the Michigan Committee on Rural Electrification.

The committee got its start in 1944 with an idea that came out of a rural electrification conference at the college. The committee was formed under the leadership of Professor Dennis E. Wright in the Michigan State Ag Engineering Department. He served as the group's first chairman.

The group met on February 3, 1944, and included Eugene TenBrink, N.J. Butler, J.D. Toner, and E.E. Twing, Jr. from the O & A Electric Cooperative. Others attending were from Detroit Edison, Consumers Power and the Agriculture Engineering Department of Michigan State College. They agreed that the committee should be comprised of six members: two from the college, two from the electric cooperatives and two from the investor-owned utilities in the Michigan Electric Light Association.

It was agreed that no operating policies of any utility or cooperative would be discussed at any educational meeting held by the committee, the college or power supplier. This was to be strictly an educational program, independent of and immune to the issues and disputes among the utility members. It functioned in that manner for some 40 years.

The power suppliers represented by the committee members served 90 percent of Michigan's farmers and the committee's work focused on agriculture's present and potential uses of electricity.

TenBrink and Butler were the co-ops' first representatives on the committee. Others who served in following years were: R. Thompson, Clarence Haslanger and Francis "Butch" Bowsman of Fruit Belt Electric Cooperative; Dolph Wolf and Vernor Smith of Tri-County Electric Cooperative, and H.E. Alverson of Southeastern Michigan Electric Cooperative.

Dues paid by each of the participating utility groups supported specific projects and activities of a designated staff person from the college, including radio and television programs to inform rural people on a wide range of uses of electricity in the home as well as in farming.

Among the early endeavors of the Michigan Committee on Rural Electrification were schools and workshops on heating and ventilation of dairy buildings, welding and other farm shop uses of electricity, auxiliary power systems, and electric heating applications on the farm. Most of the programs were presented by specialists from the Extension Service, Michigan State University agricultural departments and equipment manufacturers.

Demonstration farms were utilized by the committee and Extension personnel, primarily to determine and evaluate operating costs of various kinds of electric equipment. These covered dairy, swine, beef, poultry, potato and fruit farming uses of power. Results were published and circulated through County Extension offices, power suppliers, vocational agriculture teachers and the news media.

The committee, with the help of MSU information and media specialists, was effective in reaching Michigan farmers through radio, television and films. Producing radio and TV programs became a major activity.

The radio shows were produced through the cooperation of WKAR at the university, beginning in 1944, and continued into the 1980s under different names including, *Electricity at Work* and *Energy for Living*. In 1948, WKAR won an award for the program from *Billboard Magazine*, which said it "dramatizes life on the farm and encourages more modern methods of farming and farm living." More than 30 radio stations around the state were airing the show.

The committee also worked with the Ag Engineering Department in initiating the Electrical Technology for Agriculture program at Michigan State, an 18-month training school covering the installation of electric-powered agricultural systems, such as automatic feeding equipment, water systems, controlled environment buildings. The course of study started with the basics of electricity, and covered the wiring of many types of agriculture-related electric systems. The program continues to be popular today at MSU, with 25 students participating in every class.

Displays and short programs on electric farm equipment presented at the University's annual Farmers Week reached thousands of farmers each year. The Committee also assisted at this event with programs for farm wives on home economics, focusing on efficient uses of electricity in the home.

In the 1960s, the Committee's work expanded to include special programs and activities for 4-Hers. The young people in 4-H learned the basics of electricity and how to put electricity to work on the farm and in the home.

Dr. Truman Surbrook, a graduate of MSU, was one of Michigan State University ag engineers who served as the Committee's staff person for several years. He worked closely with the cooperatives and other utility representatives on many farm electrification areas and became one of the nation's leading experts on farmstead "stray voltage" problems.

Surbrook began investigating stray voltage questions in 1978, and his studies have helped farmers and electric utilities achieve a better understanding of this technical and troubling subject. He and his colleagues also have been working with the Michigan Public Service Commission in developing standards and investigative procedures for stray voltage.

Dr. Surbrook and Robert Fick of MSU have published a new booklet summarizing the major work of several universities and agencies on farmstead stray voltage which, says Dr. Surbrook, confirms most of the findings made here in Michigan. The need, he says, is to broaden educational efforts.

Fick works for the Michigan Agriculture Electric Council, which was organized in 1993 to resume some of the work started by the Committee on Rural Electrification, which was dissolved in 1982. Several electric utilities, including the cooperatives, are members of the new Council and provide funding for the staff person, a quarterly newsletter and special projects.

While the Committee and Michigan State University, through its Ag Engineering and Extension Service personnel, contributed significantly to the education and orientation of Michigan farmers on the uses of electricity in agriculture and in the farm home, the cooperatives also implemented their own local initiatives.

Several of the cooperatives hired what they called "power use advisors" or "electrification specialists" in the early 1950s. Some also employed a home economist to work directly with women on home uses of electricity, a much needed service in the '50s and '60s when many home appliances were new to rural families

Cooking schools and demonstrations of the latest in laundry equipment and proper use of home freezers — usually supported by appliance distributors and manufacturers — were popular in rural communities. Often, electric cooperatives sponsored cooking schools in conjunction with the annual membership meeting and women would fill the school auditorium to see the latest in electric ranges, get new recipes and maybe win an electric frying pan or mixer.

Co-op power use advisors were schooled in many facets of electricity and, where they lacked expertise, they could tap several resources including manufacturers, university and Extension personnel, and other utility people trained in specific areas. They would work directly with an individual farmer in planning a water system for livestock, an irrigation system for crops, an electrically-heated hog farrowing setup, a ventilation system for a new poultry house, or dairy parlor with automatic milkers. They also were available to help design electric heating and lighting systems for the home.

"The power use representative had a lot of different responsibilities," said Bud

Englund who worked in that capacity at Alger Delta Cooperative Electric, Gladstone, for five of his 45 years there. "We did newsletters, worked on field demonstrations, membership meetings and appliance promotions, and we did troubleshooting, sometimes bill collecting and helping get service back on in storms," explained Englund, who later served as line superintendent for 25 years.

"In those days, one person was expected to do many things. It was like being the sparkplug, the distributor and gas tank all in one job."

Wil Roisen, who retired from Top O' Michigan Electric in 1958, had five or six different jobs at the co-op but remembers his stint as power use advisor in the 1960s most fondly. "Rates were at their lowest and we were working almost every day on electric heating plans and estimates for members, plus I was doing public relations work and helping 4-H groups," he recalls.

The cooperative, like many others, had an active merchandising program and Roisen was in charge of that for a few years. "We sold a full line of appliances because we needed to build load and the rates were low. Sometimes, we would have truckload sales on electric water heaters or ranges or freezers, and the member would get a real good price."

Mike O'Meara, who was assistant manager and manager of Presque Isle Electric Co-op at Onaway for several years, remembers the "growth years" and how important load-building was in the 1950s and 1960s. "When you invest millions in a utility system and our own generating cooperative, too, it was imperative to promote the use of your product — electricity," O'Meara said.

Phil Cole, former general manager of the Cherryland Co-op and elected to its board of directors after his retirement, agrees with O'Meara in recalling what they and others regard as the "golden years" of rural electric cooperatives — golden because of the progress in bringing electricity to virtually everyone who had been without, and because of the vast improvement in the lives of rural families now using more electricity and at lower rates.

"The changes in our rural living standards in just 10 to 15 years were almost unbelievable," said Walter Cook, longtime Thumb Electric Co-op board member. "It's all because of electricity from our co-op."

Also unbelievable to many co-op members were the declining electric rates in the 1960s. It was the age of the "all-electric" home.

Some of the cooperatives were offering electric heating rates of one and half cents per kilowatt hour and general home service rates of two to two and a half cents per kilowatt hour for consumption over 400 or 500 kwh. Studies clearly showed then that "the more you use, the less the cost per unit" because after a utility covers its "fixed" costs (the lines, generators, transformers and substations), the incremental cost of delivering more power through the same facilities is small.

Later, however, as environmental restrictions pushed generating costs upward in the 1970s and emphasis was put on conservation of energy, ratemaking became a contentious issue with the regulators of electric utilities and with legislators. But in the '60s, declining rates and promotional rates were in vogue and spurred the cooperatives' growth.

Soaring kilowatt hour sales in the 1960s exceeded the expectations of everyone at the electric cooperatives, and engineers and REA officials, too. Sales of electric energy at Top O' Michigan, Thumb, Cherryland and other cooperatives were doubling in seven or eight years.

Would there be adequate power generation for the co-ops to meet the growing demands? Dick Arnold of Wolverine Electric Cooperative said that "we had everything running at all of our generating plants many days — we barely kept up." The interchange agreements with other utilities helped and, as the loads continued to grow, more power pooling agreements were reached.

Not all of the sales surge was due to additional use by the existing membership. Another form of growth was taking place — people moving to the countryside. The availability of modern, affordable electric service was a big factor in the movement.

Starting in the '50s, city folks saw rural areas as not only attractive for weekend "getaways" from the congestion and humdrum of urban life, but also as ideal places to live. Improved rural roads, better schools and lower taxes were also part of the attraction.

The influx of people to rural areas was most pronounced in northern Michigan, where lakes and ski resorts and other amenities appealed to families in search of recreation and relaxation. One of the electric co-ops that would grow beyond anyone's expectations — and today is the largest in Michigan — was Top O' Michigan, located at Boyne City and serving six counties across the top of the Lower Peninsula.

Here's what Top O' Michigan Electric's newsletter had to say on the subject in 1968:

"People are leaving Big City, U.S.A. In past years there was an exodus from rural northern Michigan. The young people like what the large cities had to offer.

"Today, history is repeating itself, only in reverse. Record numbers of Americans are moving to the country. The reasons are more space for recreation, cleaner air, quietness and tranquility. But today, thanks to clean, comfortable, economical electric power, life is easier.

"Rural electric power is everywhere — along streams, lakes, parks — and is used in homes, cottages and businesses of all types. Yes, homes in our rural areas boast all the conveniences of homes in Big City, U.S.A., plus the great outdoors. Our electric cooperative is welcoming these new families with dependable, low-cost electric power...Just like the Big City, only fresher!"

Freedom from the hassle of increasing traffic and crime in the cities could have been added to the list of reasons why people were moving out of the cities. The electric cooperatives joined with the U.S. Department of Agriculture, REA and others in promoting rural areas as a better place to live and to locate a business, adding that it would relieve the urban problems that were becoming a serious national concern in the 1960s.

Rural area development committees were formed in many states with representation from the electric cooperatives, REA, Farmers Home Administration, and other agencies that worked with rural people and local governments to improve infrastructure in rural areas. The program also was keyed to foster economic development and help bring more jobs to rural areas.

The degree of success varied from place to place. The cooperatives' efforts helped strengthen many communities, but in many instances the co-op didn't get to serve the new industry or business that moved to the area. The municipal utility or Consumers Power served most new industries. "We still realized some benefits, though, because more jobs usually meant new residences on our lines," said former Cherryland Electric Co-op manager, Phil Cole.

However, an increasingly troublesome issue for the electric co-ops was the right to serve the new rural residences and businesses — and to keep them as customers when another utility offered to connect them. There were no rules and no state law to prevent switching and customer pirating; consequently, there was open warfare between utilities in parts of rural Michigan.

"The cooperatives lost hundreds of customers to Consumers Power Company in the early 1960s," according to Bob Badner, REA Field Representative in Michigan for 36 years. "I personally saw a co-op truck pull up and disconnect a member (of the co-op), while a Consumers Power crew waited in their truck to connect the house to their line." This scene was repeated in many co-op areas.

There are many places yet today where two sets of power lines go down the same road, although rules adopted by the Public Service Commission in 1980 have stifled further duplication of power facilities. In at least one area near Traverse City, three utilities (the Cherryland co-op, the Traverse City municipal system and Consumers Power) have power lines crisscrossing,

Badner said he can still see the stacks of work orders on co-op managers' desks for disconnects, most of which were the result of Consumers Power Company's aggressiveness in urging people to switch and get a better electric rate. He said the company representatives went door to door in some areas, persuading co-op customers to switch from the co-op to Consumers Power.

Three cooperatives seemed to be the main targets of the company's pirating actions: Cherryland, O & A and Southeastern. Experiencing what some termed "competitive problems" in the 1960s, the Southeastern Michigan co-op was considering a new wholesale power supply arrangement with Detroit Edison, advocated by REA but opposed by Consumers Power, then the wholesale supplier.

REA contended the proposal with Detroit Edison, although requiring a new substation and transmission lines, would mean substantial savings to the co-op and possibly a rate reduction. In 1969, the dispute came to a head when the co-op manager was discharged and the entire board of directors resigned. REA sent personnel to Southeastern to manage the cooperative temporarily and, in a matter of months, a new manager was hired and a new board elected. Two of the new board members were Clyde Knisel and Roger Wolf.

Knisel said the co-op had service problems, "but I didn't think our rates were out of line." Wolf remembers frequent board meetings that went past midnight as the new board, with a helping hand from REA, worked out a new course for the cooperative, including the new power supply arrangement and service improvements. Both Knisel and Wolf credit Richard Stutesman, chairman of the new board, for his hard work and leadership in getting the cooperative back on a positive track. "He was a true believer in cooperatives," said Knisel. Stutesman served as board chairman for several years.

Wolf, who continued to serve on the co-op board until its merger with Fruit Belt, adds this observation: "Today, our cooperative is tops in quality of service, and people on Consumers Power lines now are wanting to get service from the co-op."

REA's concern about the fate of Southeastern Michigan and other electric cooperatives was understandable because the loss of customers posed a security risk to the government in terms of a cooperative's ability to repay REA loans. "We were very concerned about the situation in Michigan in the 1960s," said Badner. "Some of the co-ops would have faced a financial dilemma the way things were going – and, fortunately the Michigan Public Service Commission took action to stop the pirating of co-op customers."

The action of the Public Service Commission came as a result of a formal request initiated by Cherryland Electric Cooperative for the Commission to assert its jurisdiction over the electric cooperatives, as provided in state law but not previously exercised. Cherryland's attorney, Harry Running, advised the co-op's board of directors and the other co-ops in the state that going under the Commission's protective wing was the only way to survive.

Not all of the cooperatives agreed. They had been self-regulated by their boards, with oversight by REA, for almost 30 years and were apprehensive of state government intrusion. But, they agreed that if the Commission would assert its regulatory power over the territorial fights and stop the predatory practices that were continuing to plague the cooperatives, it would be worthwhile.

The Public Service Commission's position was that regulation of the cooperatives would be "all or none" and, in December of 1965, all 13 of the distribution co-ops and the two wholesale G & T co-ops became subject to Commission regulation.

The Commission quickly issued "cease and desist" orders to the utilities, putting a damper on the predatory actions of Consumers Power.

Under the leadership of Kenneth Croy, head of electric engineering at the Commission, rules were developed and implemented to settle disputes in areas where two or more power suppliers offered service to new single-phase loads, usually residential customers. These rules proved effective for the most part and brought a new, more peaceful climate to utility relations in rural areas.

Fights over new, larger three-phase loads, like a small industry locating in a rural area, continued and, again with Croy's initiative and persistence, the cooperatives and investor-owned utilities came to agreement in 1980 on a set of rules governing three-phase service extensions in rural areas.

"The Commission's rules have worked well over the years," in the opinion of John Abramson, head of the Public Service Commission's Electric Division. Utility officials, including managers of the cooperatives, generally agree and give credit to Croy and to James Padgett, then chief electrical engineer at the Commission, for effectively administering the rules.

While the 1965 action of the Public Service Commission was a step forward in settling differences between the cooperatives and Consumers Power Company, another line of fire was getting noisier and into the headlines of news media in Michigan. It centered on the generation and transmission (G & T) cooperatives, a development that private utilities didn't like 20 years prior and liked even less in the 1960s.

Harsh criticism was voiced by the vice president of Consumers Power, Birum G. Campbell, in June, 1966, when he testified before a U.S. House of Representatives Committee on a bill to create a Federal Electric Bank that would expand financing for electric co-op power projects. He said additional financing would not be needed "if they would discontinue their uneconomical and unnecessary expansion of generation and transmission facilities and discontinue making interconnections with municipalities for the purpose of selling electric energy at wholesale."

Campbell charged that the generation and transmission co-ops were making "cut-rate raids" on the municipal systems in competition with Consumers Power. He referred to Wolverine Electric Cooperative's agreement with the city of Lowell, alleging that Lowell was paying Wolverine a lesser rate than the Wolverine member co-ops paid for wholesale power.

The Consumers Power official contended that, over the past 15 years, seven Michigan co-ops (the members of Wolverine and Northern Michigan) paid $5,878,000 more for power generated by the two G & T cooperatives than they would have had they bought the power from his company. He said the co-ops paid 14.3 mills per kilowatt hour, as compared with an average of 11.8 mills paid by the wholesale customers of Consumers Power.

John Keen, general manager of Wolverine Electric Cooperative, refuted the charges of Campbell. He said that Consumers didn't want the cooperatives and municipal utilities joining together in power pools because it would give the co-ops a stronger position in bargaining with Consumers for wholesale power. And, he said, the comparisons Campbell used did not give the full picture of power costs. Keen also reminded critics of the reasons generation and transmission co-ops were created in the first place: Consumers Power and other utilities couldn't or wouldn't supply the growing needs of the rural electric cooperatives in the 1940s and 1950s. He said the Rural Electrification Act of 1936 clearly provided authority for generation and transmission loans.

The proposed Federal Electric Bank was not approved by Congress, but G & T cooperatives in several states did receive loans to build large generating plants with the goal of bringing down the cost of generating power. They called it "giant power" and it was successfully developed in Wisconsin, Nebraska, the Dakotas and some southern states, but not in Michigan.

There were two major reasons that "giant power" plants were not feasible for Michigan co-ops:

1) The 13 cooperatives were scattered in the state with great distances between several of them that would require big investments in transmission lines for the number of customers. The loads of Michigan co-ops in total would not justify a giant-size plant.

2) Lakes Michigan and Huron make it impossible to have major transmission lines that would enable power to be transported from a Michigan plant to co-ops in other states, as is the case in the Dakotas and Minnesota — and Michigan has no federal power system to help carry the power long distances.

Another ever-present factor was the hard-nosed determination of the two large investor-owned utilities in the state to control power generation and the wholesale power market to the cooperatives.

The Consumers Power executive, Birum Campbell, took aim at the generation and transmission cooperatives again in a November 1966 speech at Muskegon. There, he complained about "unfair tax advantages to these federally subsidized business enterprises."

He said the "millions of people who use federal power are not paying in their electric bills the same taxes that other Americans pay." However, he neglected to say that the Michigan cooperatives did not purchase any federal power. They never have because there is no federal power to buy in Michigan.

"If government power entities like the G & T co-ops want to expand and compete for business in the rural and non-rural areas, let them borrow money in the marketplace like anybody else," said Campbell. Perhaps he had the co-ops confused with the municipal systems. The cooperatives are not government entities; the municipals are.

Ironically, eight years later, Consumers Power and other investor-owned utilities lobbied Congress for federal assistance to their companies. In 1974 and 1975, Consumers Power was in dire financial straits because of rising fuel costs and escalating construction costs for power plants. They appealed to Congress for a federal bailout in the form of direct loans, loan guarantees and special tax credits.

Michigan Public Service Commission Chairman William Rosenburg went to bat for the utilities in 1974, recommending guaranteed federal loans for private utilities modeled after the program adopted in 1974 for generation and transmission loans for cooperatives. He insisted that "the investor-owned electric utility industry is incapable of attracting adequate capital at reasonable cost to meet the requirements of its construction programs" and that "the stark reality is that the industry has no reasonable opportunity to meet the electric power demands of this country in the long term."

The proposals for government loans and/or guarantees to the private utilities were rejected, and Rosenburg's predictions of doom and gloom did not materialize.

The investor-owned utilities waged a national advertising campaign to depict the electric cooperatives as subsidized, socialistic organizations receiving preferential tax breaks, and inferred that the cooperatives do not pay taxes. The IOU propaganda was hot and heavy in the 1960s, taking the form of magazine ads, speeches, news releases, editorials in newspapers, and television spots — almost every medium but skywriting.

As Clyde Ellis of NRECA and other co-op leaders said, it was a ploy to harass and intimidate the cooperatives and turn public officials against the REA electrification program. Author Marquis Childs commented: "Propaganda has never ceased to try to make rural electrification (by co-ops) sound like something dangerous and radical...Actually, it can be shown that virtually no federal subsidy has gone into this pay-as-you-go system."

Childs continued: "With or without government subsidy, the farmer had not been frightened by this talk...When the lights are turned on for the first time in the farm kitchen and in the cow barn, that is something tangible and real, an achievement which the farmer believes is his own and which no politician can take away from him."

The IOU's efforts may have influenced public opinion to some extent, but they did not change the facts and did not seriously harm the cooperatives. The cooperatives, through NRECA and in their local newsletters and local media, told their story and told it straightforwardly.

NRECA initiated its first-ever national advertising campaign in the mid-1960s to help the cooperatives' get their story to the general public and community leaders. It was called "Tell the Nation the Truth" (TNT).

Supported by most every electric cooperative in the nation, TNT used major newspapers, magazines and national radio to carry the story of how consumer-owned cooperative utilities not only brought electricity to the less-populous rural areas in 45 states, but have made enormous contributions to the economy, aiding development in the thousands of communities where they serve. The advertisements and radio scripts were also provided to each cooperative which placed them in local newspapers and on local radio stations.

The ads explained that electric cooperatives pay all state and local taxes other utilities pay, including real estate, personal property, unemployment, social security and sales taxes. The co-ops are not subject to paying federal income taxes unless they receive more than 15 percent of their revenue from non-members. This provision in long-standing federal law recognizes that cooperatives are not in business for corporate or individual profits but are member-owned to provide a service at cost.

As the member-owners, the cooperative's customers share the co-op's margins each year. The margins (the amount of revenue above expenses) are allocated in "capital credits" to each member who did business with the co-op during the past year. They do not belong to the cooperative.

Another important message of the TNT program was that cooperatives are not socialistic, but rather a part of the free enterprise system. Co-ops are among the most democratic organizations in America. Each is governed by an independent board of directors elected by and from the cooperative's membership. Each member-owner has one vote in election of directors and major matters such as bylaw amendments.

Several "Tell the Nation the Truth" ads focused on ways in which electric cooperatives were making a difference in their communities: creating jobs that boost the local economy, helping 4-H and Future Farmers of America groups, expanding students' civic knowledge by sponsoring youth tours of Washington, D.C., and working with community leaders to establish rural water supply systems.

The Michigan cooperatives have made it possible for more than 150 high school students to see the historical sites in Washington and watch Congress in session through the annual Youth Tour. Another 500 or more students have participated in the cooperatives' Teen Days event, where they learn how cooperatives work and the opportunities for young people in co-ops today.

One of the more intriguing aspects of electric cooperatives is how they are governed. While each cooperative has a board of directors elected at annual membership meetings, the meetings also give members the opportunity to raise questions and voice any concerns. If they are dissatisfied with the management or board policies, they have the opportunity to elect new board members and to propose changes.

As with county commissions and other local governing bodies, contested elections are not uncommon in the co-ops. As one board member described it, "It is democracy in action at the grass roots level."

The governance of rural electric cooperatives has operated under the same democratic principles since the first boards of directors were elected by the charter members in the 1930s. There have been no changes in the substance of the cooperative principles as they are reflected in each co-op's bylaws. Only the member-owners have the right to amend the bylaws.

Taxation of electric cooperatives' personal property in Michigan was an issue for the first several years. It was the subject of considerable discussion in board meetings of every cooperative in the state in the 1930s because their rural lines serving only a few customers were being taxed the same as the lines of urban utilities. The cooperatives pointed out that they had much lower revenue per dollar of investment in lines and related facilities to serve customers in rural areas, than did the utilities serving cities and towns.

They worked with the State Tax Commission to get changes that would reflect the value of the cooperatives' lines and facilities relative to their use and revenue produced. As a result, a range of "economic factors" was applied based on residential kilowatt-hour sales per mile of line, making the tax more equitable.

In 1996, personal property taxes paid by the state's electric cooperatives totaled $8,025,626. Over the course of more than 50 years, the cooperatives have paid well over $150 million in personal property and real estate taxes to the state.

When the energy crisis hit in 1973, the "war of words" and philosophical differences between the electric cooperatives and investor-owned utilities subsided. In fact, closer working relationships developed and they found themselves allies on several legislative fronts in the '70s and '80s.

While the 1950s and 1960s presented new hurdles for the cooperatives, they found they could endure challenges and move ahead by working together. Their growth was far beyond expectations. They had seen what some would call their "golden years" — but they had no idea of the storms they would face in the next decade.

**Above:** "Willie Wiredhand"—symbol of rural electric cooperatives nationally—was an attraction at co-op annual meetings in the 1950s and '60s when electricity became the number one household energy for most rural families.

**Left:** Two Top O' Michigan retirees, Eric Rasch (L) and Will Roisen, recall how the co-op grew rapidly in the 1960s, considered by many as the "golden years" for electric cooperatives.

**Bottom, right:** Bringing electric service to lake homes and hunting cabins sometimes meant running cable underwater, as seen in this Western Michigan Co-op location.
**Bottom, left:** For Cloverland Electric, extending service to islands — 38 of them — was a task started in the 1950s. Co-ops electrified some of the most remote rural areas in Michigan.

**Top:** Drawing for prizes has been a highlight of electric co-op annual membership meetings since the 1940s. In this 1963 photo, members of Western Michigan Electric come forward to claim their prizes.

**Middle:** Roger Wolf (left) and Clyde Knisel from the Southeastern Michigan Co-op board of directors.

**Bottom, left:** Bob Badner, engineer and field representative of the Rural Electrification Administration in Michigan for 36 years.

**Bottom, right:** Ken Croy, former chief of electric operations of the Michigan Public Service Commission, received the MECA Special Recognition Award for his leadership in devising rules that govern electric utilities' line extensions in rural areas.

**Top:** Trading old for new light bulbs was a service that many cooperatives provided for members. Here, Thumb Electric employees Norma Geboski and Blanche Rumptz give Keith Holdship a new supply. Photo from early 1950s.

**Below:** Michigan Committee of Rural Electrification, a joint educational program with Michigan State University, Detroit Edison, and Consumers Power, included representatives of electric cooperatives Clarence Haslanger of Fruit Belt Electric Co-op (L), Vernor Smith of Tri-County Electric (3rd from left) and Francis Bowsman of Fruit Belt Electric (R). Dr. Truman Surbrook of MSU, who worked with the committee for more than 20 years, is next to Smith (center). Bill Bickert and Bob Maddox of MSU are next to Bowsman.

Meeting with Michigan's U.S. Congressional Delegation in Washington, D.C. has been an important function for officials of electric cooperatives over the years. In this 1959 photo, Michigan co-op leaders have breakfast with Congressman O'Hara and Senators Phil Hart and Robert Griffin, seated at table in back. The co-op people were in the capital for the annual business meeting of the National Rural Electric Cooperative Association.

# Seven

# TURNING POINTS

By 1970, the electric cooperatives in Michigan were providing electric service to more than 100,000 member families and businesses in 55 counties. They were mature in many respects — capably staffed, with more dependable service thanks to "heavying up" of lines, interties with other utilities and improved maintenance. Their rates were declining as the use of electricity kept increasing.

Electric service was being made available to virtually everyone who was unserved. With electricity available in most rural areas, modern recreation facilities began springing up in many Michigan co-op areas. Ski lifts, golf courses, parks, campgrounds with electricity, conference centers and resorts joined co-op member lists.

These new electric customers were just as rural as a farm and cost as much or more to serve as a farm. Many were seasonal and not significant revenue producers for the cooperatives, but they attracted attention and prompted an action that nearly destroyed the REA program.

On December 29, 1972, President Richard Nixon announced through his Secretary of Agriculture, Earl Butz, that the REA direct loan program was terminated. The U.S.D.A. news release said that no more loans would be made under the Rural Electrification Act. Rural electric leaders remember that as "Black Friday" — the day the future of electric cooperatives nationwide was under a big dark cloud. They were stunned.

Stopping all REA loans, including those pending at the agency, would not only hurt the financially weak cooperatives serving the most thinly populated areas, such as the Upper Peninsula of Michigan, but also the co-ops in the growth areas that needed substantial amounts of capital to build more service extensions and other power facilities.

One of the growing cooperatives caught under this black cloud was Top O' Michigan, headquartered at Boyne City. The area was booming with winter sports, new lake cottages, country homes, and new businesses. At the time of the President's order, Top O' Michigan had an application pending at REA for a loan totaling $1.5 million. The co-op had 2,000 new applications for service in 1972, and anticipated as many or more in 1973 — all adding up to a construction program requiring a large REA loan. It had no alternative source for large long-term loans.

In defending his action, Nixon told newsmen that 80 percent of REA loans were going for service to "country clubs and dilettantes." That was a gross distortion, as REA or any electric co-op could easily verify.

Members of Congress were outraged at Nixon's action, one of several he announced in impounding some $8.7 billion of Congressionally approved appropriations. Agriculture Appropriations Committee Chairman Jamie Whitten of Mississippi and Rep. George Mahon of Texas accused Nixon of violating the Constitution by taking away the approved funds of fully authorized federal programs.

Top O' Michigan General Manager Roger Westenbroek met in Washington in early January 1973 with REA officials and others in the Department of Agriculture to see if there was any chance of having the co-op's loan approved and processed.

When he returned, he said the loan would not be made under the REA program and that "we still have no assurance when we will get long-term funds." He was informed by REA that the Nixon Administration was planning to make rural electrification loans under the Rural Development Act of 1972, which would mean a big increase in the interest rate to co-ops.

Meanwhile, Top O' Michigan and many other electric cooperatives had difficult decisions to make. Could they proceed with their planned construction programs or not? Where would the money come from? At what cost?

The Top O' Michigan board of directors discussed their options and decided to borrow short-term funds from the newly formed National Rural Utilities Cooperative Finance Corporation (CFC) and proceed with a drastically reduced construction program, building lines only to those applicants who were in critical need of service.

The CFC funds came at a much higher interest rate and could not be borrowed long term because the federal government held the mortgage on all of the cooperative's facilities as required in all REA loans. Westenbroek told reporters that, if the co-op had to pay market rates of interest for all future capital, there would be increases in electric rates of 10 to 20 percent over the next 10 years.

Top O' Michigan laid off 25 of their 85 employees temporarily. Another 55 people working for independent line contractors were out of jobs, too. Similar actions were taking place in many other rural electric co-ops around the country, causing deep concern on the part of local and national co-op leaders.

The radical move by President Nixon to terminate the REA direct loan program had one positive aspect: It was a call to action for the cooperatives nationwide! Hundreds of electric co-op board members converged on Washington a few weeks after Nixon's announcement and talked with their U.S. Representatives and Senators about their financing problem and possible solutions.

Annual appropriations for REA loans had become controversial in the late 1960s as pressure mounted to contain the federal budget. That had been recognized by rural electric leaders, along with the fact that the funding level wasn't keeping up with the cooperatives' growth. They discussed the concept of starting their own bank to supplement the REA funds. Resolutions were passed at NRECA regional meetings in 1966 to expedite a study and find the best options.

After failing to get legislation through Congress to create a Federal Bank for Rural Electric Systems, a special Long Range Study Committee on financing was appointed in 1967. Harlan Ruback, then manager of Top O' Michigan Electric Cooperative, was one of the 26 committee members.

After several open-forum hearings across the country and long deliberation, the committee recommended a lending institution formed by seed capital from the electric cooperatives — enough seed dollars to attract capital from Wall Street. The NRECA membership approved the recommendation and, in April 1969, the cooperatives' new financing institution, the National Rural Utilities Cooperative Finance Corporation (CFC) was chartered.

By September 1, 1969, a total of 512 electric cooperatives including several co-ops from Michigan, had paid the membership fee. CFC's first concurrent loans were made in February 1971 after successfully establishing its position on Wall

Street for bond issues. With nearly 900 member systems in 1996, CFC has experienced phenomenal growth and is the largest financing institution of its type in the U.S.

CFC was not intended to meet the total capital needs of electric co-ops. Its role was to supplement REA loans. That was strongly underscored when CFC was created. A viable REA lending program was still considered a must.

NRECA and key legislators worked tirelessly in early 1973 to draft legislation to restore the REA lending program in an acceptable form. They found Congressional support for a new REA "Revolving Fund" in the U.S. Treasury that would significantly reduce annual appropriations. The Revolving Fund was structured to receive REA loan repayments and re-loan the money to co-ops. It was agreed that most of the Revolving Fund loans would be at five percent interest and would require a concurrent loan from a private lender, like CFC, of up to 30 percent of the total amount requested.

For most Michigan cooperatives, this would mean higher interest costs on new loans, from the long-standing two percent to six percent or higher, depending upon the private market rates. Exceptions were made for "hardship" cases. At that time, the Ontonagon County Electric Co-op was one of the few nationwide that qualified for two percent loans because of its low density and financial handicaps.

Another very significant feature of the legislation gave REA the authority to guarantee loans made by other lenders, giving G & T cooperatives a way to finance large power projects.

Some 2,500 persons from electric cooperatives across the country came to Washington in May of 1973, to push for passage of the legislation. It was overwhelmingly approved by the House and Senate and, on May 11, 1973, President Nixon signed the bill into law.

It was a new day, a new era for electric cooperatives. They had solved the financing problem and were continuing to grow. Many cooperatives had reduced electric rates as power sales increased sharply in the 1960s and early '70s, but higher costs of capital and power supply would soon change the picture dramatically.

While the cooperatives' future was bright in some respects, that "Black Friday" in December 1972 was an omen for the cooperatives, foretelling a decade of dilemmas.

By 1972, the movement of environmentalism was well underway. The new U.S. Environmental Protection Agency (EPA) was implementing a series of new federal laws to protect the environment, and with each law came a myriad of rules. To comply with the rules, companies had to invest large amounts of money. Laws and regulations came at a dizzying pace from Congress and from federal and state environmental bodies, adding new standards and many restrictions to the operations and planning of power projects by electric utilities, including the cooperatives.

For electric utilities, the Clean Air Act of 1970 carried a big wallop in terms of dollars spent to buy and install pollution control equipment at generating plants. At Northern Michigan Electric Cooperative's coal-fired plant, the cost of adding emission controls and scrubbers totaled over $10 million. The new requirements equated to millions of dollars, and began to push rates upward.

If the environmental costs weren't enough to cause serious concern of utility management, a major and traumatic development in 1973 drastically clouded the future of all electric utilities in the United States: The Arab oil embargo hit like lightning in October 1973. Fuel prices shot up immediately and an oil shortage that had been nagging the United States now became a crisis. In 1972, the United States relied on imported oil, mostly from the Middle East, for almost one-third of its total supply. U.S. refineries were running at over 90 percent of capacity and new refineries were not being built.

In 1973, the growing U.S. appetite for energy far exceeded U. S. production capacity, now strapped by a barrage of environmental and social restrictions. Exploitation of U.S. coal and oil deposits was limited due to increasing costs and environmental snags, yet the use of electric power and other forms of energy continued to increase. Price controls on natural gas discouraged drilling new gas wells.

As one analysis put it: "Years of sheer neglect in planning, a failure to consider the problem of environmental pollution caused by energy production and complex international situations have all helped to create the U.S. energy crisis. Added to this is the long-held hope we have harbored that nuclear energy would quickly solve all our energy needs, which has given us a false sense of security."

Noting the expanding web of environmental restrictions on the major forms of energy production, the report said: "In a sense, what we really have today is just as much of an 'environmental and economic' crisis as an 'energy crisis'."

But the crisis was real — "the greatest issue facing the American people during the next decade," said U.S. Interior Secretary Rogers Morton. Few would disagree. President Nixon said the time had come to meet "not only the present crisis but also the long range challenge that we face." He warned that an ongoing energy shortage could jeopardize the production output of the nation's farms and factories, hamstring the U.S. transportation system and, thus, cause massive unemployment.

When Arab oil shipments to the U.S. stopped in October 1973, the impact upon the electric cooperatives of Michigan was dramatic and cause for grave concern, not only in regard to the escalating costs of oil but also the availability of adequate supplies to fuel the generators that many Michigan co-ops depended upon.

At Northern Michigan Electric Cooperative, the power supplier for three fast-growing cooperatives, the total cost of generating power in 1973 jumped 13 percent, due primarily to a doubling in the cost of fuel oil the latter part of the year. General Manager Art Steinbrecher announced that the "sharp increases in production costs together with lower than expected energy sales" put the co-op in a deficit for the year.

Steinbrecher warned in November 1973 that there might be occasional "brownouts" (reductions in voltage) in the co-op service areas that winter because of the uncertainty of oil supplies and of power that Northern normally bought from other utilities. "We are at our production limit and our outside sources are at their limits, too," he said. "I see brownouts as a very real possibility this winter."

Steinbrecher and the managers of the distribution cooperatives urged member-consumers to limit their use of electricity wherever they could, especially during peak periods in the morning and early evening. Fortunately, conservation measures and careful coordination of generating operations that winter enabled Northern Michigan to meet the demands without imposing "brownouts."

At Wolverine Electric Cooperative, power supplier to four co-ops in west central Michigan, General Manager John Keen reported fuel shortages and rising prices of construction materials were taking a toll on the generation and transmission system. In his report on 1974 operations, Keen said the price of fuel oil rose 300 percent and the cost of poles and conductor doubled.

He said natural gas was difficult to obtain and, likewise, "it was even difficult to find enough gasoline to keep our fleet of vehicles in operation." On a more optimistic note, Keen said the co-op added a second interconnection point with Consumers Power which strengthened reliability and made possible the purchase of power from Detroit Edison.

The Wolverine transmission system was being expanded with the addition of 150 miles of 69 KV line and 19 substations, allowing more interconnections with Northern Michigan and the power pool. Northern and Wolverine were now coordinating their long range power requirement studies and looking at various options for future power supply. Even though electric rates were starting an upward turn, kilowatt hour sales by the cooperatives were still increasing, partly due to continued growth of rural residences in the countryside. Decisions needed to be made soon as to how they could meet their future power supply needs most economically.

Knowing the extremely high level of oil prices and the environmental problems of coal for power generation, the management and boards of directors of the two G & T cooperatives began to consider the nuclear option. The prospect of low-priced nuclear energy was bright and REA wanted the co-ops to look closely at the nuclear alternative.

By 1975, 56 nuclear power plants in the United States were producing almost 10 percent of the nation's electricity — and, on the average, produced the electricity for 40 percent less cost than coal-fired plants and 65 percent less than oil-fired plants, according to the chairman of the Atomic Industrial Forum. But attacks upon nuclear power were being launched by environmental and public safety groups, resulting in construction delays as more safety devices and re-engineering were needed. Still, a national public opinion survey in 1975 showed a surprisingly large majority of Americans (63 percent) favored the building of more nuclear power plants, while 19 percent were opposed and 18 percent were uncertain.

In 1976, Detroit Edison announced its plan to build a 300-megawatt nuclear power plant near Monroe. Named Enrico Fermi II, the plant's total cost was pegged at $950 million in the original proposal. The G & T cooperatives — Northern Michigan and Wolverine — had engaged the firm of Southern Engineering to conduct comprehensive studies of the alternatives for future power. Backed by REA engineers, Southern strongly recommended that the co-ops purchase a portion of Edison's Fermi II.

REA Administrator David Hamil came to Michigan to discuss the co-ops' participation in the nuclear venture with the boards of directors of Northern and Wolverine. Convinced that the nuclear option would provide the cheapest power, Hamil and his staff were persuasive in talks with the boards and offered to guarantee a sizeable Federal Financing Bank (FFB) loan to the cooperatives for buying a piece of Fermi II.

Engineers Al Hodge and Bob Daverman of Daverman & Associates conducted power requirements studies and reviewed the projected costs of the plant. Based on the cooperatives' load growth patterns over past years, they agreed with Southern's conclusions. The cooperatives took action in early 1977 to purchase 20 percent ownership in the plant for approximately $220 million.

Almost immediately construction costs of Fermi II started rising. Delays were incurred. New regulations for safety were imposed. By 1978, the total cost shot up to $1 billion and, in another two years, it doubled to $2 billion. This meant that the investment of the two co-ops for their share more than doubled and the amount of REA-guaranteed loan funds increased accordingly.

There were more delays and added requirements that pushed the Fermi II costs even higher. To make matters worse, inflation was rampant and load growth of electric utilities, including the cooperatives, was slowing down. The inflationary trend not only drove prices of materials up, but interest rates as well, including the FFB lending rate to the G & T co-ops. It all added up to a debt of more than $700 million for the two cooperatives in the Fermi plant, and their share of the plant's output was reduced from 20 percent to less than ten percent based upon an agreement reached with Detroit Edison in 1983 to cap the cooperatives' investment. Later agreements would be made that removed the cooperatives' ownership entirely and reduced their REA/FFB debt.

By 1980, however, it was apparent that the co-ops' involvement in the Fermi II nuclear project presented a problem of unprecedented dimensions to the two power supply co-ops and their seven member co-ops. How did the cooperatives get themselves in such a bind?

There were skeptics and some who opposed the Fermi II nuclear venture back in 1976 and 1977. One of the skeptics was Roger Westenbroek, who was general manager of Top O' Michigan Electric, largest of the seven member co-ops. "I was afraid we were going into it without having all of the questions answered, and many of the assumptions were arguable," said Westenbroek, an electrical engineer who worked for co-op and municipal utilities for over 40 years. "Our load growth patterns were changing in some ways, the economy didn't look good and there were some questionable points regarding nuclear power that were downplayed."

Phil Cole, general manager of Cherryland Electric Cooperative, said he shared some of those questions, but the "politics" of the situation at that time resulted in a decision to go along with REA's recommendations.

The crisis created by the commitment of Northern Michigan and Wolverine in Fermi II put new pressure upon the two G & T co-ops to merge. There were many discussions in the early 1970s, but the boards concluded that there would be no significant benefits. It was a different story in 1981 when a special joint committee was formed to study and make recommendations.

REA had insisted on the study and, as Bob Badner, longtime REA field representative in Michigan, put it, "REA was strongly in favor of the two merging because of substantial savings to be realized." The two G & T co-ops were among the smallest in the nation and they both faced the financial dilemma of Fermi II's debt.

With the guiding hand of Barrie Lightfoot, a board member from Cherryland who was engaged to coordinate the merger study, and with the support of most board members from Northern Michigan and Wolverine, the two cooperatives took formal action in December, 1982, to merge and the new Wolverine Power Supply Cooperative was born.

The assistant manager of Northern Michigan, Ray Towne, served as interim manager, and most of the former Northern Michigan and Wolverine employees went to work for the "new" Wolverine, with headquarters in Boyne City. Plans were made for the co-op to move to Cadillac, a more central location for the seven member co-ops. In 1985, Wolverine moved into a new office building and dispatch center five miles east of Cadillac. John Keen, manager of the "old" Wolverine, retired just prior to the merger, and Clyde Johnson, manager of Northern Michigan, was not rehired when the new co-op was created. That was part of the merger agreement.

Ray Cristell, manager of a municipal power agency, was selected as general manager of the merged cooperative. He and Wolverine's attorney, Richard Lang, and Assistant Manager Ray Towne, with the help of the Michigan Public Service Commission and attorney Al Ernst, began the task of forging a new agreement with Detroit Edison — one that would enable the financially troubled co-op — avoid bankruptcy and keep its power costs from soaring.

Wolverine and Detroit Edison reached an initial agreement in December 1983 to cap the co-op's investment in Fermi II. As the cost of the plant continued to rise, the cap reduced the percentage of the plant's capacity owned by the co-op, thereby increasing the co-ops' projected cost per kilowatt significantly. Inside of another year, the cost of the plant zoomed to more than $3 billion and the cooperative resumed negotiations with Detroit Edison to find further remedies.

In August 1985, Detroit Edison agreed to purchase portions of the cooperative's Fermi II ownership in amounts equal to Wolverine's quarterly debt payments to REA. Any hope for the cooperatives' future in Fermi II vanished when the costs of the plant jumped again in September 1985 to $4.2 billion. In October 1986 the two utilities outlined an agreement for Wolverine to sell its entire share in Fermi II to Detroit Edison, effective January 2, 1990, for $550 million. Edison also agreed to make the quarterly debt payments to REA until the sale date and the cooperative agreed to purchase increasing amounts of energy and capacity from Edison through the year 2025.

Realizing the extremely high debt service costs — about $1 million per month in interest costs on the $780 million owed REA — and seeing no other viable options, the seven member cooperatives that comprised Wolverine voted in October 1987 to approve the sale of Wolverine's ownership in Fermi II to Detroit Edison for $550 million, the amount of Wolverine's debt that Edison agreed to assume. REA and the U.S. Department of Justice approved the deal, which left Wolverine owing some $200 million to the Treasury and no ownership in the plant.

"We worked out the best possible deal we could and I believe we gained some positive results overall," said Ray Towne, who took over as manager of Wolverine in December 1987. "We believed it was the right decision because the alternative of bankruptcy had too many unknowns and was not a path we wanted to take." He credited Roger Fischer, who was chief of staff at the Michigan Public Service Commission, for helping to get all of the parties together in reaching a workable solution to a very serious problem.

Another key player in developing strategies to resolve the Fermi II crisis was Al Ernst of the Dykema Gossett law firm. Ernst has served as legal counsel for the Michigan Electric Cooperative Association since 1979 and also did legal work for the two G & T co-ops. "It was a team effort and it is to the credit of the Wolverine board members that we persisted in developing a workable arrangement rather than filing for bankruptcy," said Ernst.

Wolverine's only other joint venture was the purchase of a small interest in Consumers Power Company's Campbell #3 coal-fired plant in 1980 for $3.6 million. Fortunately, neither Northern Michigan nor the "old" Wolverine co-op were part of Consumers Power's Midland nuclear project, which was aborted after lengthy delays and skyrocketing costs.

The cooperatives had looked into the prospect of buying a share of the Midland plant in the early 1970s, but Consumers said it wasn't open to co-ownership. The cooperatives joined with the municipal power group in an antitrust action against Consumers and were awarded a settlement in 1979. Practices of Consumers Power in applying for a license from the Atomic Energy Commission had led to an investigation by the U.S. Department of Justice. The Justice Department said that the Commission should hold hearings to determine whether granting a license to the company "would create or maintain a situation inconsistent with the U.S. antitrust laws." The co-ops and municipals were accepted as intervenors in the proceedings, resulting in the settlement.

Power generation and nuclear energy weren't the only issues of the 1970s. Environmental legislation in Congress and a wave of "utility reform" proposals on national and state levels caused new concerns among co-op boards and management.

The Public Utilities Regulatory Policy Act (PURPA) passed by Congress in 1978 had many repercussions on utilities, including the mandate that utilities buy power from non-utility generators that use renewable resources or cogeneration. This included small privately-owned hydro facilities and wind power generators.

Interest and inquiries about wind power surged. The Michigan cooperatives in 1980 cosponsored research on wind power at Michigan State University, conducted under the supervision of Dr. Gerald Park, head of the MSU Electric Engineering Department. Results showed that wind power was not economically feasible in most Michigan locations. The co-ops would not be able to rely on a steady supply of power from wind-driven generators, Dr. Park concluded.

With the government's emphasis on conservation following the 1973 oil embargo, REA borrowers were urged to eliminate promotional activities which encouraged greater use of electric energy and to initiate efforts to conserve energy. By 1977, methods for reducing demand for power during peak hours of the day and seasons of the year were being strongly advocated among cooperatives. In January, 1979, REA issued its new conservation policy requiring all new loan applications to include a board policy proclaiming the co-op's commitment to energy conservation, a report on its efforts to conserve energy in its own facilities, and a report on how the co-op helped members make the most efficient use of electric energy. This brought on home energy audits conducted by the cooperatives and private contractors, and informational programs on how to save energy in the home and in commercial buildings. Although some questioned the overall impact or success of such efforts, REA announced at the end of 1979 that the rate of growth in kilowatt-hour sales had been cut from 6.3 percent in 1978 to 2.9 percent in 1979.

REA Administrator Robert Feragen also urged development of supplemental energy sources, such as solar and geothermal. Many electric cooperatives began promoting geothermal heat pumps, a form of heating and cooling that uses Mother Nature's earth as a heat sink. Michigan co-ops became actively involved in the 1980s recommending geothermal heat pumps to co-op members. Several thousand rural Michigan homes now use this form of heating.

Another factor in reducing the use of electricity in the late 1970s and early 1980s was the rising price of a kilowatt hour. The oil shortage and its cascading impacts upon the U.S. economy forced utilities across the country to raise rates and, in many cases, not just once but two or three times within a few years.

Coal-fired generating plants were still the major source for electric energy and environmental protection measures added substantially to the cost of generation. The rate hikes became controversial and hotly contested in some areas. Consumer groups formed, some in active protest to the increases. In Michigan, the Citizens Lobby and PIRGIM (Public Interest Research Group in Michigan) built their organizations and became active in the Michigan Legislature in the 1970s.

Among Michigan cooperatives, there were members who expressed discontent with rates, but more vehement were those who opposed nuclear power and who advocated that co-ops develop alternative energy sources. But one such move — Wolverine's proposal for a wood-burning generating facility — was stopped by a citizens' group and the Attorney General.

A special committee of Michigan legislators was appointed in 1974 to investigate utility ratemaking practices and make recommendations to the Legislature.

State legislators were also drafting and introducing bills to put more stringent environmental protection laws on the books that would add still more costs to electric utilities.

"We saw all of this building up in the Legislature and, on top of it, more issues at the Michigan Public Service Commission concerned us, so we started serious discussion about the co-ops forming a full-time statewide association," said Roger Westenbroek, former manager of Top O' Michigan. "We had an association but it had no staff and no mission or goals. I made it a priority to get a new operative statewide organized that could effectively work for us on legislative and regulatory issues and help us communicate with our members and the public."

Opinions of the managers and board members among the 15 cooperatives, including the two power supply co-ops, about a staffed statewide organization varied. Some voiced concerns as to the cost and some questioned the need. Westenbroek, backed by Lyle Wilson of the Alger-Delta cooperative, Jack Holt of Cloverland, and a few others, responded that if all the co-ops would join, the dues to support a staffed association would not be prohibitive.

Officials from REA, NRECA and other statewide associations spoke at meetings of Michigan co-ops. They explained how the statewide organizations functioned, not only within a state, but at the national level as well. Over the years, electric cooperatives in 32 states had formed full-time statewide associations. Most had staffs of 10 to 25 persons. While the discussion continued among the Michigan co-ops, Westenbroek had hired a lobbyist to be paid temporarily by Top O' Michigan. "We needed professional representation in Lansing and we selected the former State Senate Majority Leader, Milt Zaagman of Grand Rapids."

Although it was evident not all the Michigan co-ops would sign a charter for a new association, Westenbroek had tentative commitments from six other cooperatives. He called a meeting for June 1, 1978, to formally organize the Michigan Electric Cooperative Association (MECA). Top O' Michigan's legal counsel, Nathaniel Stroup, prepared Articles of Incorporation and a set of bylaws for MECA. Those who signed the Articles of Incorporation of MECA at that meeting and the cooperatives they represented included:

■ Lyle Wilson and Roy Hawkinson, Alger Delta Cooperative Electric Assn.
■ Harry Pechta and John Holt, Cloverland Electric Cooperative.
■ C. Victor Lyon and Michael O'Meara, Presque Isle Electric Cooperative
■ Joseph Glenn and Carl Hoffman, Southeastern Michigan Electric Cooperative
■ John Rockershousen and Philip Cole, Cherryland Electric Cooperative
■ Truman H. Cummings, Jr. and Roger Westenbroek, Top O' Michigan Electric Company
■ John Tyndall and Frank P. Anderson, Western Michigan Electric Cooperative
■ Emma Reinbold and Clyde L. Johnson, Northern Michigan Electric Cooperative

Soon after the new statewide was chartered, four other cooperatives joined the association: Fruit Belt Electric Cooperative, Thumb Electric Cooperative, Oceana Electric Cooperative and Tri-County Electric Cooperative. Wolverine Electric Cooperative, the G & T, also decided to join when the statewide went into operation in January 1979.

Lyle Wilson was elected the association's first president, and was succeeded in October 1979 by John Kutter of Thumb Electric Cooperative. John Rockershousen of Cherryland Electric was elected vice-president, and Frank Anderson of Western Michigan, secretary-treasurer. Truman Cummings of Top O' Michigan and Warren St. John of Cloverland also served on the executive committee.

The other two Michigan co-ops — O & A Electric and Ontonagon County Rural

Electric — later became members of MECA, Ontonagon in 1981 and O & A in 1995.

"The formation of MECA was a major turning point in the progress of Michigan's electric cooperatives," said Bob Badner, retired REA field representative who worked 36 years with the Michigan co-ops. In many ways, the co-ops had been disjointed, often going in different directions and, at times, it was a nightmare trying to move forward and resolve issues, especially at the Public Service Commission, whose actions and decisions had big impacts upon the cooperatives.

"I encouraged Roger Westenbroek and others who wanted a coordinated, united approach to solving problems to go ahead and organize," said Badner, who was held in high esteem by the cooperatives. "I regard the start-up of the new statewide association as one of three or four major decisions that put the Michigan co-ops on a path of progress during my years (1960 - 1996) working with them."

In Badner's judgement, the other turning points were: 1) the cooperatives' decision to be regulated by the Michigan Public Service Commission in 1965, which gave them some security against further loss of customers to Consumers Power, a troublesome problem for years; 2) the 1982 merger of the two G & T power supply co-ops, Northern Michigan and Wolverine, which meant substantial savings and much more efficient, coordinated operation of generation and transmission facilities; 3) the decision to buy a piece of Detroit Edison's Fermi II nuclear plant and the subsequent actions to sell the co-ops' share of ownership back to Edison. "It was a fine concept but so many unforeseen factors came into play," said Badner of Fermi II.

The new statewide organization wasted little time getting into operation. The MECA board of directors selected me as general manager, and I began my duties in January, 1979.

I had 20 years of experience with electric cooperatives, including two years with a G & T co-op, 15 with a distribution co-op, two with a statewide association and one year with the National Rural Electric Cooperative Association. I also had organized an association of rural community water systems in South Dakota and served as its executive director for two years.

The MECA office was established in Lansing, scene of much of the association's work with state legislators and the Michigan Public Service Commission. MECA retained Milt Zaagman, former state senator, as its legislative consultant. Both Zaagman and I registered as lobbyists for MECA.

We were into the legislative arena even before we had an office," said Kuhl, "because important issues were being debated that could significantly impact our cooperatives. One was a comprehensive wetlands bill that could have dictated costly restrictions and procedures for electric utilities, and we were very pleased to have our proposed amendments accepted. That made the new law workable in rural areas."

Another early and memorable win for the new statewide was the exemption of electric cooperatives from a bill that created an intervenors fund from revenues of electric utilities. Two cents of every dollar of revenue would go to the fund for use by intervenors in rate cases at the Public Service Commission.

Bob Fredericksen, MECA legislative committee chairman who was manager of the Oceana co-op, came to the hearing with a head of steam, and he emphatically articulated several valid reasons to exempt the co-ops.

One compelling reason was that no one had ever filed to intervene in a cooperative's rate case at the Commission. The legislators heard him loud and clear and agreed with the exemption. Other utilities today pay into the fund, but for cooperatives, it didn't make sense because co-op contributions would go to groups in rate cases of the big utilities.

Legislative work, including liaison with Michigan's members of Congress, was one of the top priority functions outlined by MECA's first board of directors. Rolfe Wells, the lone member of that board still serving in 1996, said that, in addition to legislation, the board felt that giving close attention to regulatory matters at the Public Service Commission and providing training programs for co-op employees were important to the co-ops.

"These were the most crucial needs common to all of the cooperatives and it made sense to have one coordinating body be on top of the issues and conduct the work," said Wells. "Costs have gone up like they have in everything else, but having one unified work force through MECA is the most efficient and effective way to do these things."

**Above right:** Roger Westenbroek, former manager of Top O' Michigan Electric, is congratulated by MECA President Lyle Wilson, who presented the Special Recognition Award to Westenbroek in 1981 for his leadership in organizing the statewide association. MECA was chartered in June, 1978, by eight cooperatives. **Above left:** Born in the political arena, the Rural Electrification program has been the subject of legislation year after year. But with active support from the grassroots and Congress, REA stayed alive and viable. Calling on their U.S. Representatives during the 1984 Congressional session were (L to R): Bob Neterer, manager of Fruit Belt Electric, Raymond Kuhl, manager of the Michigan Electric Cooperative Association, Rolfe Wells, Fruit Belt board president, Willard Haenke, Tri-County Electric board member, and Art Biehl, Top O' Michigan Electric board member.

Tornadoes and ice storms are big troublemakers for Michigan's electric cooperatives, causing millions of dollars of damage over the years. Both of these photos were taken in the Western Michigan Electric service area, hit by an ice storm in 1967 and a tornado in 1971. A statewide emergency assistance plan among co-ops sends crews and equipment to help restore service in hard hit areas.

**Top:** Buying a share of Fermi 2 nuclear power plant proved to be near-fatal financially for the Northern Michigan and Wolverine Power cooperatives in the 1970s. Cost of the Detroit Edison plant skyrocketed before completion but the co-ops worked out a series of agreements resulting in Edison buying back the co-ops interest in exchange for a long-term power supply deal.

**Middle (left):** Signing papers for the merger of the "old" Wolverine and Northern Michigan G & T co-ops into Wolverine Power Supply Cooperative are, seated (L to R): Willard Haenke, Don Harmon, and Norm Newby of the old Wolverine, with attorney Dan Hesslin looking on.

**Middle (right):** Dick Arnold, who managed power plants for Wolverine Cooperative and its successor for several years, remembers working 90 hours a week to keep all the generators in running order during the 1973-74 oil crisis that gripped the nation.

**Bottom (left):** Two key players in the Northern Michigan-Wolverine merger were Barrie Lightfoot (left), of Cherryland Electric Co-op, who chaired the coordinating committee and Ray Cristell, manager of the merged co-op.

**Bottom (right):** Ray Towne served as assistant manager of Northern Michigan and the merged Wolverine Power Supply Cooperative before being named manager in 1983. He retired in 1995.

**Left:** Jewell Gillispie of Beaver Island describes new submarine power cable to Top O' Michigan engineer Clayton Slocum and manager Roger Westenbroek. Island residents are members of the co-op and previously depended upon diesel-powered generation.

**Below:** New rules adopted by the Michigan Public Service Commission in 1980 have helped prevent duplication of power facilities and disputes over service to new prospective customers. The Commissioners who took the action were (L to R) Eric Schneidewind, Dan Demlow, (chairman), and Edwyna Anderson.

**Below:** An example of duplication of power lines before approval of the 1980 MPSC rules is shown in this photo of a rural location south of Traverse City where Cherryland Electric Cooperative and Consumers Power both provide service.

**Above:** George Allard, one of Western Michigan co-op founders, was one of state's first representatives on the national rural electric association board of directors.

# MOVING FORWARD TOGETHER

The cooperatives found that an association, given a set of goals and priority work areas, can tackle many tasks with a small staff. After starting on the job as general manager of the association in January 1979, I established the MECA office in south Lansing. With four employees on the staff by the end of 1979, I proposed a budget of $268,000 for 1980. Thirteen cooperatives were paying dues which were based upon the number of meters served.

One of the first positions filled was Director of Safety and Job Training, responsible for establishing and conducting a year-round program to instruct and advise line workers and other employees of the cooperatives on safe work practices and procedures.

Workshops were set up to cover a wide range of technical subjects, and "hands on" line worker schools became annual events. As the workload expanded to include developing safety standards, performing on-site safety inspections, and coordinating a statewide emergency work plan, a second person was added to Safety and Training.

Robert Palmbos, Director of MECA's Training and Loss Control Department, started with MECA in 1979. He and Michael Stelter, Training and Loss Control Consultant, presented thousands of programs for employees at the cooperatives, and help coordinate a dozen or more annual workshops and line schools, plus the continuing development of safety standards and work procedures. Stelter led a study that developed a comprehensive set of guidelines for use of rubber gloves in working on energized lines. The manual is used nationally.

Palmbos was instrumental in establishing a new Utility Technicians School at the Alpena Community College. He worked with Frank Talentino, former Operations Manager at Cloverland Electric Cooperative, Chuck Shefler of the college and others in developing a curriculum for men and women who want to become line workers. With the close support of Edison Sault Electric, Alpena Power, Corey Somes and other equipment suppliers, and the electric cooperatives, the program was initiated in 1990 and has graduated 125 students in five years. "This program creates a pool of qualified people ready to step into apprentice line jobs at co-ops and other utilities," said Palmbos.

Palmbos believes that improving the quality of the customer's electric service by upgrading employee training is the underlying objective of MECA's loss control and training programs. "The most important thing we've been able to do through our educational programs is consistently and steadily improve the quality of work performed in terms of safety, efficiency and technical skills," he said.

Another valuable service coordinated through MECA is the Statewide Emergency Work Plan, which dispatches line crews to help cooperatives when storms cause major service interruptions. The MECA plan outlines procedures, available equipment and other details important when a cooperative needs assistance. "The cooperatives exist to provide the best possible quality electric service, and our emergency plan is always ready to swing into action quickly when a cooperative needs help in restoring service," said Palmbos.

Ice storms, tornadoes and severe wind storms are not strangers to Michigan. Palmbos says the emergency assistance plan is utilized once or twice almost every year. In 1984, MECA recruited nearly 100 line crews from cooperatives and contractors to assist five co-ops in the south central part of the state hit hard by an ice storm. "That was the worst we've seen since the statewide plan has been in place," said Palmbos.

In the summer of 1995, vicious thunderstorms hit the Detroit area and, for the first time, the cooperatives were asked to help Detroit Edison restore service. Crews from six co-ops assisted the Detroit utility in making repairs.

MECA has also initiated and presented seminars on "Disaster Preparedness" to inform the co-ops on procedures and communications to use in the event of a major catastrophe such as an earthquake, flood or tornado. A guidebook helps co-ops establish their own plans.

The MECA founders also gave emphasis to communications and informational programs, primarily to help the cooperatives inform their member-consumers of new and more efficient uses of electricity, rural issues and developments of interest, and legislation that can impact them.

A special committee was appointed in 1980 and recommended a statewide publication, one that MECA would compose and publish with a section of pages for each cooperative's news. The result was the birth of *Michigan Country Lines*, a bimonthly publication that was launched in tabloid format in November, 1980.

Michael Buda was employed as Director of Communications and Marketing in January, 1980, and was named editor of *Country Lines*. I served as executive editor. We converted the publication to a magazine format in 1985, providing more pages for each cooperative's news and information, and also adding the regular column, *Right At Home*, by Jim Hough, former columnist in the *Lansing State Journal*.

Reader surveys and mail have shown Hough's column to be the most popular part of the magazine. According to the surveys, more than 82 percent of member subscribers read three out of every four *Country Lines* issues. Each issue has special features and a regular column on efficient uses of electric energy.

MECA's magazine, which has grown in circulation from 100,000 in 1980 to over 200,000 in 1996, won the coveted National Rural Electric Cooperative Association "George Haggard Award" three times — in 1987, 1990 and 1991— for "the most lucid, forthright and effective presentation of the ideals and objectives of cooperative rural electrification." Michelle Smith and Daniel Watts, former associate editors, have shared the honors with Buda.

Appointed editor of *Country Lines* in September, 1996, was Gail Knudtson, who has been associate editor and communications specialist with MECA since 1992.

Buda's job at the statewide has covered marketing, economic development, youth programs, public relations and assisting with legislative work. He was instrumental in forming the Michigan Geothermal Energy Association (MGEA) in 1993, serving as chairman for two years and then as executive director. More than 50 geothermal contractors, manufacturers and distributors have joined with several Michigan utilities in the MGEA to develop standards, training programs and marketing plans. "It is a vehicle that helps ensure that geothermal heating and cooling systems meet or exceed performance expectations," says Buda.

In the Fall of 1996, Buda was named MECA's Director of External Affairs with more responsibilities in government affairs.

Through MECA, the cooperatives have sponsored more than 500 high school students to participate in the annual Teens Days, a three-day experience at the Kettunen 4-H Center where they learn about co-ops and electricity. One hundred fifty students have seen the sights of the nation's capital and learned about their federal government, thanks to the annual Washington, D.C., Youth Tour sponsored by the electric co-ops and MECA, along with NRECA.

The Youth Tour to Washington also gives the students the opportunity to meet some of Michigan's Members of Congress. They have also made visits to the White House and the Supreme Court.

One of MECA's most important activities each year is coordinating personal visits of officials of the electric cooperatives and the MECA staff with Michigan's two U.S. Senators and 16 Representatives in Washington. This has been one of the most beneficial functions of the statewide association since we started in 1979. I've counted 68 trips to the nation's capital in my 17 years at MECA. Our initiatives and timely discussions with Michigan's Congressional Delegation have been in close support of our national association's legislative goals, and we have led the efforts on some issues, including REA financing, rights-of-way for cooperatives, taxation, transmission access and other energy policy issues.

Most of MECA's legislative work is with the state legislature in Lansing. The Michigan Legislature is one of the few in the United States that operates year-round. To keep informed on a daily basis and to be ready to take necessary actions, the association has engaged a legislative consultant. The first ten years, MECA contracted with Milt Zaagman. In recent years, Robert Noordhoek of Public Affairs Associates has been MECA's representative.

Before taking positions on major issues, we consulted with the MECA Government Relations Committee. There can be 200 to 300 bills introduced each year with potential impact on electric cooperatives.

An innovative program was initiated in the mid-1980s by the MECA Government Relations Committee under the leadership of Tom Hanna, Top O' Michigan general manager. In conjunction with one of the member cooperatives, MECA invited a state senator or state representative from an urban area to visit the cooperative's area, see firsthand how a co-op utility functions, and talk with rural community leaders.

The program's first participant was Representative Alma Stallworth of Detroit, who chaired the House Public Utilities Committee for several years. "It was an eye-opening experience that gave me a much better perspective of the rural infrastructure and how the electric cooperatives have brought modern living standards to our rural areas," Rep. Stallworth commented after her tour of Cloverland Electric Cooperative.

A dozen state legislators have been on visits to Cloverland, Alger Delta, Ontonagon, Cherryland, Top O' Michigan, Presque Isle, Oceana, Western Michigan and Thumb electric cooperatives. "These were not 'pleasure trips.' They were serious informational visits for legislators who were not familiar with rural areas or electric cooperatives, and it is important to us that they understand our unique problems and needs," said Hanna.

MECA's efforts to work more closely with legislators were vital when the state's laws on cooperatives were revamped in 1985. One specific revision adopted upon MECA's recommendation was to allow electric cooperatives to retain unclaimed patronage refunds and deposits after five years, rather than send the monies to the state. This has saved the cooperatives hundreds of thousands of dollars.

Other legislative initiatives of the statewide association have enabled the co-ops to provide liability protection for individuals who serve on their boards of directors and to permit the newly merged Wolverine Power Supply Co-op to qualify for tax abatements when the co-op built its new headquarters and dispatch center near Cadillac.

Within the first six years of MECA's operation, we estimated that our legislative achievements would result in savings of more than $5 million to the cooperatives. In addition, the association had established working relationships with the Michigan Public Service Commission, where the co-ops had much at stake in terms of rules and regulations, costly procedures and ratemaking issues, all of which translated into significant dollars for each cooperative.

A major problem still unsolved in 1979 was the matter of territorial disputes in areas where two or more power suppliers clash over which utility has the right to serve the prospective new customer. This had been addressed by the Commission in regard to "single-phase" customers, but not the larger "three-phase" commercial and industrial loads. A special committee was appointed in 1979 by the Public Service Commission that included Roger Westenbroek and me from the cooperatives and several from the investor-owned utilities. Ken Croy, of the Commission's electric division, headed the committee.

After several months of work and negotiation, the group agreed upon the principal elements of a comprehensive set of rules, the essence of which is that the utility "closest to" the prospective new customer in a rural area has the right to serve, except that where two suppliers are within 300 feet or more than a half mile from the new load, it is the customer's choice. The rules, adopted by the Commission and put into effect in 1981, have more detailed provisions and, in general, have served to prevent unnecessary and costly duplication of facilities by the investor-owned and co-op utilities.

The MPSC rules have been fairly administered by the Commission staff and, while they are not a panacea for every situation, they have enabled the cooperatives to serve loads rightfully theirs that they would not have otherwise secured. This was a big step forward not only for the co-ops but for sensible economics, because the rules have worked to prevent costly duplication of very expensive utility facilities.

James Padgett of the MPSC electric division was responsible for administering the territorial service rules, and was commended by MECA for his work in a Special Recognition Award. Other MPSC personnel have received similar MECA awards: John Abramson, head of the electric division; the late Ken Croy, formerly with the electric division; and Daniel Blair accounting specialist with the division.

The cooperatives' progress in regard to regulation by the Public Service Commission can be attributed largely to Albert Ernst, who was selected in 1979 to represent MECA in its work with the Commission and other legal matters. Ernst, a partner in the law firm of Dykema Gossett, has been a key person for us through the years in achieving a productive, coordinated working relationship between the cooperatives and the Commission. The co-ops made tremendous progress in terms of cutting costs and having issues decided in a fair and timely manner because of Ernst's aggressive and effective work.

The longtime REA Field Representative in Michigan, Bob Badner, said that because of MECA and the work of Al Ernst, the cooperatives have approached the Commission with one clear voice and made innumerable gains. "His competence has made a huge difference in the advancement of Michigan's electric cooperatives financially," said Badner.

One of the early and most important gains advocated by Ernst and MECA was a simplified and less costly ratemaking procedure that was especially helpful to the smaller cooperatives in the state. The Commission tried the new mechanism with Ontonagon County Rural Electric Association in 1981, approved it, and since has permitted nine other co-ops to use it.

Called TIER ratemaking (for Times Interest Earned Ratio), the procedure cuts the time and need for expert witnesses and other work ordinarily required in utility rate cases, thus saving thousands of dollars for each cooperative when a rate change was needed. The procedure was later adopted by several other states upon learning of the Michigan cooperatives' success with it.

"We blazed the trail and have demonstrated to the Commission that the co-ops, being owned by their customers, are not interested in ripping off the member-consumers," said Ernst. "Any way we can cut costs brightens the prospect of reducing rates or holding them stable."

It is impossible to give an estimate of the overall savings that the Michigan cooperatives have realized through MECA's work at the Commission and in the Legislature, but "we know it's in the millions, probably tens of millions of dollars," said Ernst.

Most significant, in Ernst's opinion, has been the credibility that the cooperatives have earned through MECA over the years. "That's true at the Commission and in the Legislature, and it is a real strength of the electric cooperatives. We have built understanding and trust among public officials."

Building political muscle was also part of the statewide association's goals soon after its start in 1979. The Action Committee for Rural Electrification (ACRE) was a growing political action group formed at the national level in the 1960s, but had only 25 to 30 Michigan members, the MECA board of directors formed a state ACRE Committee and a PAC fund under state law.

Within a few years, membership in Michigan's ACRE program reached 200. With leadership from Top O' Michigan's Tom Hanna, Oceana's Bob Fredericksen, Cloverland's Bernard Doll, Fruit Belt's Rolf Wells, Wolverine's Ray Towne, and Bob Matheny and Carl Morton from Tri-County, the ACRE membership doubled to 400 in 1989 and topped 500 in each of the years since.

"The participation itself indicates the importance and value of people joining together to support those legislators who are supportive of electric cooperatives and the issues vital to us," said Doll, who has been an ACRE member since he came on the Cloverland board in 1976. "Politics is part of the real world in which we work. We have a lot at stake and, in my view, we have no choice but to be a voice in the political process and ACRE gives us a voice that is heard."

The electric cooperatives' PAC is much smaller than those of the large investor-owned utilities, but it gives us a voice and the presence that is needed in our open democratic system of government. The Michigan ACRE has supported as many as 50 to 60 candidates for the state legislature and sometimes has supported gubernatorial candidates.

Part of an individual's dues to Michigan ACRE goes to the national ACRE which is one of the larger rural-based political action committees in the nation. The national ACRE has supported many of Michigan's members of Congress. For the number of cooperatives in the state, Michigan has one of the highest ACRE participation rates in the country and has been recognized for its achievements. In 1997, MECA established a new, separate political action committee called M-ACRE. It is functioning to step up support for state legislative candidates.

Another area in which the cooperatives found they could work together and realize big savings was workers compensation insurance. The co-ops were paying almost double the rate of other electric utilities for the insurance to cover lineworkers, and the insurance companies wouldn't make an adjustment.

In October, 1981, a Self-Insurance Fund for the Michigan electric cooperatives was formally organized and put into operation. All of the state's co-ops, except one, came into the plan within a year. The premium was reduced from $8.99 per $100 of payroll for outside workers to less than $6 the first year, followed by other reductions and $700,000 in refunds of premiums to the co-ops. Conservatively, the cooperatives saved over $3,000,000 in the five years of the Self-Insurance program.

Due to a series of unprecedented accidents involving five fatalities at four cooperatives over a 17-month period, the MECA Self-Insurance Fund could not obtain reinsurance (backup coverage by another carrier) and was forced into inactive status in October 1986. Two of the deaths resulted from electrical contacts, but three occurred in freak accidents.

The MECA Self-Insurance Fund had a separate board of directors and was administered by the MECA staff. Handling of claims and the reporting and analysis of losses were contracted with an outside agency. "We had a very sound and successful program and I'm sure we would still be functioning if we could have found a reinsurer after that string of terrible accidents," said Betty Gordon, who served on the Self-Insurance board for several years. She has also been active on the MECA board for many years.

Although some accidents involving line work at Michigan co-ops have occurred since the 1985-86 tragedies, none have involved deaths.

In MECA's early years, the manager and staff worked with other co-op groups and farm organizations to build support and unity on issues that affected cooperatives or rural people in general. I served on the boards of the Michigan Association of Farmer Cooperatives, the Michigan Agriculture Association and the Michigan Alliance of Cooperatives. Mike Buda and I helped organize the Alliance, which embraces all types of cooperatives, in the state. Buda served as president of the Alliance for several years in the '80s.

The Alliance developed educational programs on cooperatives. It reverted to part-time operation in 1994 with Joel Welty as executive director, and continues to foster cooperative education and co-op networking.

The history of the Michigan Electric Cooperative Association since its beginning in 1978 is the story of the strengthening and maturing of Michigan's co-op utilities. Unity of rural people in the 1930s enabled the cooperatives to get started and develop; unity of the cooperatives through their statewide association enabled them to pool their resources and become more effective, competitive utilities.

The extent to which the co-ops share resources and work together in a coordinated manner will determine their future. There is no question that they have more strength and considerably more resources by working closely together, the cooperatives will need all of the strength they can muster to successfully compete in the changing utility world.

Succeeding me as MECA general manager in 1996 was Michael Peters, who came to the Michigan post from the Illinois Association of Electric Cooperatives, where he was corporate counsel and was involved in legislative work. He was previously employed by the Kansas Electric Cooperatives, where he started his career in rural electrification.

In its first 18 years, MECA has grown to a staff of eight persons. When O & A

Electric Cooperative joined MECA in 1995, the board of directors expanded to 28 — two from each cooperative. The board reverted to 26 members in 1997, when the O & A and Oceana cooperatives merged to become the Great Lakes Energy Cooperative, and was cut to 24 members in 1998 with the merger of Fruit Belt and Southeastern Energy Co-ops into Midwest Energy Cooperative.

Several committees of board members, managers and co-op employees participate in making recommendations for MECA's annual work plans and budget.

One of the committees played a big part in planning and presenting quality training and educational programs for employees and board members of the electric cooperatives. The Committee on Human Resources, first organized in 1979, has made valuable input over the years in reflecting the needs of the cooperatives' work force and boards for specific educational opportunities.

"The Human Resources' programs have been wide-ranging, targeting every group of co-op employees, upgrading their skills and knowledge so they can perform more competently in serving the member-customers," said MECA's Bob Palmbos, who helped develop and coordinate the programs.

Through the statewide, educational programs have also been provided for board members, many of whom are elected to the board with little knowledge about electric cooperatives. One of the most popular programs has been the biannual MECA Directors Conference where as many as 70 and 80 people from the cooperatives' boards attend two days of solid discussion about virtually every aspect of the co-op utility business.

MECA also scheduled and coordinated many management and director training courses in Michigan offered by NRECA. An increasing number of board members have earned certificates by completing the basic series of NRECA courses, and several have participated in the advanced training program.

"As the electric utility business becomes more complex and more competitive, requiring more knowledge and savvy on the part of management and boards, these opportunities for education and development are increasingly important," in the view of Martin Thomson, who was a board officer for years at the Presque Isle cooperative and is now the co-op's general manager.

"Board members have heavy responsibilities for planning and policy-making — all the major decisions—along with the general manager...We need the training and tools to do the best job possible for the member-consumers," said Thomson. "We are no longer coddled or insulated by a government agency. We carry the full burden in mapping our future."

In the case of Presque Isle Electric & Gas Co-op, what Thomson said is especially true because, in 1995, the cooperative elected to pay off its REA loans in total, at a discount, to have more flexibility in their business decisions. A major step taken by the co-op was its decision to go into the natural gas business. Thomson said the decision was based on the potential market and service needs in the area.

Presque Isle's move reflects a trend for more diversification in the services of electric cooperatives. While that movement is not directly attributable to specific training or educational programs, it does reflect greater awareness of the customers' needs and wants. Formal and informal education has been a big influence in bringing these changes.

An affiliate of the statewide association that has played a quiet but supportive role of the cooperatives in recent years is the Michigan Rural Electric Women's Association. Wives of co-op managers and board members had met socially in earlier years, according to Shirley Smith, wife of the late Vernor Smith, longtime manager of Tri-County Electric Cooperative.

One of the duties of the women's group, Shirley recalls, was "initiating" those who came to Michigan meetings from Washington, D.C. "This often included cutting off their ties — that lightened up what otherwise was rather dry, serious talk," she said.

The women's group became involved in activities of the national women's association of electric cooperatives and saw the opportunity to be of more help. The group helped raise funds for the ACRE program through sales of cookbooks and other items, and a major project in recent years has been awarding college scholarships to sons and daughters of electric co-op members.

First president of the Michigan chapter of the National Rural Electric Women's Association was Betty Barth, wife of Fruit Belt Electric Co-op director Andy Barth. Marge Fredericksen, wife of Oceana Electric manger Bob Fredericksen, was vice-president. Ruth Bowsman, wife of Fruit Belt manager Butch Bowsman, was secretary-treasurer.

President of the Michigan Electric Cooperative Women's Association in 1996 was Delores Damm, wife of Thumb Electric Co-op board member Martin Damm. Lois Sandbrook, wife of Tri-County Electric board member Richard Sandbrook, served as vice president.

Emma Reinbold, from the Top O' Michigan board of directors and also the MECA board, represented the Michigan women's group on the National Rural Electric Women's Association in the 1980s. In recent years, Jean Chapin of Tri-County Electric served as Michigan's representative. Mrs. Chapin has also been an officer of the state group. Her late husband, William Chapin, served on Tri-County's board of directors for 26 years and was the first board chairman of the newly merged Wolverine Power Supply Co-op in 1982-83.

People like Jean and Bill Chapin invested countless hours to the advancement of rural electrification in their community and the state. They, like so many other co-op members, generously volunteered over the years to support their electric cooperative in activities that helped strengthen rural communities and make rural Michigan a better place to live and work.

The success of the rural electrification program over the past 60 years can be summed up in a few words: the determination and hard work of people at the grass roots — people of commitment!

## MICHIGAN MAN TURNS DOWN CONSIDERATION
## AS REA CHIEF

A Michigan man was close to becoming the Administrator of REA in Washington in the early 1980s. Elwyn Olmstead, board member from Western Michigan Electric Cooperative, represented Michigan on the National Rural Electric Cooperative Association board of directors for six years in the 1970s and apparently made some good impressions.

After he had retired from the co-op and NRECA boards, he received a phone call while he was vacationing in Florida. It was a prominent U.S. Senator, Jesse Helms of North Carolina, to ask Olmstead if he would consider being appointed the Administrator of REA in Washington. Olmstead said it came as a big surprise and he told Helms he would have to give that some thought.

Senator Helms chaired the Senate Agriculture Committee, so he had influence as to who would be the next Administrator. He called again a few days later, urging Olmstead to send his resume for consideration to the appointment. Olmstead was still undecided, and Helms called a third time. Olmstead told him he was flattered and appreciated the opportunity, but he respectfully declined.

"I wasn't that fond of Washington and I really didn't want a full-time job. I was starting to enjoy retirement and just didn't want to take on that kind of commitment," said Olmstead.

## "THE NEXT GREATEST THING"

This story has become legend after the book entitled *"The Next Greatest Thing"* was published by the National Rural Electric Cooperative Association in 1984. A farmer in the Tennessee Valley area back in the early 1940s, whose place had recently been connected to the electric cooperative line, said this in testimony at his country church:

"Brothers and sisters, I want to tell you this. The greatest thing on earth is to have the love of God in your heart, and the next greatest thing is to have electricity in your house."

Another legendary experience reported in *"The Next Greatest Thing"* concerned a farmer who was told that his farm was "too far from the power line" to get service from the co-op. A few days later, he returned to the office waving his $5 membership fee. "I moved my house," he exclaimed in triumph.

**Top (L):** Action Committee for Rural Electrification (ACRE) was organized through the statewide association (MECA) to support legislators who are supportive of the cooperative's interests. ACRE membership topped 500 in 1993. Boasting 100 percent membership from their cooperatives were (L to R): James Shull, Oceana; Carl Morton, Tri-County; Tom Hanna, Top O' Michigan; Robert Kran Jr., Western ; Ray Kuhl, MECA; Phil Cole, Cherryland; Walter Cook, Thumb; and Craig Borr, Wolverine.

**Top (R):** State Rep Alma Stallworth was the first of several urban legislators to visit electric co-ops through a MECA program. She toured Cloverland Electric's generating facility near Dafter with Cloverland manager Don Wozniak in 1987. Stallworth chaired the House Committee on Public Utilities for eight years.

**2nd row (L):** Michigan Electric Cooperative Association's Special Recognition Award is present to Bob Daverman (center), a Grand Rapids engineer who worked with co-ops during six decades. Presenting the award at the 1985 MECA annual meeting is board chairman Leon Smith. At right are MECA manager Ray Kuhl and wife, Jackie. **2nd row (R):** Asparagus from Michigan is sampled by U.S. Senator Carl Levin at a breakfast sponsored by Michigan's electric cooperatives in Washington, D.C. MECA general manager Ray Kuhl (R) cited Senator Levin for being one of the state's most consistent supporters of electric co-ops.

**Above (L):** Michael Buda, MECA Director of External Affairs. **Above (center):** Robert Palmbos, MECA Director of Training and Loss Control Services. **Above (R):** Bill and Jean Chapin of Tri-County Electric, leaders in the Michigan rural electrification program.

Michigan Electric Cooperative Association board of directors in 1981, representing 14 member cooperatives including (L to R): Don Clark, Alger Delta, Emma Reinbold, Top O' Michigan; Don Grimes, Southeastern; Mel Basel, Presque Isle; Rolfe Wells, Fruit Belt; Harold Hansen & Frank Anderson, Western; Joe Glenn, Southeastern; Mike O' Meara, Presque Isle; Francis Bowsman, Fruit Belt; Vernor Smith, Tri-County; Tom Hanna, Top O' Michigan; Leon Smith, Thumb; Jim Clarke, Tri-County; Phil Cole, Cherryland; Matthew Kokx, Oceana; Mike Krause, Thumb; Bob Fredericksen, Oceana; Jack Holt, Cloverland; Clyde Johnson, Northern Mich.; John Rockershousen, Cherryland; Lyle Wilson, Alger Delta and Willard Haenke, Wolverine. Not pictured: Warren St. John, Cloverland; Truman Cummings, Top O' Michigan; and Norm Newby, Wolverine.

Al Ernst, MECA legal counsel.

**Above:** Governor Jim Blanchard was given a kerosene lantern when he signed revisions to Michigan's co-op law in 1986. L to R: Mel Basel and Ray Towne, representing Wolverine Power Supply Co-op; Leon Smith, Thumb Electric Cooperative, MECA board Chairman; Tom Hanna, Top O' Michigan manager and chairman of MECA's Legislative Committee; and Raymond Kuhl, MECA manager.

Bob Noordhoek, MECA legislative consultant.

**Left:** Through the Michigan Electric Cooperative Association, the cooperatives sponsor Teen Days each year at the Kettunen 4-H Center, and a Washington D.C. Youth Tour.
**Bottom, left:** At Teen Days, students learn about lineworker's tools and their trade and see live demonstrations of the danger of contact with power lines.

# PEOPLE OF COMMITMENT

Farmers tired of toiling in the dark. Women weary of being slaves to the scrub board.

Powerless people. Young people, old people, men and women of the soil who could see a better life, if only they could get electricity.

With steely determination and clear purpose, hundreds of men and women decided to take risks into a field unknown and virtually untried — electrification of rural areas on a broad scale.

These were the pioneers, the pathfinders for what would soon become one of the most successful self-help programs in the United States.

There was no mold, no tried and proven formula, no guarantee of success in this venture. The government had ideas and the financial assistance needed. But should the rural people put full faith and confidence in this New Deal agency called REA? Uncertain of the steps to take or of the ultimate results of their efforts, they elected to pursue the goal of getting electricity.

The gritty organizers would gather in farm homes, town halls, schoolhouses and at country crossroads as often as necessary to lay the foundation for their electric cooperatives. They devoted countless hours to the cause with no assurance of success. They were committed.

Along the way, the cooperators were inspired and urged on by leaders like John M. Carmody, Administrator of REA in Washington. In a letter to one Michigan cooperative group, he said: "The success of an enterprise such as an electric cooperative depends almost wholly upon the spirit of the people in the community. Electricity is a great boon to humanity, but it doesn't come by magic. It comes by the process of hard work."

Thousands of rural people got involved in the process, helping get sign-ups and right-of-way, hauling poles, digging holes for the poles, pulling wire, spotting meters, going to meetings and learning how to get their co-op into operation.

While there were few women's names on the first boards of directors of electric co-ops, women were often the decision-makers in signing up for service, using their coveted egg money for the $5 fee. Canvassers learned quickly that it was smart strategy to talk to the farm wife. As an REA newsletter put it, "Often the wife would pay the sign-up fee before the organizer had finished arguing with her husband."

In many cases, women were active in recruiting others to sign up and to give their okay to right-of-way because the men were in the fields working long hours for survival in the Depression days. Women really had more incentive than their husbands to get the electricity flowing because women knew that electricity would relieve many of their backbreaking chores: washing clothes, ironing and pumping water.

Some of the pathfinders became intricately involved in the organizational work — talking with REA officials about loan funds, discussing feasibility with engineers and negotiating with contractors. They soon found themselves signing incorporation papers, officially forming the cooperative, and becoming the co-op's first board of directors. Across the state of Michigan from 1936 to 1940, 91 people signed as incorporators of the 14 electric cooperatives. (All are listed in the individual histories of the cooperatives elsewhere in this book.)

The electric co-op board members gave new meaning to being a director on a utility's board of directors. They did not receive $500 or $1,000 per board meeting, not even $100 or $10. In most cases, the co-op director's fee for the official monthly meeting was $3 or $5, and many meetings were attended without any compensation.

Here's how Top O' Michigan's attorney, Leon Miller, described the co-op directors when he spoke at the cooperative's annual meeting October 1, 1938, in Boyne City:

"I want to tell you (the members) something about this board of directors. They cannot blow their own horns. It would be unseemly of them to do so. They became directors one year ago today. Before that time, some of them had worked for weeks, some for months, some of them even for years, traveling all over the state endeavoring to bring about this electrification. It is still out of their own pockets. It always will be because there is no way to get it back...All this they have done for something like $30 a piece...prior to October 1 last year, they had a lot of meetings for which they did not get anything. Now, they receive $3 for attending the board meeting, but there is a catch to it: there are several meetings in the month, but they can be paid for only one."

The responsibilities of a board member in the early developmental and construction years of an electric cooperative seemed to multiply as time went along. First it was a matter of obtaining the necessary right-of-way, drafting bylaws, approving memberships and working with REA about the financing. But, the directors soon saw their job enlarge.

It was up to the board, in consultation with REA, to make decisions on virtually every aspect of construction and financial matters, and to find sources of power supply. Setting the electric rates to be fair and equitable for all members was not an easy task. And, of course, answering questions and resolving problems of co-op members fell upon the shoulders of directors.

Then there was the job of setting up records and proper accounting methods to conform with REA directives, and the continuing challenge of learning the REA standards as they evolved. Probably the most important responsibility of all was hiring the co-op manager or "project superintendent," as they were usually called in the first few years. An ongoing duty of the board has been establishing policy so that management and employees would have guidelines on how to operate the cooperative.

Those basic responsibilities of electric co-op boards of directors remain the same today. Principally, they are to establish policy, set goals, approve budgets and major work plans, select the general manager/CEO, provide general direction for the cooperative's future course, and conduct membership meetings and affairs as required.

However, to be an effective board member today, one needs to have broad knowledge in the electric utility field as well as savvy about cooperatives. People newly elected to electric co-op boards are not expected to possess all of the know-how. Educational opportunities for today's co-op directors are plentiful and most directors take advantage of them.

A series of training courses is made available to them through the National Rural Electric Cooperative Association and statewide associations. Many other sources, including universities and community colleges, offer programs helpful to co-op directors, as does the Michigan Alliance of Cooperatives and other co-op organizations.

But back in the 1930s and 1940s, board members learned the hard way — by "trial and error" on the job. As Cy Clark, the first manager of the Ontonagon co-op put it, "They didn't know the difference between a kilowatt and a kilowatt hour, but they learned fast."

Those pioneer directors couldn't help but learn the basics of electric power distribution because they were getting information from REA and engineers almost daily. Some took correspondence courses through the Rural Electrification Administration — courses on electricity, wiring, accounting, management and power generation and distribution.

Mary Bailey, of Mancelona, daughter of Top O' Michigan charter board member Martin Schaff, remembers how intense her father's interest was in electricity and putting it to work. "He put his heart and soul into getting the co-op started and took several correspondence courses, and then did many farm wiring jobs," Mrs. Bailey recalls.

One characteristic of co-op boards in Michigan has changed over the years. Of the 91 incorporators of Michigan's electric cooperatives in 1936-1939, only two were women. In 1996, 15 women were serving on the boards, including one as board president, three as board secretary and two as board treasurer.

The women's role in electric cooperatives has expanded from the days when they were stereotyped as secretaries and bookkeepers; some worked as home economists helping co-op members put electricity to efficient use in the home. Now, women are involved in professional, technical and management positions at many cooperatives.

And, what about their participation on the boards of directors — is that just a facade? Not from the experience of Michigan female board members.

Emma Reinbold, of Pellston, the first woman on Top O' Michigan's board as well as the Wolverine Power Co-op board and the statewide association (MECA) board, expressed the feeling of many in saying, "I believe there should be a woman on every co-op board. We think a bit differently and we have definitely something to contribute."

Emma contributed immensely to the rural electrification program in Michigan, taking an active part in Wolverine power supply decisions and statewide legislative matters over several years. Her dedicated service earned her the Special Recognition Award from the Michigan Electric Cooperative Association in 1984.

Another who helped shape the statewide association was Bernadine Qualmann from the Alger Delta Cooperative Electric Association. She served longer than any other woman on the MECA board —12 years, leaving in 1993. She continued to serve on the Alger Delta board.

Michigan holds the distinction of having one of the first African-American women to serve on an electric cooperative board of directors in the United States. She is Constance Dukes, of White Cloud, who has been a member of the O & A Electric Co-op board for 20 years, serving as secretary of the board in 1996. With O & A's recent merger with Oceana Electric Co-op, she is now a member of the Great Lakes Energy Cooperative board.

Mary C. Hawley, longtime director on Oceana's board, was one of the first Hispanic-American women on an electric co-op board. She was serving as secretary-treasurer of the co-op before the merger.

Beth McDonald, of Bad Axe, is the first woman elected to the Thumb Electric Co-op board since Ruth Brandmair in the 1930s. With two years' experience on the board, she believes commitment is the key. "Everyone brings a unique viewpoint to the board discussions...it's a matter of working together with common purpose."

A relative newcomer to the Fruit Belt Electric Cooperative board, Sue Vomish, of Dowagiac, says that her first year on the board was "one of the most interesting and educational years of my life." She considers women as strong advocates of cooperatives and co-op principles, and supports the challenge of educating young people and new co-op members about electric cooperatives.

Three women are members of the Cherryland Electric Cooperative board. Two have served as board president: Betty Gordon, of Lake Ann, and Betty Reynolds-Maciejewski, of Traverse City. Betty Gordon has been active in the Michigan Electric Cooperative Association as an officer of the MECA board and as chairperson of the MECA Self Insurance Fund. She also served on the Long Range Planning Committee and Government Relations Committee.

The third woman on Cherryland's board is Elizabeth Worden, of Thompsonville. She has served more than 12 years on the board, several as the treasurer. "Women were the driving force behind the co-op movement years ago," says Worden, who sees more management jobs for women.

Betty Gordon, the first female on Cherryland's board, points out that the co-op has a policy of providing educational opportunities for women employees, encouraging them to move up the ladder. The cooperative has a female office manager and others who are in marketing and engineering.

As to her perspective on female board members, Gordon believes the trend will continue. "Our cooperatives face complex issues and need the diversity of input and viewpoints to succeed."

Another who envisions more women on co-op boards is Sally Knopf, of Rogers City, who has served two terms on the Presque Isle Electric & Gas Co-op board. She has been secretary of the board and is one of Presque Isle's representatives on the Wolverine Power Supply Co-op board. "Although board members and the manager may have been uneasy when I first came on the board, I think we have a good working relationship today," Knopf says.

A concern shared by many of today's board members — men and women — is how to interest more young people in serving on the boards. "The cooperatives need new ideas and fresh thinking," says Mel Basel, retired director from the Presque Isle board.

Others echo that feeling, and some co-ops have experienced an influx of younger people on the board. Fruit Belt Electric Cooperative, Cassopolis, lost four veteran directors in a three-year period and as Rolfe Wells, former Fruit Belt board president, said, "the new younger persons on our board give the co-op a new aggressive spirit."

Bill Parsons, retired from the Top O' Michigan co-op board after 24 years of service, does not consider age a problem. "Most directors are truly committed to the cooperative and have the member-consumers foremost in mind regardless of age," said Parsons.

Jim Clarke, retired from the Tri-County Electric Cooperative board after 22 years of service, says the board must "keep the pulse of the membership." The Tri-County co-op does this through personal contact, district meetings and member surveys.

"Today's board member faces tougher issues than ever before, except perhaps the co-op founders." That's the thinking of Carl Eagle who has served on the Cloverland Electric Cooperative board since 1961. He points to the growing financial, political and competitive pressures in the electric utility world, emphasizing that management and board members must work together to deal with them effectively.

Don Wozniak, manager of Cloverland, agrees that today's director needs to be financially astute and, he adds, "customer oriented." Martin Thomson, manager of the Presque Isle Co-op, feels strongly that the board member "must be a good listener because he or she is the conduit for the member-consumers to influence the cooperative so that we make the right moves in serving their needs."

Thomson said that the input of co-op members as to their energy needs is what convinced the cooperative to enter the natural gas business in 1994.

A former manager of the Cloverland Electric Cooperative, John Holt, said "the cooperative is only as good as the employees." He recognized the significant investment in each employee and he regarded employees as the organization's most valuable asset. He conducted a special Employees Recognition Dinner each year.

There's no question that in an electric utility, the employees — in the plants, in the office and out in the field — literally energize the utility. Even with today's technological advances, their role and their performance is critically important to the quality of service.

"It is service excellence that we strive for every day," says Bob Matheny, general manager of Tri-County Electric Cooperative, Portland. The co-op gets continuous feedback on the quality of its service and customer satisfaction levels by providing easy-to-use postcard responses to members.

"We need to know if our programs and services are meeting the expectations of the co-op members. The degree to which they are or aren't tells us a lot about the performance of our employees, who are the ones providing the services," Matheny explains.

Since the start of rural electric cooperatives in the 1930s, one of the most vital and most visible jobs is that of the lineman. To most co-op members, the lineman has been the face of the electric co-op, whether he's climbing a pole or in his truck calling the office for an answer to a member's question. In those early days, a lineman did many jobs. "We learned to do most everything at the co-op," said Edwin "Bud" Englund who worked for the Alger Delta Electric Co-op from 1939 to 1977. "It was by necessity because we only had three or four employees." He later worked as the co-op's line superintendent for 25 years.

Line work was a rough, demanding job in the early years of electric cooperatives. "We worked all day and night many times," said Harry Pauley, lineman and later manager of the Presque Isle Co-op.

When Wayne Bumstead, of O & A Electric Co-op, started in line work in the 1960s, he asked one of the linemen what was the toughest part of the job and the fellow said "climbing the pole." After Wayne got up the pole, the other lineman in the crew said, "no, the worst is coming down the pole."

Bumstead said a big part of learning to be a lineman is giving attention to safety. "There's no margin for error in working on power lines," said the veteran lineman.

Frank Talentino, who retired after 46 years in line work and operations at Cloverland Electric Co-op, readily agrees. He's proud of the fact that Cloverland was the first cooperative in Michigan to be awarded National Safety Accreditation by the National Rural Electric Cooperative Association. "You have to continuously emphasize safety in working with electricity," says Talentino.

Paul Juriga, retired lineman from Fruit Belt Electric Co-op, said that in his first 10 years there was a lack of safety procedures — "nothing like you have now." He started doing line work in 1937 when, as he described it, "it was all muscle, physical work."

Most linemen agree that their work is demanding but exhilarating. "You are a lineman 24 hours a day, 365 days a year," said Jurgia, noting the possibility of storms and equipment failures any time of the year. "You know people are counting on you to get the power back on as soon as possible." With a smile, Clarence Marttila, line crew foreman at Houghton for Ontonagon Rural Electric, put it this way: "We've come a long way the last 30 years or so. We used to climb every pole. Now we use bucket trucks. It's a lot easier, but it sure spoils the image of the rugged lineman."

Lyle Johnson, who started as a "grunt" for 60 cents an hour in 1946 at Cherryland Electric Co-op, said virtually all lineman training was on the job until the 1950s. As to safety, he said an accident that fractured his skull caused the cooperative to develop written safety rules and require all line personnel to wear hard hats.

Bill Thomas, line superintendent at Cherryland for several years, put strong emphasis on line safety and served on the statewide Safety and Training Committee. Herm Fedawa, retired from Tri-County Electric, also was active on the safety committee and gave safety top priority. "There's no alternative to a good safety program in power line work," said Fedawa.

A common trait of electric co-op linemen back in the early days and continuing today is their familiarity with the rural community and the rapport with the people they serve. "There's a trust built between them and the co-op members," is how Frank Talentino of Cloverland described it.

Jackie Bates, retired from Top O' Michigan co-op after 46 years in the office and as dispatcher, said that "the line workers are tops...they work in the worst of conditions to get the power back on and most people don't see that, but I think they really appreciate it."

As written in *"The Next Greatest Thing,"* a book commemorating REA's 50th anniversary, the lineman "became the co-op's representative out on the land and along the lines...the lineman earned the farm family's trust and respect...their feats of courage and endurance in winter storms, hurricanes, tornados, and floods have become commonplace, almost expected."

This poem says it well:

*"So here's to the lineman, son of a gun!*
*He'll go without sleep for a week,*
*Working for you 'til every bit's done,*
*So the feeders can carry their peak.*
*Here's to the lineman!"*

Linemen and other field personnel of Michigan's electric cooperatives are known as "Good Neighbors" for another reason. In the course of their jobs, they cover a lot of ground driving down country roads and often use their two-way radio to report accidents or call for emergency assistance. Trained in first aid and CPR, the line workers have saved many lives over the years.

Ten Michigan co-op employees were recognized with "Good Neighbor Watch" awards in 1996 by the Michigan Electric Cooperative Association. There are dozens of others involved in helping people and law enforcement during the year that go unreported. It's part of the day's work.

Across America, more than 50,000 people work for electric cooperatives in hundreds of different jobs. One mark of the typical electric co-op employee, regardless of the specific job, has been loyalty. When employed in a full-time position, people tend to stay for 20, 30 or 40 years with a cooperative.

Greater mobility and more opportunities in our society today make this kind of longevity less likely. Movement from one electric co-op to another is now commonplace for management and professional people.

When the cooperatives were first getting into operation, there were extraordinary examples of employee loyalty. The first bookkeeper for Western Michigan Electric Cooperative, Marguerite Lorenz, worked four months before getting a paycheck because the co-op had to wait for REA funds and had no other income while under construction.

She stayed with the co-op and later was one of the organizers of the Michigan Electric Cooperatives Accountants Association, a group that has met each year to exchange information and learn new procedures and bookkeeping requirements.

A sense of commitment and determination developed, similar to that of the co-op organizers. Employees felt the challenge to succeed and, with few exceptions, they quickly became dedicated to the cooperative's future.

In the formative years, many employees attended meetings and workshops on their own time. They would drive considerable distances to learn how to do their jobs. It was all new to them and to the cooperative.

"There were always new procedures and changes in our billing methods," said Margaret Conrad, who worked 41 years at Fruit Belt Electric Cooperative, several as billing supervisor. The biggest change, she said — and many other co-op office people agree — was when the co-op switched to computers. For most cooperatives, that was in the 1960s.

Technology has changed how the electric cooperatives do many things, but it has not changed the fundamental purpose and focus of the co-ops: to provide the customer with the most dependable electric service at the least possible cost consistent with sound business principles. In short, it is CUSTOMER SERVICE.

The board members of yesterday and today, and the managers and the hundreds of employees, are to be commended for their commitment to serving the co-op member-customers. These tried and true cooperators, from the shores of Lake Superior to the rolling countryside of southwest Michigan, have built a system of delivering rural electric power that is second to none.

They built a network of cooperative power in Michigan and 45 other states. And it all began with the gritty people of the 1930s who started lighting their houses and barns "on their own power."

Now, thanks to those rural electric pioneers, 30 million Americans are "on their own power." They are co-owners of their co-op utility.

Clyde T. Ellis, rural electrification pioneer and first general manager of the National Rural Electric Cooperative Association, made this statement when he looked back on the accomplishments of the early electric cooperators:

"The wires which tied the houses of rural people together also seemed to unite their spirits. Beginning in the early days and growing through the years, there has been some unusual quality about the rural electrification program which has drawn people of diverse political and social views together in a common purpose. The people who work for our program feel they're working in a cause or a crusade which many of them cannot define."

Sixty years after the rural electrification pioneers built the cooperatives from the grass roots, their crusading spirit lives on. The feeling of unity among an ever-more diverse people continues to be manifested even in the face of new challenges and constant change in the electric utility industry. Thanks to the rural electric co-op pioneers and thanks to all the cooperators who followed, the light of cooperation is still shining brightly in Michigan.

---

## "Keeping Up With the Times"

I've never had much patience with the men who tell us women to buy things for the home just because their neighbors have them, and they do not want to be outdone.

That sounds so petty, doesn't it?

But when I go home to think the matter over after I've exploded in the face of some man who insists on telling me why women buy the things they do, I have to admit there is just enough truth in those statements to give them toe hold.

I might be willing to admit that seeing an electric refrigerator in Kath Norbert's kitchen first set me thinking I had to have one myself, but I refuse indignantly to listen to any suggestion that I wanted a refrigerator because she had one. That wasn't it at all.

I remember very well the day I first saw that refrigerator. Six of us were at Kath's for lunch. I won't say she'd given the luncheon in honor of the refrigerator, but it did get most of the attention. In the first place, she hurried us out to the table the very instant she was ready, so we could see the frozen cream cheese stuffing for the pear salad before it had a chance to melt.

And as soon as we had finished the last crumb of the chocolate ice box cake, we all trooped into the kitchen to see this new machine for ourselves. It made a great impression on us, standing there big and white and clean looking.

We opened the doors; we examined the ice trays, we listened respectfully to the motor. Then we began racking our brains for a place to get a little extra money.

"Is it cold all the time?" I asked.

"Yes, it's the same day or night." Kath's voice was proud and happy. "It's somewhere between 40 and 50 degrees. That's what the government calls the safety zone for food...I can keep things from day to day that we had to either eat or throw out before...and, oh, the children like to drink the cold milk and eat the frozen custards. I can get them to eat more salads, with the greens cold and crisp."

Behind our exclamations of wonder and admiration, we were all counting the steps we'd save and the strength we'd save and the time we'd save if we had electric refrigerators, too. Of course, we all wanted one the minute we saw Kath's standing there in the kitchen. But don't let any man tell you it was just because Kath had one. That just introduced us to it...

...In one sense we did, all of us, buy refrigerators because Kath had one. But land sakes alive, it wasn't because we had any feeling of jealousy or rivalry. We wanted refrigerators for what they would do for us, and Kath just showed us what that was.

I can't help but feel a little cross when men say that about us, for after all, we aren't trying to keep up with the times.

-- *Author unknown (from yesteryear)*

# MECA AWARD WINNERS

The Michigan Electric Cooperative Association inaugurated the MECA "Special Recognition Award" in 1979 to honor individuals who have made significant contributions to rural electrification in Michigan. Fifty-two men and women have been selected for the award over the past 18 years.

Members of co-op boards of directors who have received the award are: William Parsons, Top O' Michigan; Lyle Wilson, Alger Delta; Willard Haenke, Tri-County; Emma Reinbold, Top O' Michigan; Rolfe Wells, Fruit Belt; James Clarke, Tri-County; Leon Smith, Thumb; Melvin Basel, Presque Isle; Bernard Doll, Cloverland; Walter Cook, Thumb; Wayne Nordbeck, Cherryland; Elwyn Olmstead, Western Michigan; William Chapin and Jean Chapin, Tri-County; Raymond Berger, Alger Delta; Kenneth Bennett, Cloverland; Rolfe "Junior" Wells, Fruit Belt; and Harold "Doc" McCaughrin, Top O' Michigan.

Recipients who were managers of cooperatives: Carl Hoffman, Southeastern Michigan; Roy Hawkinson, Alger Delta; John Kutter, Thumb; Roger Westenbroek, Top O' Michigan; Harry Pauley, Presque Isle; John Keen, Wolverine; Francis Bowsman, Fruit Belt; Frank Anderson, Western Michigan; John Holt, Cloverland; Robert Fredericksen, Oceana; Philip Cole, Cherryland; Raymond Towne, Wolverine, Robert Neterer, Fruit Belt; Thomas Hanna, Top O' Michigan; and Jack Stickney, Western.

Others given the award: L.A. Cheney, executive secretary of the Michigan Association of Farm Cooperatives; Robert Feragen, REA Administrator; Robert Badner, REA Field Representative in Michigan; Kenneth Croy, Michigan Public Service Commission; Bob Bergland, Executive Vice President of NRECA; Al Hodge and Bob Daverman, consulting engineers; U.S. Representatives Don Albosta, Guy VanderJagt, Bob Traxler, and Dave Camp; J.R. Rudolph, former employee of Fruit Belt who served on the MECA board; Frank Talentino, former Operations Manager of Cloverland; Mark Harper, Cooperative Finance Corporation; Theresa Erschens, former MECA employee; John Abramson, James Padgett and Dan Blair, staff of the Michigan Public Service Commission; Dan Hesslin, attorney for Western Michigan; Raymond Kuhl, former manager and Executive Vice President of MECA; and Dr. Truman Surbrook, Michigan State University; U.S. Senator Carl Levin; and Lt. Gov. Connie Binsfeld.

## "A CELEBRATION OF SUCCESS"

Robert Feragen, the eighth REA Administrator, wrote a poem with the above title, published in *The Next Greatest Thing*, which chronicled 50 years of cooperative rural electrification. The book was published by the National Rural Electric Cooperative Assoc. in 1984. Here are two excerpts:

*"Take time to celebrate,*
*Having caution for what is true*
*of times past and people of the land.*
*Take care, as if in prayer, to mark well our passage*
*across half a century of America's brightened way.*
*Hard won, our country lights are beautiful with prospect,*
*reality surpassing the dream.*
*Our achievement greater than our strength:*
*Not the glory of light alone,*
*but the radiance of minds and souls,*
*And the promise and power of hope."*

*"What was built is not for us alone, nor for our children only,*
*The legacy is the future we make possible:*
*Cooperation arising from each community,*
*built upon the democratic dream.*
*From rural electrification for and by the people*
*comes a gift to all the nation:*
*A landscape peopled for freedom,*
*Rural America binding all America.*
*Weight the prize by no balance sheet*
*But in the heart."*

## RETIREMENT RULES

When Vernor "Smitty" Smith retired in 1983 after 30 years as manager of Tri-County Electric, his wife, Shirley, put together a few "rules" for his retirement. Here are a few:

"Go to the doctor every year for a checkup. You'll know you'll need medical attention when you get winded playing chess or when your mind makes contracts your body can't meet."

"Stay out of my kitchen, except to make popcorn."

"Draw up a chart showing which half of the household chores you intend to take over. I will want you to help around the house...For instance, I'll want you to become familiar with the washer and dryer — you know, those two white enameled things in the utility room? They do not load and unload themselves."

"Have your glasses checked, then subscribe to a second newspaper because we are going to have lots of conversation time from here on, and news will help fill it. Be sure the papers have good crossword puzzles so we can both have one."

Shirley and Smitty enjoyed 10 years of retired life together before Smitty passed away.

Women with ties to Michigan electric cooperative history (L to R): Margaret Conrad, Fruit Belt; Emma Reinbold, Top O' Michigan; Constance Dukes, O & A Electric; Betty Gordon, Cherryland; and Mary Bailey, Top O' Michigan.

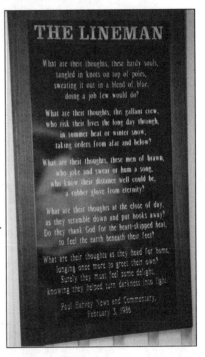

**Above:** Frank Talentino, a leader in line safety and training programs, retired from Cloverland after 46 years in line work and managing system operations. **Below:** Paul Juriga, longtime lineman for Fruit Belt Electric Cooperative.

**Above:** No matter what the weather, restoring service is the number one priority of electric cooperatives and their line crews.

**Below left:** Four of Cherryland Electric Cooperative's first linemen with the co-op's first service truck, a 1940 Ford. (L to R): Lyle Johnson and Bob Lambert. Front: E. Stibitz and and E. Lehn. **Below right:** The lineman's image has changed with bucket trucks and other new equipment, says Clarence Marttila, lead lineman at Ontonagon Country Rural Electric Association.

**Above:** A unique way of commemorating the 50th anniversary of REA in 1985 was the cross country journey of Scott Hudson, former board member of Cherryland Electric Cooperative, by horse and buggy. Hudson and his Belgian draft horse, Carter, travelled over 1,300 miles north through the Upper Peninsula and south to Tennessee. He published a book entitled *Neighbors--Electric Burro on the Road to Bogota* describing his adventures and his concept of electric cooperatives. "One thing that surfaces again and again as we travel the co-op countryside is the unique spirit that existed as REA got off the ground. People were doing for themselves, hand in hand with the government," wrote Hudson.

**Above top to bottom:** Co-op leaders Martin Thomson of Presque Isle, retired Cloverland manager Jack Holt, and longtime Cloverland director Carl Eagle.

Early 1940s photo shows Louise Snyder (L) bookkeeper from Oceana Electric and Marian Baker, Tri-County Electric bookkeeper (standing), at a regional meeting in Washington, D.C. They helped form the Michigan Electric Co-op's Accountants Association. The other two women are from Ohio.

**Above, left:** (left to right): Tri-County Electric manager Bob Matheny, former Congressman Howard Wolpe, Tri-County board chairman Carl Morton, and the NRECA executive manager Bob Bergland chat in Washington during an NRECA Legislative Conference. **Above, right:** MECA offices in Okemos. MECA provides educational programs, legislative services, and communications for the state's electric co-ops.

# ALGER DELTA COOPERATIVE ELECTRIC ASSOCIATION

It was a rocky start for the pioneers of the original co-op project in Delta and Alger counties. After futile attempts to get power companies to bring electricity to their farms and homes, the half dozen or so men from the Trenary-Rock-Perkins area decided to look into the new REA program.

They got legal assistance from Charles Lewis and filed papers with the State to incorporate in September of 1937. But months went by as the men continued to investigate power sources and confer with the Rural Electrification Administration in Washington.

Julius Sivula, first president of the cooperative and also project coordinator during construction, was relentless in pursuing the first REA loans and in negotiating with power companies for the co-op's power supply.

When one of the major suppliers was first contacted, Sivula was quoted 5 cents per kilowatt hour — higher than many retail rates. The price was later negotiated down to 1-1/4 cents per kwh.

> Incorporated  Sept. 2, 1937
>
> Original Incorporators:
>
> Harry Hall, Rock
> Julius Sivula, Trenary
> Elmer Peterson, Perkins
> Albert Whybrew, Rapid River
> Paul Sappanen, Rock

On December 8, 1938, the first power was turned on to members in the Trenary-Rock-Perkins area. One substation with three 37-1/2 KVA transformers served the load, which was very small by today's standards. As former Alger-Delta Line Superintendent Edwin "Bud" Englund explained, "Many farmers then just couldn't afford to get the farm wired right away and, for many, use was limited to lighting and maybe an electric iron or washing machine."

The delays in getting places wired was still a problem in 1939 as minutes of a board meeting in August of that year show that almost half of the farms signed up for service were not yet wired and ready to be connected. REA officials met with the board to devise a plan that would expedite connections on the first section of lines built. Also jeopardizing the co-op's progress was the loss of 50 or more prospective members to the Wisconsin-Michigan Power Company.

At the same meeting, sparks flew over the co-op's proposed "Section B" in Menominee County where the M & M Traction and Power Company was soliciting customers in the area to be served by the co-op. "The company's activities in Menominee County seem to indicate that M & M is doing all in its power to interfere with the cooperative's plans," said Sivula who took issue with other reports defending M & M.

When the Menominee area was added to the system in 1940-41 and the Stonington area was added later the co-op faced the knotty problem of power supply again. In addition, the M&M Power Company said it planned to extend electric service to 300 or more farms in Menominee County. But Sivula and the board persisted and built 135 miles of line to serve 500 members in the county.

Other areas were added later to the Alger Delta system, including the Isabella-Nahma vicinity, Cornell and LaBranche, Big Bay and Grand Marais, the latter not connected to the system until 1956 after a year's work in building 26 miles of line and a substation. The number of member-consumers in the Grand Marais area has tripled to more than 600 since 1956.

By 1964, the cooperative was serving over 4,000 members, almost half of them seasonal consumers using a monthly average of less than 50 kilowatt hours. Many farm members were using 500 to 700 kwh per month — 10 times the amount they used 20 to 25 years before.

Assets of the co-op totaled $2.3 million in 1964. Owing REA $2 million, member equity in the co-op was less than 10 percent. It has since grown to more than 30 percent.

1964 is remembered as the year of the "big blow." Tornado-like winds struck a large area and the entire Alger Delta system was knocked out for several hours. Crews came from Presque Isle Electric Cooperative to help restore service.

The cooperative grew to 7,000 members and over $8 million in assets by 1984. The staff of 21 included nine linemen, plus four men on right-of-way and brush clearing. Don Clark was manager.

Two "giants" in Alger-Delta's history whose leadership kept the cooperative moving forward when it faced difficult challenges were Raymond Berger and Lyle Wilson. Berger served on the board 45 years, most of those years as chairman. Wilson's service spanned more than 30 years, and he represented the state's co-ops on the National Rural Electric Cooperative Association board of directors in the 1960s.

**First Board of Directors:** Julius Sivula, Frank Heino, Paul Sappanen, Edward J. Johnson, Algot Gustafson

**Early Co-op Project Superintendent/Managers:** Harry Hall, Julius Sivula, Frank Sahlman (Menominee Co.)

**Other Early Leaders:** Arthur Berger, Emil Lampinen, John Barstow, Henry Demille, Lawrence Smith, George Grabowski, Wesley Zeratsky, Semer Thorsen, Charles Turan, William Vinette, Harry Sederquist, Alfred Sands, Henry Gustafson, John Koski, Folmer Olson, Henry Glaser, Joseph DeCremer, Herbert Lockhart and Samuel Hannon

**First Project Attorney:** Charles E. Lewis

**First Lines Energized:** December 8, 1938

**First Annual Membership Meeting:** 1939

**First Employees:** Orva Makela, Wy Nieuwenkamp and Edwin "Bud" Englund

**First Office:** One room at Rock, MI; moved to Escanaba in 1939 and to Gladstone in 1941

Wilson also was instrumental in forming the Michigan Electric Cooperative Association and was elected its first president in 1978. He realized the co-op's critical need to have unity and coordination in working with the State Legislature and the Public Service Commission.

The Michigan Electric Cooperative Association honored Berger and Wilson were honored by with its "Special Recognition Award" for their many years of dedicated work in the advancement of electric cooperatives.

Dealing with power companies to obtain bulk power supply in adequate amounts and at reasonable cost was always a priority for the Alger Delta Cooperative. In the early years, some of the contracts severely limited the supply and there was uncertainty about meeting the co-op's growing needs.

In recent years, power has been purchased from two Wisconsin utilities, UPPCO and the City of Marquette. The wholesale rates increased in the 1970s and 1980s, but negotiations in the 1990s have resulted in reductions and consequent retail rate drops from 11 cents per kilowatt hour to a little over 8 cents per kwh.

The office of the cooperative was moved to Gladstone in 1941. Employees moved into a new building there in the Fall of 1948. In 1996, the co-op's staff of 18 employees served more than 8,660 member-consumers.

Dan Roberts was appointed to succeed Don Clark as general manager when Clark retired in 1992. Sam Moulds of rural Marquette was elected board chairman upon Ray Berger's retirement.

- Lineman's pay at Alger Delta in 1940 was 40 cents per hour, and 50 cents per hour when climbing.

- Net income to the co-op in 1940 was $108.92. Total revenue in 1939 was $5,392. As of August, 1939, only 145 member-consumers were connected on 122 miles of line.

- Line loss (amount of electric current transmitted but not delivered/sold) was 30% in 1940. It has been reduced to less than 10 percent in recent years.

- Bottom rate in 1940 went up to 3 cents per kilowatt hour for use over 200 kwh; minimum was $3 for 40 kwh.

- The board of directors was expanded to nine in 1940; directors were paid $2.50 for attending meetings. Raymond Berger's 45 years on the Alger-Delta board, including 38 years as the chairman, is a record among Michigan's electric cooperatives.

- Bud Englund worked for the co-op from 1939 to 1977, excepting for a stint in the U.S. Army Air Corps. He was a lineman, power use adviser and operations superintendent, and has been involved in 50 of the cooperative's annual meetings where he conducted the prize drawings.

- The co-op's 1939 annual meeting was conducted in Finnish, which was the language of most of the members at that time.

## TELLING IT LIKE IT WAS:

"When I came on the board in 1948, we were barely making it financially, and we had problems with outages and getting folks to use more electricity, but farmers soon put the power to work in many ways. Today, we have excellent service and I think we as country people live as well or better than city people, thanks to the cooperative and REA."—*Raymond Berger, who served 45 years on the Alger Delta Board of Directors*

"This cooperative serves one of the most sparsely-populated areas in the state but with good employees and a very dedicated board of directors always trying to serve the members' best interests, we have succeeded and made progress beyond the dreams of those who started the co-op."—*Roy Hawkinson, former Manager of the Alger Delta cooperative*

"It was a struggle to get the co-op going — most everything was a struggle in those days. Many farm people could only pay a dollar (of the $5 sign-up fee) because of the terrible Depression, and they would pay the balance later. Some couldn't afford to hook up and pay an electric bill."—*Edwin "Bud" Englund, former Alger Delta employee of 45 years*

"We didn't have hot line tools in those early years, so sometimes you'd hear and feel a little sizzling in your hand working on a line. I was 'put to sleep' once on a pole, but luckily it wasn't serious. We really didn't have a safety and training program until the 1950s."—*Bud Englund*

"The first REA engineers in the 1930s deserve the credit for designing lines and devising construction methods that made large-scale rural electrification possible — and we have to also praise our loyal co-op linemen who work in all kinds of weather to keep the lines in service."—*Lyle Wilson, former Board member and officer, deceased*

"One of the most earnest and enthusiastic believers in cooperatives I've known on the board in 45 years was Lyle Wilson from the Stephenson area. He represented Michigan on the national electric co-op association board for a few years, and he was a strong advocate of forming the Michigan Electric Cooperative Association in 1978. It was fitting that he was elected the first president of MECA."—*Raymond Berger, former Board Chairman*

"We've heard the opinions of a few people saying we should sell the cooperative to a power company, but I think our record of service and the recent rate reductions give sufficient cause for members to want to keep the organization that they and their neighbors have built over 55 years."—*Dan Roberts, General Manager of Alger Delta Electric Cooperative*

113

**Right:** Former Alger Delta board president Lyle Wilson signs REA loan papers. **Above:** Former Alger Delta manager Wy Nieuwenkamp (L), longtime board chairman Ray Berger (center) and attorney Clair Hoehn. **Below:** Alger Delta board of directors in 1948 or '49.

**Below left:** Co-op manager Wy Nieuwenkamp (left) checks right-of-way work for a new power line that brought electricity to American Playground Device Company when it moved to Delta County in the 1950s.
**Below right:** Safety Award presented to Alger Delta manager Nieuwenkamp and staff in 1958 by Employers Mutual Insurance. (L to R): Roy Hawkinson, Wilfred Salo, Robert Anderson, Wayne Cassell, Wy Nieuwenkamp, Rudolph Scrock, Edwin Casimir, Phillip Cretins, Ed Pilon (behind Bob Schmidt of Employers Mutual) and Bud Englund.

**Above, top row, L to R:** Retired employee, Bud Englund, and Julius Sivula, one of the cooperative's founding fathers. **Above, bottom row, L to R:** Sam Moulds, former board chairman, and former manager Roy Hawkinson.

# CHERRYLAND ELECTRIC COOPERATIVE

Cherryland Electric Cooperative was one of the last electric co-ops in Michigan to get officially incorporated and under construction. Max Goin, Frank Burkhart, and Eino Lehto were among those who spent many days and evenings for a year or more talking with people about the REA and how they could get electricity by organizing their own cooperative.

The group held its first official meeting July 27, 1938, at Traverse City, and named Frank Burkhart chairman. In November of 1938, the co-op submitted its first REA loan application in the amount of $372,000 to build 300 miles of line and a substation.

On May 25, 1939, the first lines were energized bringing power to 60 members. The board negotiated with Michigan Public Service Company (later sold to Consumers Power) for power supply and that was the cooperative's sole source of power the first several years.

Without any service area rules or state law, the cooperative and the power company tangled over territory. As the co-op built more lines, the company extended its rural lines and served customers the co-op intended to serve. Many of them were uncertain about the co-op's future and its rates.

> **Incorporated July 27, 1938**
>
> **Original Incorporators:**
>
> Eino Lehto, Copemish
> Frank Burkhart, Traverse City
> Ray C. Johnson, Thompsonville
> Max Goin, Lake Ann
> Morgan McDermott, Traverse City
> E.G. Cowan, Copemish
> Dr. Robert Flood, Northport

That was cause for concern at REA cooperative. If the co-op would lose prospective members where it had lines mapped out, the economic feasibility of the project would be seriously threatened. To be feasible and make the REA loan payments, the co-op needed to realize at least $11 revenue per mile of line.

One of the original board members, Morgan McDermott, now deceased, said that the co-op did not have the minimum number of members nor the assured revenue per mile cinched, "but once the lines were up, it was easier to get sign-ups." Hard to believe now, but some folks then were skeptical of electricity's value.

As Bob Lambert, one of the co-op's first linemen and later its manager, remembers, Cherryland had less than 500 members connected when he started with the co-op in June of 1941. Then World War II hit and construction came to a standstill. Only a few farms, where short extensions of line were needed, could be connected — and that was up to the War Production Board.

By 1946, when Lyle Johnson started with the co-op in line work, Cherryland was serving nearly 2,000 members. By September, 1948, electricity was flowing to 2,739 members over 554 miles of line.

The average use in 1948 was only 115 kilowatt hours per month and the average monthly bill was $5.13. Line loss was 20 percent, which was typical in those days over long spans.

The cooperative bought a house and garage at 213 Bay Street in Traverse City in 1945, and six years later built a new headquarters in Traverse City. Today's headquarters building, facilitating a staff of 50, was built in 1973 in Grawn, a few miles southwest of Traverse City.

When Bob Lambert was appointed manager January 1, 1962, the cooperative was serving 5,308 members.

Competition with Consumers Power was "dog-eat-dog" in Lambert's words. Cherryland lost members who switched to Consumers Power for a better rate. The battle for new loads came to a head when the co-op and Consumers went to court disputing which utility should serve the new Platte River fish hatchery.

Cherryland won the court case and Cherryland's attorney, Harry Running, then recommended that the co-op be regulated by the Michigan Public Service Commission so the Commission could set rules to stop customer switching and resolve disputes over new loads. The Commission agreed it would exercise its authority over the cooperatives, and in 1966 all 13 Michigan electric co-ops became subject to the Public Service Commission.

**First Board of Directors:** the orignal incorporators

**Early Co-op Project Superintendent/ Managers:** Neil Chesebro, Harry Hall.

**Other Early Leaders:** Don Gray, Harry Lautner, Veikko Nordbeck

**First Project Attorney:** Wilfred Lewis

**First Lines Energized:** May 25, 1939; Dedication Ceremony June 10, 1939

**First Annual Membership Meeting:** August 24, 1938

**First Employees:** Irv Stibitz, Ernie Lehn, Bob Lambert (later served as manager), Lyle Johnson

**First Office:** 122 Front Street, Traverse City

While the move to regulation helped in respect to "single-phase" loads (the typical residential customer), fights ensued over the larger loads such as shopping centers outside city limits and new industries. It wasn't until 1980 that the cooperatives, the investor-owned utilities and the Commission came to agreement on rules for the larger loads. The MPSC rules on service extensions and their enforcement were important to Cherryland because of the area's fast and continued growth over the years.

A solution to the problem of power supply to meet the growth in kilowatt hour sales was the creation of Northern Michigan Electric Cooperative in 1949, a "Generation and Transmission" (G&T) co-op formed by Cherryland, Top O' Michigan and Presque Isle cooperatives. The G&T co-op built a coal-fired generating plant near Boyne City and acquired other generating facilities as well as purchasing large blocks of power from other utilities.

Cherryland board member Wayne Nordbeck served as chairman of Northern Michigan's board of directors in the mid-1970s when the decision was made to buy a piece of Detroit Edison's Fermi II nuclear generating plant. "All of the studies showed it to be the most economical power for the future, but several developments changed that picture and we then worked out an agreement with Edison to sell back our share."

When Phil Cole assumed the manager's position in 1976, the Cherryland cooperative was serving 11,000 members. In 1979, the co-op installed its first inhouse computer to do all of the billing and other data processing tasks.

Cole and John Rockershousen, Cherryland board member, were two of the original incorporators of the Michigan Electric Cooperative Association in 1978. Rockershousen, now an employee of the co-op in charge of marketing, said he regards the founding of the statewide association as a "turning point" for co-ops in Michigan.

"MECA has provided great communications tools, most notably the *Country Lines* magazine, which goes to all Cherryland members and contains important information about our cooperative and major developments around the country," added Rockershousen.

A change in the cooperative's bylaws in 1984 increased the size of the board of directors to nine. Three of the nine directors on the board in 1996 were women; one serves as president —Betty Reynolds-Maciejewski; one as secretary —Betty Gordon; and one as treasurer —Elizabeth Worden.

Over its 58 years of operation, the cooperative has issued patronage capital refunds to members totaling more than $7,000,000. Cherryland has become a leader in quality of electric service, strongly emphasized by its general manager, Bruce King, who came to the co-op from an investor-owned utility in Maine in 1993.

In the past 20 years, the cooperative has more than doubled the number of member-consumers served. In mid-1996, the count was 24,256.

One of Cherryland's past newsletters presented this perspective on "Who Is the Cooperative?"

"The co-op is people...you and your neighbors. But especially people who try to see clearly, who feel deeply and who like to be self-reliant...they see that the whole community benefits by people working together."

Under the management of Bruce King, the co-op has down-sized and made budget cuts, enabling two rate reductions. Goal-setting and empowering employees has helped improve efficiency and productivity, says King. "We want to be totally customer-focused — that's what we're here for."

King chaired a special committee of the Michigan Electric Cooperative Association in 1995 to study and provide recommendations on the position of the co-ops in regard to deregulation and restructuring. "We intend to continue to put quality of service to the member-customer first and successfully compete in the changing utility industry," says King.

## TELLING IT LIKE IT WAS:

"In swampy areas, we had to dynamite the poles into the ground and sometimes the charge would blow the top of the pole off and we'd run like heck so it wouldn't fall on us. Those days, like storms, I don't miss."— *Lyle Johnson, lineman in the 1940s and later Line Superintendent and Distribution Manager.*

"Getting our statewide association organized in 1978 was important to our cooperatives because it gives us much more strength in legislative and regulatory matters, and a terrific magazine (Country Lines)."— *Wayne Nordbeck, member of Cherryland board of directors the past 30 years.*

"At the time of the decision (1976), nuclear power from Fermi II looked to be the cheapest but I had serious doubts about the numbers. It was a good move when we got out of it."— *Phil Cole, former Cherryland manager who was elected to the co-op's board in 1995.*

"I remember working 40 hours straight without sleep in one storm making repairs, and we didn't have the tools to work with then that linemen have today — and no bucket trucks. It was all climbing in those days."— *Bob Lambert, one of the co-op's first employees and manager from 1962 to 1976.*

"Consumers Power threatened to stop selling power to Cherryland in the late 1940s, so we got busy and started our own power supply co-op, Northern Michigan, and it's a good thing we did because our kilowatt-hour sales increased beyond expectations in the 1950s and 1960s."— *Wayne Nordbeck, longtime Cherryland board member and former chairman of Northern Michigan Electric Cooperative board of directors.*

## READY FOR 21st CENTURY: CHERRYLAND OFFERS ONLINE SERVICE

The Cherryland Electric Cooperative, headquartered at Grawn near Traverse City, has formed a new subsidiary to expand Internet service to co-op members and others in the area of Grand Traverse, Leelanau and Benzie counties.

Subscribers to Cherryland Online Service will have access to World Wide Web, E-Mail, interactive chat rooms, interactive games and other options. "We feel the region is ready for a provider who has a proven track record, is reliable, customer-focused and delivers quality service, said John Rockershousen, Cherryland Marketing Manager. The Internet is the way people will do business in the next century."

■ In 1941, Bob Lambert started with the co-op doing line work —often 60 to 70 hours a week — for a salary of $80 per month.

■ $25 War Bonds were given as annual meeting prizes in 1944 and the co-op board in July, 1944, approved purchase of four $1,000 War Bonds to help the war effort.

■ The two-way radio system, first installed in 1950, was a big factor in making line work safer and easier, said Lyle Johnson, who started with the co-op in 1946 and became Line Superintendent.

■ In the Cherryland area, the lines of the cooperative and of Consumers Power and the municipal system of Traverse City intermingle at some crossroads, the result of "open competition" before MPSC rules. Duplication of facilities and public safety have been major concerns of the Commission and legislators.

■ The name "Cherryland Rural Electric Cooperative Association" was adopted upon the suggestion of Morgan McDermot at the first board meeting July 27, 1938.

■ Cherryland has issued capital credit refunds to members regularly in recent years. The returns in 1994 and 1995 totaled $1.1 million. That is in addition to rate cuts of 3 percent in those same years.

**Top right:** Safety Award presented in 1962 from Employees Mutual to Cherryland Manager Bob Lambert (center). On the left are retired manager, Harry Hall, and Eino Lehto, board president. Line foreman Lyle Johnson is on right.
**Below left:** Wayne Nordbeck (L) who has served on the Cherryland board since 1967, and John Rockershousen, a former board member who became the co-op's marketing manager.

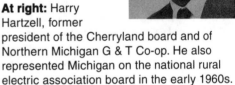

**Above:** Lyle Johnson (L), retired lineman who had been with the co-op since 1946, and on the right, Phil Cole, former manager of the co-op, now a member of the board.
**At right:** Harry Hartzell, former president of the Cherryland board and of Northern Michigan G & T Co-op. He also represented Michigan on the national rural electric association board in the early 1960s.

**Above:** 1997 Cherryland board of directors, left to right: Wayne Nordbeck, Phil Cole, John Porter, Terry Lautner, Betty Gordon, Bill Hoxie, Betty Reynolds-Maciejewski, Elizabeth Worden, Laverne Maginity.
**At right:** The original Cherryland board in 1938. Top row (L to R): Morgan McDermott, Ed Cowen, Eino Lehto, and Frank Burkhart. Bottom row: Ray Johnson, Max Goin, and Dr. Robert Flood.

# CLOVERLAND ELECTRIC COOPERATIVE

The pioneers who incorporated the Cloverland Electric Cooperative in July of 1938 had actually met several times in 1937 to lay the groundwork for the organization. The Dafter Township Hall, just a mile from the cooperative's present headquarters, was the scene of the group's first organizational meeting in 1937.

After the charter was approved, it didn't take long for work to begin on the system because contact had already been made for an REA loan. The loan came through on August 27, 1938, and the first poles were set less than a month later. The $427,000 loan was to finance 350 miles of line and several substations.

Before the first lines were energized, a dedication ceremony was held October 17, 1938, and Michigan Governor Frank Murphy addressed the 650 people attending. Murphy told the crowd that the progress of the Cloverland cooperative and its board of directors "is giving you electricity which you never would have gotten until the private utilities saw a profit in rural electrification."

Murphy took pride in having removed the barrier imposed by the state in 1936 when electric co-ops were not allowed to be legally incorporated, thereby preventing any REA loans in Michigan. His Attorney General, Raymond Starr, issued a ruling that enabled the co-ops to get charters and apply for the REA funding. He also appointed Joseph Donnelly, from the Upper Peninsula, to the Michigan Public Utilities Commission, and Donnelly actively supported the cooperatives in their early stages of development.

> **Incorporated July 29, 1938**
>
> **Original Incorporators:**
>
> Howard McKelvey, Engadine
> Edward Doll, Dafter
> George Raynard, Pickford
> Albert Schopp, DeTour
> Emile Savoie, Dryburg
> Russel Brown, Sault Ste. Marie
> David Liukko, Dafter

Energizing of the lines in March of 1939 brought power to 1,090 co-op members. They paid a minimum of $2.50 a month for 30 kilowatt hours, 4.5 cents per kwh for the next 50, three cents for the next 120, and 1.5 cents per kwh for use over 200. Loans were made available to members for wiring their premises.

By 1951, average kilowatt hour use per member was 133 per month, and 3,300 farms and residences were receiving service. Within the next five years, those numbers increased to 200 kwh per month and 5,500 members.

Power supply arrangements were made with the Edison Sault Electric Company, which continues to provide a portion of the cooperative's needs. As Cloverland grew to more than 3,000 members in the early 1950s, the board decided to build a diesel generating plant at Dafter and transmission lines to deliver the power. The capacity of the plant was boosted in 1959 and 1960 with more diesel units.

The diesel generating units were economical until the Arab oil embargo of 1973 when oil prices skyrocketed. According to former Cloverland manager Jack Holt, the co-op's cost jumped from 11 cents per gallon in 1972 to over $1 per gallon in 1975.

The cooperative's membership reached 8,000 by 1968. To assure adequate and dependable power supply, interconnections were made with Consumers Power Company and jointly-owned transmission lines were built by the co-op and Edison Sault. The system includes 170 miles of 69,000-volt and 138,000-volt lines.

The cooperative paid almost a half million dollars in property taxes in 1995.

The cooperative has more than 2,000 miles of distribution line in Chippewa, Luce and Mackinac counties after starting with just 100 miles energized in 1939.

In 1953, the Cloverland board and management decided to tackle a challenge. Manager Roy Wells and Area Foreman Frank Talentino formulated plans with REA and consulting engineers to bring electric service to the islands of Sugar, Neebish and Drummond. They devised a system to install cable underwater and succeeded in providing electricity from the cooperative not only to these three islands but another 35 over the next 10 years.

Cloverland brings electric service to more islands than any other electric co-op in the nation. The largest is Drummond Island where resorts, a large limestone plant and hundreds of private homes and cottages are served.

Talentino was promoted to Line Superintendent and later Operations Manager before his retirement in 1995 after 46 years with the co-op. His innovative work and leadership in power line safety is widely known, and a scholarship in

**First Board of Directors:** the original incorporators

**Early Co-op Project Superintendent/ Managers:** Harley Peasley, George Raynard, Harvey Kapphahn

**Other Early Leaders:** Clifford Roberts, Frederick Taylor, Chester Crawford.

**First Project Attorney:** Paul L. Adams

**First Lines Energized:** March 9, 1939; Dedication Ceremony October 17, 1938, when first poles set.

**First Annual Membership Meeting:** 1938

**First Employees:** Harley Peasley, Connie King

**First Office:** 521 Ashmun St., Sault Ste. Marie

his name was instituted in 1994 at Alpena Community College's new utility technician's course.

Cloverland's board of directors took on other challenges through the years, including a controversy over personal property taxes — that is, the tax on the power lines, transformers, and meters. Records show that the Cloverland board made contact with each township supervisor "to see about securing a reasonable assessment of the lines." The issue was later resolved allowing for economic differences in co-op service areas.

The cooperative's staff moved into a new office building in the summer of 1971. It is located on Highway M-28, just west of I-75. The Cloverland staff totals 48 including line crews at DeTour, Dafter and Newberry. In 1995, the co-op's revenue reached $11,541,000 from 15,500 members.

Don Wozniak, who came to the co-op as office manager in 1979, was appointed manager in 1985. He believes that cooperatives, like Cloverland, have demonstrated unique expertise in serving rural areas. "It's our niche now and into the future," says Wozniak.

He and Board Chairman Bernard Doll are active supporters of the statewide and national associations.

Wozniak was president of the Michigan Electric Co-op Association in 1995-96, and Doll represented Michigan cooperatives on the national board for 12 years.

■ In March of 1939, the Cloverland board approved purchase of a standard Ford coupe with a box in the rear for $745.73 and a 1939 Chevrolet pickup truck for $696.10.

■ When Mrs. Russel Brown was hired for right-of-way work in September, 1938, getting easements from some landowners was not easy — adding the "woman's touch" was an appropriate move.

■ Beginning in the 1950s, "Willie Wiredhand" promotions encouraged co-op members to buy electric ranges, clothes dryers, water heaters and freezers with offers such as 100 kilowatt hours free when you bought one of the appliances.

■ Edward Doll was elected the first chairman of Cloverland's board of directors in 1938. In 1995, his son, Bernard Doll, was elected board chairman. Bernard succeeded his father on the board in 1976.

■ Longest serving Cloverland board member was Howard McKelvey, from 1938 to 1978.

■ George Raynard, who was one of the cooperative's original incorporators in 1938, lived to the age of 105. He died in January, 1998. His son, William, served on the board in the 1980s.

■ Back in 1966, Manager Roy Wells did a "co-op walkathon" — he and a few coworkers covered every mile of line in the cooperative's service area to provide precise details for system maps. The co-op then had about 1,900 miles of line serving 7,700 members.

# TELLING IT LIKE IT WAS:

"I will never forget the fight that I and Howard McKelvey, our board president, had with REA in Washington getting approval for a loan to bring service by cable to the first three islands we serve."— *Former Manager Roy Wells, who led the successful efforts to serve several islands in the 1950s.*

"You can have electricity before the snow flies."—*Joseph Donnelly, Michigan Public Service Commissioner to 100 farmers at Dafter meeting in 1938. He was off by a few months. The first power flowed in March, 1939.*

"I think I dug more than a thousand holes by hand in my early years with the co-op....One thing I'm most proud of is that Cloverland was the first co-op in the state to earn National Safety Accreditation in 1973."—*Frank Talentino, who retired after 46 years with Cloverland, the last 25 as head of operations.*

"The cooperative is only as good as its employees."—*Former Manager Jack Holt, who held an employee recognition event every year.*

"I don't think you can beat Cloverland Electric Co-op for quality of service. That's the only reason we are in business — to serve the customers, our members."—*Carl Eagle, Cloverland board member since 1961.*

"Electricity is the fuel of the future — clean, safe and the most efficient."—*from Cloverland newsletter article reporting on USDA tests of electric and bottle gas appliances.*

"A power company line went right by our place before we got Cloverland going, but the company (Edison Sault) wanted $1,000 to connect our farm, and my father said that was too much."—*Bernard Doll, board member since 1976 when he succeeded his father.*

**Above left:** Retired after 46 years with Cloverland, Frank Talentino with wife, Fran, at his namesake power station. **Above right:** Manager Don Wozniak, manager, who has been with the co-op since 1980. **Below left:** The office of the co-op in the 1940s in Sault Ste. Marie. **Below right:** Well-deserved awards for service on the Cloverland board were given to (left to right): Howard McKelvey, Albert Schopp and Edward Doll–all members of the original board of directors in 1938.

**Below:** Cloverland linemen learn the techniques of using hotline tools in hands-on training in early 1970s. The co-op has been a leader in power line safety and job training.

# FRUIT BELT ELECTRIC COOPERATIVE

The founding fathers of what was visualized as a large cooperative stretching from Berrien, Cass and St. Joseph counties all the way north to Ottawa county were anxious to get the co-op incorporated and qualified for a loan from the Rural Electrification Administration. When the state approved the charter in June, 1937, the Fruit Belt board of directors filed for a loan of $125,000 to build 98 miles of line.

One of the early resolutions adopted by the board was a declared policy of conciliation and cooperation with existing utilities, including the Indiana & Michigan Power Company. The co-op board met with officials of this company in October, 1937, to discuss power supply and an agreement on service territories.

The co-op contracted for its first wholesale power from Michigan Gas & Electric Company in March, 1938. Within a few months, controversy began when the company alleged that the co-op was serving farms in its territory. The co-op and the farmers involved countered that the power company had previously refused to connect the farms without large payments that the farmers could not afford. The farmers stayed with the co-op.

> Incorporated June 25, 1937
>
> **Original Incorporators:**
> R.B. Walker, Middleville*
> Johannes Naber, Holland*
> Ethel Gibbon, Decator*
> Dean Clark, Buchanan
> W.F. Leach, Cassopolis
> Verne Bates, Mattawan*
> Claude Van Dyke, Hudsonville*
> Ray Mohney, Three Rivers
>
> *resigned when Van Buren and other counties north were considered outside the Fruit Belt area.*

Meanwhile, the cooperative's first project manager, Lynd Walkling, was discharged by the board and Robert Thompson hired to get the project moving. Efforts to get right-of-way easements were expedited and construction started in early 1938. A big celebration was held July 30-31 when the first lines were energized bringing electricity to 300 farms and homes.

The group of leaders from Van Buren County had decided to organize a separate cooperative, and laid plans for construction with their own REA loan. Both cooperatives proceeded with work in 1938 and 1939, and the two boards held a joint meeting in June of 1939 to discuss consolidation. Agreeing upon economic advantages, they put it to a vote of the membership of each cooperative. Only one member voted no.

The two officially became Fruit Belt Electric Cooperative on April 17, 1940, and construction continued to serve 3,000 or more members that year. The co-op also moved forward with plans for its own generating plant and, in August of 1940, three 670 horsepower diesel generating units were put into operation at Cassopolis. In 1941, two more diesel generators were added.

An interesting article in one of the area newspapers on August 8, 1940, commended the management of Fruit Belt and stated that "they offer the territory served by them a most desirable location for industrial plants and enterprises of various character and add materially to the attraction of the community."

A news item in the Cassopolis newspaper in June of 1939 told of the big REA Farm Equipment Show coming to the area July 3-4. Large crowds attended the demonstrations of farm and home electric equipment, conducted by experts from the Department of Agriculture and manufacturers. The show, which travelled many states, featured electric feed grinders, elevators, hay drying, automatic milkers, water systems, irrigation systems and other farm uses of electricity.

The Fruit Belt cooperative progressed rapidly, serving almost 6,000 members by 1947 and, in 1957, topping the 10,000 mark. Average monthly use was 354 kilowatt hours in 1957 at an average cost of 2.55 cents per kilowatt hour. Total revenue was $999,620 — more than 87 percent of it from farm members.

The cooperative shut down its diesel plant in 1951 and entered into a contract with Indiana & Michigan Electric Company for all of its power supply. Looking at other alternatives in 1976, the co-op decided to join the Wabash Valley Electric Power Cooperative, a generating and transmission (G & T) cooperative in Indiana. Wabash Valley later filed for Chapter 11 bankruptcy when it invested $280 million of REA loan funds in a nuclear power plant (Marble Hill) that was cancelled during construction by the Indiana governor's order.

Fruit Belt continues to buy its wholesale power from Wabash Valley. The G & T co-op won a legal battle with REA over the amount of debt it owes to REA; as a result, its rates for wholesale power were not increased.

Over the years, Fruit Belt has

**First Board of Directors:** Dean Clark, Buchanan; W.F. Leach, Cassopolis; Ray Mohoney, Three Rivers; Rolfe L. Wells, Dowagiac; Ralph W. Hain, La Grange Twnp. Two additional directors were elected at the cooperative's annual meeting in February, 1938: Manning Kingsbury, Cass County, and Leon Bivvens, St. Joseph County

**Early Co-op Project Superintendent/ Managers:** Lynd Walkling, Robert Thompson

**Other Early Leaders:** Myrl Moyer, Ralph Pashby, and the following board members of the Van Buren Electric Co-op that merged in 1940 with Fruit Belt: Otis Klett, Keeler; Calvin Millard, Decatur; Berlin St. John, Hartford; Fred Stiver, Schoolcraft; Cyril Latus, Hartford; Earl Passmore, Paw Paw; Joseph Lupekas, Decatur

**First Project Attorney:** William L. Fitzgerald

**First Lines Energized:** July 30, 1938. Two day celebration July 30-31

**First Annual Membership Meeting:** June 26, 1937

**First Employees:** Robert Foreman, Paul Juriga, Virginia Knoll, Francis Bowsman, Gene Spencer, Jack Playford

**First Office:** First National Bank building, Paw Paw, then relocated to Cassopolis in late 1937

been a leader in advocating efficient electric heating systems — for the past 20 years, it has promoted geothermal heat pumps. The co-op's heating and air conditioning load, combined with relatively high use of power on farms the co-op serves, puts the co-op near the top in Michigan on kilowatt-hour sales per member.

In 1996, the Fruit Belt cooperative served almost 25,500 members over 2,600 miles of line. The staff of 70 is headquartered in a newly remodeled building at Cassopolis. General Manager is Jon Bellgowan, formerly an electric co-op manager in Minnesota. He succeeded Robert Neterer who passed away in 1994. Francis "Butch" Bowsman, Clarence Haslanger and Clarence Staples preceded Neterer.

Bellgowan has instituted several changes at the cooperative, including a major remodeling and addition to the office facility. He has also put new emphasis on energy marketing and customer services. In 1997, the co-op announced a new 24-hour telephone service to accommodate customer requests and inquiries.

"We believe that we have what it takes for our cooperative to be the utility of choice in the increasingly competitive electric utility world," says Bellgowan.

## TELLING IT LIKE IT WAS:

"We will continue to upgrade and improve our system as demand indicates, so that members will not have to cope with brownouts or blackouts."— *Francis "Butch" Bowsman in his first report as co-op manager in 1974 (when energy crisis arose).*

"The cooperatives need to stick together and be strong...they're like a ripe plum to the big utilities and we don't want Fruit Belt to be picked off."— *Margaret Conrad, retired from the co-op after 41 years in customer service and billing.*

"It was tough going in those first years....we worked long hours and farmers helped haul poles and dig holes, all by hand...but it was worth it when you saw the changes in life on the farms."— *Paul Juriga, retired line foreman who started with the Van Buren co-op in 1937 and worked 42 years for Fruit Belt.*

"I went with my father sometimes when he'd go to get sign-ups and easements, and I remember quite often it was the farm wife who was the one to say 'Yes' because she saw so many things that electricity would do to lighten her workload."— *Rolfe "Junior" Wells, member of the Fruit Belt board for 25 years.*

"We are dedicated to serving the customers — the member-owners of this cooperative — in every way to meet their expectations. That's the way it should be in a co-op — we have no other reason to exist."— *Jon Bellgowan, general manager of Fruit Belt .*

■ At the first organizational board meeting in June of 1937, R.B. Walker of Middleville was named chairman and Johannes Naber, vice chairman. Later that year, when the proposed service area was revised, Rolfe L. Wells of Dowagiac was elected chairman. His son, Rolfe, Jr., also served as board chair from 1989 to 1995.

■ Donald Dickerson and Emil Knoska each served more than 40 years on the Fruit Belt board of directors. Dickerson was board chairman for several years and Knoska was secretary-treasurer.

■ Acknowledging that the war had curtailed expansion of the co-op's service, Fruit Belt Manager Robert Thompson announced in August, 1942, that the co-op "will focus its efforts on furnishing power to produce and conserve foods needed to win the war." He explained that some farms may qualify for electric service where line extensions are approved by the War Production Board.

■ Energy theft was a problem for the cooperative in the 1970s and '80s. J.R. Rudolph, power use specialist for the co-op, developed detection methods that led to arrests. His work and efforts of the Michigan Electric Cooperative Association led to passage of a state law providing for prosecution and penalties for energy theft.

■ The cooperative was recognized in 1966 for eight years of work without a disabling injury. Accidents involving power line contact are, unfortunately, also part of the co-op's record and the other 13 co-ops in Michigan. Safety has been given high priority through a statewide program the past 20 years.

■ Bill McKenzie, who started working part-time at Fruit Belt in 1947, retired in September, 1996, longest serving of any Fruit Belt employee. He continued to do production work on Fruit Belt's pages in *Country Lines* magazine on a part-time basis. Bill has had responsibilities for the cooperative's newsletter almost from the start. He's been dispatcher and, for many years, worked in data processing.

■ Rolfe "Junior" Wells, whose father was one of Fruit Belt's founders, is the longest serving member on the Michigan Electric Cooperative Association board; in 1997, he was the only remaining director from the original MECA board.

■ Manning Kingsbury, member of the Fruit Belt board in the 1940s, represented Michigan on the National Rural Electric Co-op Association board 1946-47.

■ Marion Wolkins of Union wrote to Michigan *Country Lines* magazine in 1985, telling of his experience in 1938 and 1939 working for a contractor building REA lines: "We dug holes six feet deep with a spud and a spoon shovel. We dragged the poles from the road to the holes by hand and we set them by hand with pike poles...My brothers, Johnny and Lee, and I worked for 40 cents per hour, and one cent of each dollar was taken out for Social Security." Their parents, Mr. and Mrs. John Wolkins, lived on a farm near Union in southwest Michigan for 25 years before they got electricity. Thanks in part to their sons, they got electric service over REA-financed lines from Fruit Belt in 1939.

**At right:** Electronic data processing was new at Fruit Belt in 1968. Barbara Adam Masica (left) and Carol Truex Bowman were the first office workers to use the machines. **Below left:** Bill McKenzie observed his 40th year with the co-op in 1987. **Below middle:** Gene Farnsworth, retired line superintendent. **Below right:** Clarence Haslanger, who managed the co-op in earlier years.

**Below:** Fruit Belt board of directors in 1958. Left to right: Arlo Lutz, Leah Carroll, Harry Barrett (president), Ray Mohney, Donald Dickerson (vice president), Emil Knoska (secretary-treasurer), J.E. Monette, Leon Phelps, and James Hoff, attorney for the co-op. **Inset:** Harold Zimmerman, who was also a member of that board.

# O & A ELECTRIC COOPERATIVE

In Ottowa and Allegan Counties in 1936, some 1,500 farms did not have central station electric service.

Farmers, including Dale Jewett, got tired of waiting and looked into the new REA program. They knew it offered farmers the chance to get electricity by organizing their own utility.

Jewett worked with the County Agent to make a survey of farmers' interest in forming a cooperative. Although there were some naysayers, most were willing to give it a try.

"We were ready to go," said Jewett, "but the Michigan Utilities and Securities Commission blocked us from incorporating." It was a political barrier, involving a major farm organization in the state and the private utilities. Their stand was: no REA funds in Michigan.

After Governor Frank Murphy took office in 1937, the Attorney General ruled the co-ops should be recognized as legal entities and O & A was officially chartered by the state. Murphy had campaigned in support of the REA program.

Early in 1938, O & A applied for a $165,000 REA loan for line construction,

> *(merged with Oceana Electric Cooperative as Great Lakes Energy Cooperative Jan. 1, 1997)*
>
> **Incorporated  December 28, 1937**
>
> **Original Incorporators:**
> Johannes Naber
> Eugene TenBrink
> Roman L. Seplinski
> Bert D. Roelofs
> Dale H. Jewett
> George E. Bolks
> Claude Van Dyke

followed by another loan of $975,000 in August of 1938 for additional lines and a generating plant. But, a big unanswered question was where could the cooperative find a source of power at a fair price?

The decision to install diesel generators at a site near Burnips came after discussions with the city of Zeeland and other possible sources failed to assure an adequate power supply. Another nagging problem was getting all of the necessary right-of-way easements and township franchises. This slowed construction progress and it was October, 1938, when the first 180 miles of line were energized with power from the Burnips plant.

According to Jewett, Consumers Power quickly built lines down the same roads as the cooperative, taking customers that the co-op would have served but couldn't until an entire section was ready to be energized. "The power company even built lines where O & A had set poles," said Jewett.

The O & A board had a "thorough discussion" in April, 1938, on the activities of Consumers Power in building "spite lines" and pledged to expedite the co-op's construction program. And, a month later, the board talked of "fighting the Consumers Power propaganda as to the rates to be charged by the cooperative."

Rates set by the board in August established a $2 monthly minimum and a follow-on rate of 1.5 cents per kwh for use over 200, similar to the other co-ops in Michigan.

Many of the fledgling electric cooperatives were being threatened by the predatory activities of Consumers Power. Seeing the need for the cooperatives to unite "for their mutual protection and advancement, the O & A board of directors declared their "unqualified support" for what was to be called "The Michigan Association for the Protection and Promotion of REA Cooperatives" and authorized O & A to join for $25.

Eugene TenBrink was the co-op's representative to the association which gathered and reported information on the progress of the 13 cooperatives in the state and answered criticisms and innuendos of the private utilities. It dissolved and another statewide organization was established later.

TenBrink was also one of the first co-op representatives on the Michigan Committee on Rural Electrification, organized in 1946 by Detroit Edison, Consumers Power, the cooperatives and Michigan State College to assist rural families in applying electricity safely and efficiently in their homes and in farming operations. It was a successful program for 35 years.

Some farmers were using electricity to do a wide range of jobs on the farm, calling it the cheapest hired hand they could get. But others were slow to invest in the equipment and needed to see how it would improve production and pay off.

World War II stopped construction except for short line extensions to farms approved by the War Production Board. O & A built 30 such extensions, and couldn't resume a full construction schedule until 1947. Its service area had been extended northward through a narrow portion of Muskegon County and into Newaygo, Lake and Osceola counties. What started as a two-county co-op grew to a system serving parts of 12 counties.

By 1948, the cooperative was serving power to 5,000 members and had a second diesel generating station — this one located at Hersey. Earl Murley, manager, and Carl Johnson, president of the cooperative, recognized the need for a coordinated plan for power supply with other co-ops in the west and central parts of

---

**First Board of Directors:** the original incorporatrors

**Early Project Superintendent/Managers:** Claude Van Dyke (killed in accident April, 1938); Roman Seplinski; Bruce Watkins; Powers Luse; Harry Wolfe.

**Other Early Leaders:** George Johnson, Carl Johnson, Henry Mulder.

**First Project Attorney:** Tom Robinson

**First Lines Energized:** October 8, 1938

**First Annual Membership Meeting:** 1938

**First Employees:** Claude VanDyke, Les Brown

**First Office:** Zeeland (moved to Newaygo in December, 1938)

Michigan.

"It didn't make economic sense to build more small isolated plants and run them only in peak times," said Murley. "We needed to tie our plants together and get a coordinated plan for the future."

Teaming with Tri-County Electric Co-op in 1949, they organized the Wolverine Electric Cooperative as a generation and transmission co-op and, with REA's approval, started receiving loan funds to bolster the generating plants and built high voltage lines to connect power supply points. The move not only made economic sense but also improved system dependability.

John Keen, who was assistant manager at O & A, became assistant manager of the new Wolverine G & T and later promoted to manager.

A vicious sleet and ice storm hit the O & A system in December, 1948, disrupting service to members in all parts of the co-op's area. A new two-way radio system also helped the crews restore service, but damage was so widespread that it took five days to get all the lines back on with the help of Western Michigan co-op crews.

With many lakes in its area, O & A experienced the influx of people building vacation homes and hunting cabins in the 1950s and '60s — most of them seasonal users. New rate schedules were adopted for the seasonal members who comprised almost half of the co-op's membership.

The cooperative's assets in power facilities — less than $100,000 in 1938 — passed the $2 million mark in 1950. However, deficits in operations as of December 31, 1950, totaled $199,647 and the long-term debt to REA was $2.3 million. As the cooperative grew in consumers and kilowatt-hour sales in the 1950s and '60s, the deficit was erased.

In 1959, Ken Bumstead was promoted from office manager to manager. He and Board Chairman Carl Johnson were opposed to regulation of the cooperative by the Michigan Public Utilities Commission, but all of the co-ops were put under the Commission's control in 1966 to resolve territorial disputes and stop customer switching, which had resulted in duplication of facilities in many areas of the state.

Territorial battles between O & A and Consumers Power did not cease, however, even after new rules were adopted by the Commission in 1981 to settle service disputes over "three-phase" commercial and industrial customers. Since Bob Hance's appointment as manager in 1988, the cooperative has competed with Consumers for more than a dozen prospective larger loads and has been successful in each case.

Not all have gone to the Commission. Some of the larger loads, like the Donnelly Corporation facility at Newaygo, were added because the customer chose the co-op. "We offer and provide a better value to the customer," is how Hance explains O & A's success. "Some years back, we decided to stand up to the big guy (Consumers) and tell the prospective customer what we had to offer."

In 1995, the cooperative served over 30,000 members and sold 230 million kilowatt hours of electricity — an amazing record of growth since the modest start in 1938 with a few hundred members. Most impressive is the doubling of electric energy sales over the past five or six years, resulting from the new industrial loads.

Hance and the board are very pleased that their efforts in working with Newaygo and the new industries have resulted in creating more than 500 jobs in the area. That's a big economic boost to the community.

The cooperative took a giant historic step in 1996 when the membership voted overwhelmingly for a merger with Oceana Electric Co-op, and the Oceana membership likewise approved by a wide margin. The new entity is known as the Great Lakes Energy Cooperative, with Hance as general manager and headquarters in

Newaygo. An office also is maintained in Hart.

Hance sums up the co-op marriage this way: "It's a new day in the electric utility world. Cooperatives need to look at ways to become stronger, more competitive. This (merger) was a perfect fit."

With 40,000 member-consumers, the new Great Lakes co-op is the second largest electric cooperative in the state.

■ When the seven founders of the cooperative were trying to lay the foundation of the co-op in 1937, they decided to meet every Friday night at the farm home of Johannes Naber, with discussions often going past midnight.

■ The O & A board not only encountered problems with Consumers Power Company in the first years of construction, but had problems with engineers and a contractor and delays at REA. They persevered and saw all their efforts pay off when the lights came on October 8, 1938.

■ Les Brown, electrical advisor and for O & A for many years, started with the co-op in 1938 and was appointed Superintendent of Maintenance and Construction, and also served as acting manager in the late 1940s. He was also on the radio, giving information on electricity use and electrical safety.

■ Well-attended annual membership meetings are part of O & A's history and most of them have been held outdoors, such as the 1951 annual meeting at the White Cloud state park with 2,800 in attendance.

■ Average use of electricity in 1950 was only 147 kilowatt hours per month, but it climbed rapidly in the 1950s and '60s as the co-op actively promoted electric water heating, electric cooking, home freezers and many farmstead uses. Average use in 1995 was nearly 700 kwh per month.

■ Of the 50 people employed by O & A, 23 are involved in line work with crews in three locations for quick response to outage calls.

## TELLING IT LIKE IT WAS;

"I've seen many changes over the years, but I think one of the most important has been to improve the member billing system when we engaged Central Area Data Processing, which is a cooperative comprised of many electric co-ops, to do all of our billing."— *Pat Forbes, O & A Office Manager who started at the co-op in 1965 as receptionist.*

"Lots of people back 40 or 50 years ago thought the electric co-ops to be short-lived, but they were wrong and I think they just didn't realize the hard work and determination rural people were willing to put into their own electric utility business."— *Wayne Bumstead, lineman who started at the co-op in 1953 as a custodian.*

"The electric cooperative has meant a new life on the farm for thousands of families, and I think our new merged co-op (O & A and Oceana) will give us as good, if not better, service than we have today. We've come a long ways and I'm glad to have been part of it."— *Bill Vissers, member of O & A Board of Directors for over 20 years.*

"With the new Great Lakes Energy Cooperative, we can provide members with virtually all of the energy forms and sources that they want, including propane gas. It's like one-stop shopping."— *O & A Manager Bob Hance speaking about the merger with Oceana Electric.*

"We need to create awareness and recognition that O & A and electric cooperatives provide the best service for their market areas that can be provided. The big utilities just don't care about these rural areas."— *Mike Wood, retired auto executive who joined the board in 1995.*

**At right:** Construction of O & A power lines resumed after Word War II. Here, manager Earl Murley inspects new lines. Airplane was used for line patrol to spot any defects.

**Below left:** Merger of O & A and Oceana co-ops in 1996 created Great Lakes Energy Cooperative with headquarters in Newaygo. Great Lakes' board members, back row, left to right: Richard Walsworth, Richard Birkman, James Shull, Paul Byl, Carl Fortelka and Leon Ford. Front row: Don Marsh, Constance Dukes, Burton Scott, Michael Wood, Peter Boss and Wallace Hoffman.

Veteran lineman Wayne Bumstead who started with the co-op in 1953.

**Below:** 1959 Wolverine Electric Co-op board of directors included two O & A board members, Carl C. Johnson (second from left) and Eugene TenBrink (third from right). Johnson was chairman of the Wolverine and O & A boards for several years. Others in the photo are: Glen Chase and Harry Burmeister from Oceana Electric; I.E. Royer and Howard Pung from Tri-County; Harold Storz, attorney from Portland and John Keen (far left) Wolverine manager.

# OCEANA ELECTRIC COOPERATIVE

Former County Agriculture Agent James Thar and Loyal Churchill, a realtor from Hart, talked with farmers in Oceana County in 1937 about the new REA program that was getting started in some areas of Michigan and they arranged for REA representatives from Washington to come to Hart to explain the program.

After more discussions in January, 1938, it was decided that a meeting would be held to investigate possibilities of building "electric projects throughout Oceana and Mason counties," according to co-op records.

The first informational meeting was held March 4, 1938, in the courthouse at Hart with officials from REA and the Michigan Public Utilities Commission. It was concluded that, if a cooperative was legally formed and enough applicants for service signed up, REA would loan funds at the cost of money to the government.

Several area farmers, including Charles Kokx, were enthusiastic about the idea as shown by a unanimous vote at the March 4 meeting to move forward.

An organizational meeting was called for April 1 and a board of 10 persons elected to proceed with the necessary steps to incorporate. Kokx was elected chairman of the group and Churchill, secretary-treasurer. The name, Oceana Electric Cooperative, was selected.

*(Merged with O & A Electric Co-op as Great Lakes Energy Cooperative in January, 1997)*

**Incorporated  June 21, 1938**

**Original Incorporators:**
Charles Kokx, Weare
R.L. Aldrich, Crystal
Harry Burmeister, Benona
Glen Chase, Leavitt
Jesse Davis, Golden
William Wenk, Ferry
Roger Southwick, Elbridge
Charles Omness, Claybanks
Clarence Babbit, Hart
Loyal Churchill, Hart

At a meeting of the board of directors on June 24, 1938, the cooperative's bylaws were approved and the membership fee set at $5. Board meetings were frequent that summer in preparation for construction plans.

Bob Daverman, engineer from Grand Rapids, was engaged to work on the project.

When the first REA loan to Oceana was approved in July, construction got underway on the first 240 miles of line. Farmers in the area were hired to work on the project, digging holes and hauling poles. Right-of-way problems sometimes meant delay but the board of directors remained optimistic.

With REA's approval, the board set up a rate schedule: $2.50 minimum monthly charge (for 30 kilowatt hours) for farm residents and an $18 minimum for the seasonal users (nine months or less).

By March, 1939, the lines of the first section were completed, transformers and meters installed and the big day of energizing arrived. The newspaper report stated: "Current was first turned on to the south main line on March 10 and every connection worked perfectly, according to Loyal Churchill." Within a few weeks, the first 800 members had service.

Churchill and the board made additional loan applications to REA for constructing more lines in Oceana County and, within the next year, a loan of $112,000 was approved to build 110 miles. Work got underway in May, 1940. Although the war stopped most construction, the co-op was serving 1,553 members over 370 miles of line in early 1944.

Oceana members' use of power was minimal in the early 1940s, averaging less than 100 kwh per month. Despite the low revenue, the cooperative realized a net margin of $10,019 for the year in 1943.

Power was originally purchased from the Michigan Public Service Company. In 1941, the co-op began buying power from Western Michigan Co-op, Scottsville.

Harley Johnston succeeded Churchill as manager in 1946. He believed in a frugal, efficient operation, holding maintenance costs down to keep rates competitive. His successor in 1978, Bob Fredericksen, initiated programs to clear right-of-way and upgrade many parts of the system to bolster service dependability.

"We cut line loss from the 12-15 percent level to six percent, saving thousands of dollars, as well as improving service reliability," said Fredericksen. He also started a newsletter to the co-op's members and became actively involved in the state-wide association (MECA), serving as its board chairman two years and head of the legislative committee in 1980-81.

Fredericksen retired in 1991 and returned for a brief stint when his successor, Harry Ruth, resigned. Both Fredericksen and Ruth pushed economic development in Oceana County, helping create jobs and more kilowatt-hour sales. The co-op also promoted load management with its power supplier, Wolverine Power Co-op. Oceana was one of three co-ops that formed the original Wolverine Electric Cooperative in 1949 to assure an adequate supply of power.

Over the years, the Oceana cooperative operated with one of the smallest staffs for co-ops its size across the country: one employee per 600 member-consumers. In 1995, the board gave serious study to a merger with one or more other co-ops. A landmark decision was made by the Oceana board of directors and the co-op's membership in 1996 when they voted to merge with the O & A Electric Cooperative of Newaygo effective January 1, 1997.

"Looking at the potential savings and how well the two co-ops fit together in providing services that people want today, I'm convinced it is a wise decision," said Richard Walsworth, Oceana board member who was a leader in advocating the merger. He had seen the co-op grow to 10,000 member-consumers, but he said he believes that's still small in the changing utility world where competitiveness is vital.

The consolidated co-op, known as Great Lakes Energy Cooperative, is second largest in the state with 40,000 member-consumers. The office in Hart is maintained with a staff and the same services.

## TELLING IT LIKE IT WAS:

"Not knowing if the project would be a flop or a success, we didn't rent an office (in 1938)...we worked out of Mr. Churchill's home for several months. My desk was their dining room table."—*Louise Snyder, Oceana's first employee.*

"Charles Kokx, our first board president and Loyal Churchill, our first manager, were two fine men. They stood for the common people to get electricity for all of us out in the country."—*Clarence Babbit, member of the original board of directors.*

"Back in 1937 and '38, my father (Charles) put most of his time into getting the co-op started, and I took care of the farm. He was going in every direction to settle right-of-way problems and almost anything else that came up."—*Ray Kokx, whose farm north of Hart was one of the first to get electricity from the co-op.*

"At the present time, the Oceana Cooperative is proving a good investment, paying its own way and proving an asset of untold worth to farmers of the county."— *Muskegon Chronicle, June 13, 1940.*

"Getting the Wolverine G & T co-op started in 1949 was the right thing to do and timely because we were in desperate need of more power and couldn't depend upon the utilities who were fighting us."—*Bob Fredericksen, former Oceana manager and Wolverine accountant prior to Oceana.*

"Oceana has been a success, but a larger co-op can spread the overhead costs and do more to control costs and stabilize rates while still providing top quality service. I believe this is a good marriage."— *Richard Walsworth, Oceana board member commenting on the Jan. 1, 1997, merger with O & A.*

■ Two women have served on the Oceana Electric Board of Directors for the past 20 years, Donna Blackmer of Hart and Mary Hawley of Shelby. Hawley was secretary-treasurer for several years.

■ A news item in 1940 related that "after the electric co-op lines were energized, a number of members who had installed electric milk coolers were getting a bonus of 10 cents per hundred weight for their milk because they were able to deliver it at a temperature of 50 degrees or lower."

■ The first member to receive power from the co-op in 1939 was the largest user, a farmer who used electricity to incubate and brood turkeys in large volume. His operation consumed close to 1,000 kilowatt hours per month. Most members were using only the minimum of 30 kwh that first year.

■ Loyal Churchill's visit to REA's office in Washington in 1938 not only produced the needed funds for Oceana to get started, but became a classic story retold many times. You'll find it in chapter 3 "Trials and Tribulations."

■ The cooperative built a new office and warehouse facility in 1983 at the south edge of Hart. In 1990, the co-op added a subsidiary — Oceana Energy Company — to sell and service heating systems.

■ The popular REA Farm Electric Show was a big hit at Crystal Valley county park June 17-18, 1940, where farm families saw demonstrations of a variety of equipment as well as a "cooking duel" and a special feature on "Ingenious Uses of Electricity." The travelling REA show helped millions of farmers across the country put electricity to work productively and safely.

**First Board of Directors:** Same as incorporators
**Early Co-op Project Superintendent/Manager:** Loyal Churchill
**Other Early Leaders:** James Thar, Gustave Aue
**First Project Attorney:** Gerald M. Meehan, Hart
**First Lines Energized:** March 10, 1939
**First Annual Membership Meeting:** August 2, 1938
**First Employees:** Loyal Churchill, Louise Snyder
**First Office:** The home of Loyal Churchill, then moved to the basement of bank on Main Street in Hart

**At left and below:** Men and women from Oceana and Mason Counties flocked to the REA Electric Show in June, 1940, to see demonstrations of electric appliances and equipment for the farm. The travelling show attracted tens of thousands in 30 states.

**At right:** Founding father of Oceana Electric Co-op, Charles Kokx (with pitchfork). **Below:** Co-op board of directors and manager in 1985. Front row, left to right: Clare Shull, Mary Hawley and Donna Blackmer. Back row: Wallace Hoffman, Richard Birkman, Paul Byl, manager Bob Fredericksen, and Richard Walsworth.

**Above:** Loyal Churchill, first manager of Oceana Electric.

# ONTONAGON COUNTY RURAL ELECTRIFICATION ASSN.

Undaunted by the challenge of doing what a multimillion dollar utility company couldn't or wouldn't do, four men put on paper a daring plan to bring electricity to the western Upper Peninsula of Michigan.

It was 1937 and they — along with thousands of other rural people — had waited long enough to get out of the kerosene age and into the electric age. Even the little village of Ontonagon had central station electric service dating back to 1895.

After months of talking and surveying, John Franti, Elmer Rautio, Otto Halme and Jalmer Lehto decided to take the first official step and filed incorporation papers creating the Ontonagon County Rural Electrification Association. On September 30, 1937, the new cooperative was legally born.

August Hautamaki of Trout Creek joined the board soon after incorporation. Others who helped get the co-op organized and off the ground were Lawrence Walsh, who became the co-op's attorney, William Davidson, who was named project superintendent, and Isadore Weze.

> Incorporated  September 30, 1937
>
> **Original Incorporators:**
> John E. Franti, Ewen
> Elmer R. Rautio, Green
> Otto Halme, Ontonagon
> Jalmer Lehto, Mass

As Bruce Johanson wrote in his book, *This Land, The Ontonagon*, this was a group of men "with a vision to venture" given the low density of farms in the area which made economic feasibility questionable.

A news article told how the group had put together "good, live-wire committees" of area farmers to help get sign-ups and easements. They paved the way, and REA approved the co-op's first loan soon after the incorporation papers were filed. In April of 1938, the Ontonagon board applied for another $850,000 loan to extend lines into parts of Houghton, Baraga and Keweenaw Counties.

A big event attracting hundreds of people to the Ontonagon Township Community Building on May 8, 1938, was the dedication and energizing of the cooperative's first lines. Governor Frank Murphy and Public Utilities Commissioner Joseph Donnelly were guest speakers. Donnelly, a native of Ontonagon, championed the cause of rural electric cooperatives in Michigan after Murphy was elected in November of 1937. The co-ops had been stymied by Governor Fitzgerald's administration.

Governor Murphy turned on the power to some 200 homes in Ontonagon county that day. "It was indeed a memorable and exhilarating occasion when we energized those first lines," said Elmer Rautio, who served on the board several years. "Then we could see that all our efforts were worthwhile."

As Ontonagon historian Bruce Johanson said in his book, putting the electric co-op together was especially difficult because of the area's geography: "the population seems to live in clumps helter-skelter," due to the fact that the federal and state governments own much of the land and rural folks are separated by these large tracts of land. Ordinarily, REA allowed just one substation with feeder lines going out to serve co-op members. But, in the case of Ontonagon, it would take at least five substations because of the scattered, non-contiguous areas.

"It took a great deal of convincing (REA) on the part of the local co-op officers that five substations were necessary to save on line construction costs," said Johanson. As the co-op grew to almost 4,000 members by 1995, it had 900 miles of line in 13 separate areas.

The Ontonagon cooperative has the least number of consumers per mile of line of any co-op in Michigan: 4.6 members per mile, and that includes seasonal consumers. That sparsity, combined with total dependence on other utilities for power supply, led to relatively high electric rates compared with other Michigan utilities.

Ontonagon's first power supply was from the Copper District Power Company in the northern part of the county and from Wisconsin-Michigan Power Company in the south part. Today, most of the power is purchased from Upper Peninsula Power Company (UPPCO) and Wisconsin Electric Power Company (WEPCO).

The cooperative's first annual meeting was held August 9, 1938, with about 80 members present. Annual meeting notices and some of the reports were printed in Finnish as well as English because of the large population of Finnish people in the area. Over the years, most board members have been Finnish.

At the 1940 annual meeting, the board expanded to seven. New members were John Perttula, John Rova, Carl Liimatainen, John A. Carlson, Fred Wuovi and Edward Relto.

Cy Clark had been hired as co-op manager and, in 1941, he joined the Coast Guard, and board members did the day-to-day management until Clark's return in 1945. Clark worked as manager until his retirement in 1973. The cooperative's office building is named in his honor.

Most of the cooperative's subscribers used only the minimum amount of electricity the first few years, restricting their use to lighting and an iron and radio. As

**First Board of Directors:** same as original incorporators, and August M. Hautamaki of Trout Creek

**Early Co-op Project Superintendent/ Manager:** William Davidson and Cyril M. Clark

**Other Early Leaders:** John Perttula, John Rova, Victor Katajamaki, William Kohtala, Carl Liimatainen, Edward Relto, Fred Wuovi

**First Project Attorney:** Lawrence Walsh

**First Lines Energized:** May 8, 1938

**First Annual Membership Meeting:** August 9, 1938

**First Employees:** William Davidson

**First Office:** old Hawley building in Ontonagon

Bruce Johanson stated in his book, "It took a great deal of salesmanship and promotion on the part of the co-op to introduce to the rural dwellers the vast potential of electric power. Finally, a few more daring customers tried electric water pumps and soon the old windmills were standing idle."

Two of the co-op's board presidents over the past 45 years, Uno Kemppainen and Carlo Heikkinen, took firm stands against critics of the co-op who were elected to the board and advocated selling the co-op. Although the co-op has never received an offer, the dissident directors stirred controversy with letters to the editor and emotional statements at annual meetings.

"It was a conflict of ideology, whether we should continue as a cooperative or become customers of an investor-owned power company, and the vast majority wanted to stay as a co-op," said Heikkinen, who had managed a co-op grocery store for 14 years. Cooperatives were also part of his education, having participated in programs at the University of Wisconsin Center for Cooperatives.

The cooperative has achieved a "comeback" of sorts, upgrading its service, reducing line loss and getting in better shape both physically and financially. Since Jim Morgan became manager in 1982, members' equity in the co-op has jumped from 1 percent to 15 percent. He retired in 1995 and Tom Haarala succeeded him.

"We have brought rates down and instituted a special commercial/industrial rate, and we have improved our financial position," Heikkinen added. 'We need to keep increasing kilowatt hour sales to make up for the loss of farm members and, with new lakeshore homes and other development, I think we will have 5,000 members within the next five or six years."

■ The village of Ontonagon had electric service in 1895. The *Ontonagon Herald* reported in March, 1906, that the town was in darkness due to a dynamo burning out in the light plant..."it worked good until it was taxed beyond its capacity." In the rural areas of the county, the *Herald* said, "the kerosene lamp was still king of the night."

■ Many farmers in Ontonagon County agreed to dig their own power pole holes for which they were paid the staggering sum of $1 per hole (2 feet by 6 feet), and they were all hand dug in the 1930s and '40s. —*from Bruce Johanson's book,* This Land, The Ontonagon.

■ Joseph M. Donnelly, former Michigan Public Utilities Commissioner who helped electric cooperatives get organized as legal entities, was given special recognition by the Ontonagon cooperative at the co-op's 1970 annual meeting for his role in making rural electrification possible in Michigan and his assistance in founding the Ontonagon co-op. Donnelly, who became a judge at Houghton, was a native of Ontonagon County.

■ Cyril Clark, longtime Ontonagon manager who started with the co-op in 1938, couldn't understand very much Finnish, but he said he learned some words like "switchbox" and "outage." Most board matters in the early years were discussed in both English and Finnish. Cy's son, Bob Clark, is line superintendent at the co-op.

■ Ontonagon has the fewest employees of any Michigan electric co-op: 13, including the manager.

According to Haarala, who has been working at Ontonagon since 1983, sales of electricity have increased about 4 percent in 1994 and 1995. He, too, sees more development in the area. That, combined with lower power supply costs as a result of "open access" to power from different sources, should bode well for the cooperative.

Gordon Jukuri, who succeeded Heikkinen as board chairman, also has optimism about the future of the co-op. "Much depends upon what happens in our service area and how the economy goes," said Jukuri. "We recently purchased a small part of UPPCO's rural service area near Houghton when the Coast Guard closed its station, adding McLain State Park and some residences to our system. It all helps."

Two rate reductions, one in 1995 and another planned for 1996, also brighten the picture for Ontonagon.

## TELLING IT LIKE IT WAS:

"The completion of the Ontonagon Rural Electrification project will bring smiles to the faces of 600 farm women in the county...Electric washing machines are rapidly replacing gasoline motors and the old-fashioned washboards. Wash days are about to become happy days!"— *The Ontonagon Herald, May 7, 1938.*

"In 1937 and '38 and '39, the rural people had to be educated about electricity...it was an education for me, too, because a co-op utility was a new creature. I am amazed at the progress of the co-op since those days."— *Cy Clark, Ontonagon manager from 1938 to 1973.*

"Biggest change for linemen over the years was getting the bucket truck, which has meant a lot less climbing — but, you know, it has spoiled the image of the rugged lineman."— *Clarence Marttila, Ontonagon line foreman at Houghton who's been with the co-op 30 years.*

"Our Ontonagon cooperative would be hurt if we lost the REA (now RUS) lending program...We need the 5 percent loans to keep costs down so we can get our rates in line with the others, and we are just about there. We had a rate reduction in 1995 and we are planning another."— *Carlo Heikkinen, L'Anse, former chairman and vice-chair of the Ontonagon board of directors.*

"We were dedicated to improving the quality of service in the 1980s and we did it. I think Ontonagon has a good future...one plus has been the co-ops working together at the state and national levels to keep the financing program so we can continue to improve system dependability."— *Jim Morgan, Ontonagon manager from 1982 to 1995.*

**At right:** Retired Ontonagon manager Jim Morgan who came to the co-op in 1982.

**Above left:** Uno Kemppainen, longtime leader of the cooperative's board of directors. **Above right:** Tom Haarala, who succeeded Morgan as manager.

**Above:** (L to R) Donna Siren and Wendy Tandlund, familiar faces in the co-op office.

**Below:** To get an adequate supply of power to all of the co-op members in a dozen separate areas, feeder lines were built. These 1940 photos show new lines being constructed and one of the co-op's newly-built substations.

# PRESQUE ISLE ELECTRIC & GAS CO-OP

Amid political ploys to keep "REA" out of the state, a group of farmers and a County Extension Agent met in the Fall of 1936 at Metz in Presque Isle County to discuss plans for forming a cooperative to bring electricity to their area.

As the Presque Isle newspaper later reported, "For anyone to believe that the farmers were capable of such an undertaking was considered to be foolhardy in 1936, but the charter members had the courage to face all criticism, opposition and ridicule, to overcome all obstacles placed in their way to prevent a rural electric cooperative from being established."

Led by County Agent Jack Brown, the group met and formed a committee. In a meeting at the farm home of Allen Taylor in February, 1937, the first board of directors was chosen. After Governor Frank Murphy took action in early 1937 to enable electric co-ops to organize, the board incorporated Presque Isle Electric Cooperative and promptly applied for an REA loan.

> *Formerly Presque Isle Electric Cooperative*
>
> **Incorporated  March 22, 1937**
>
> **Original Incorporators:**
> Otto Grambau, Posen
> Frank Smith, Posen
> Hilmer M. Olsen, Hawks
> Edgar C. Rambadt, Rogers City
> Carl Sorgenfrei, Rogers City
> Leonard Poch, Rogers City
> Herbert F. Paull, Hawks

Within a few months, the Presque Isle board authorized a contract with Laird Construction to build the first 63 miles of line. A special and historic event was scheduled for the setting of the first pole, believed to be the first REA-financed power line pole in Michigan.

It was on September 22, 1937, that the pole-setting ceremony was held in the village of Posen, where a state historical plaque marks the place where construction of the first rural electric co-op power line in Michigan began. It is also significant because the lines built that fall were the first energized by a cooperative in the state — just in time for Christmas of 1937, brightening the farm homes of 82 Presque Isle families.

The first power supply came from the Norway Dam of Alpena Power Company. The line extended to Cathro, Bolton, Posen, Metz, Hawks, Hagensville and Moltke. Alpena Power Company, headed by Philip K. Fletcher, had pledged support of the co-op project.

Speaking at the September 22 dedication ceremony, Fletcher said: "We of Alpena Power are in this project because we are interested in the development of our part of Michigan...for four generations we have tried to help along the same lines. Let's put it all into one pot today — power company and you people — to make northeastern Michigan and our area the best in Michigan."

Joseph Donnelly of the Michigan Public Service Commission praised Alpena Power for its cooperation which, he said, "is of a type not usual in southern Michigan" where he said Consumers Power has held up progress of the cooperatives.

Also commended for his work in getting the project underway was County Agent Jack Brown. State Representative Frank Buza and Agriculture Extension Leader C.V. Ballard credited Brown with giving the impetus and guidance the fledgling co-op needed. Brown worked closely with the board in making decisions the first few years, including right-of-way and design of the electric rates.

In 1943, Brown was presented the distinguished service award by the National Association of County Agricultural Agents for his work in rural electrification and community development.

Formal dedication of the co-op's first power line was given by U.S. Representative John Luecke. "Today, electricity is bringing us music and word from all parts of the world by a mere turn of the radio dial. It furnishes power for every known job and, today, you have the beginning of use of that power for your farms," said Luecke.

"The farmer wants electricity. He needs it more than they do in the city and the day has come when he is about to be served...This day makes history for you because a better and brighter future is in store for all."

The cooperative soon extended lines into Cheboygan and Montmorency counties and, by 1943, it was serving electricity to 2,900 farms and rural residences. Energy consumption was totaling about 300,000 kilowatt hours per month — an average of just over 100 kwh per member. Farmers were using electricity for pumping water, grinding feed, milking and lighting barns and poultry houses, even chick brooding.

On the farm of Edgar Rambadt, co-op board member, electricity was being used to do the milking, power grain elevators, pump water, light the barns and run the barn ventilation system, plus the lights in the house and a refrigerator, stove, food mixer, radio and iron — all for about $7.50 per month. Potato farmers made good use of electricity for ventilation of storehouses and for water-spraying their potatoes, a significant boost to wartime potato production.

More than half of the power in the early 1940s came from the Tower hydro plant and the co-op's new diesel plant added at Tower. The rest was purchased from Alpena Power and Michigan Public Service Company. Presque Isle acquired

---

**First Board of Directors:** same as the original incorporators

**Early Co-op Project Superintendent/ Manager:** Albert Hall, Gust Kleber

**Other Early Leaders:** Jack Brown, County Agent

**First Project Attorney:** Carl R. Henry

**First Lines Energized:** December 23, 1937.

**First Annual Membership Meeting:** November 23, 1938.

**First Employee:** Alice Wozniak

**First Office:** Posen

the Tower hydro when it purchased the Onaway Light and Power Company in 1941. A small plant was also added when the co-op bought the Atlanta Power system.

The cooperative constructed a new hydro power facility three miles down river from Tower. Named Kleber Dam for retiring Manager Gust Kleber, the addition enabled the co-op to meet demands for a few years.

Use of electricity was growing rapidly in the late 1940s, and power supply again became a question.

In 1948, Presque Isle joined with the Top O' Michigan and Cherryland cooperatives in forming Northern Michigan Electric Cooperative, a generation and transmission co-op that was given the responsibility of providing the three co-ops with all of the power needed. Presque Isle's power facilities were turned over to the new "G&T" cooperative.

Otto Grambau, one of the founding fathers, served as chairman of the board for 25 years, and represented Michigan on the National Rural Electric Cooperative Association board of directors for six years. Succeeding him as chairman was Bernard Kline, who served on the board from 1939 to 1977. Kline was elected president of the new Northern Michigan G & T cooperative.

By 1955, the Presque Isle co-op was providing service to 9,500 members in parts of seven counties over 2,500 miles of distribution line. Its annual report showed some $594,800 paid back to REA on principal of loans, plus $504,000 in interest.

Harry Pauley, who came to work for the co-op as a lineman in 1943 and succeeded William Reutter as manager in 1971, told of the postwar growth years. The co-op sold water heaters by the truckload and hired college students to sell electric frying pans and small appliances door-to-door. "We needed to build load to make it finan-

■ A resolution from the village of Millersburg, dated October 1, 1938, expressed appreciation to the Presque Isle Electric Co-op for "the benefits which have come to the village through the establishment of the new electric service of the cooperative." Special thanks were extended to County Agent Jack Brown, project superintendent Albert Hall, State Rep. Frank Buza and U.S. Rep. John Luecke.

■ A newspaper headline in 1961 stated that only one in six new "REA Customers" is a farmer, which was true in Michigan as thousands of people built cabins and vacation homes in the countryside. Presque Isle Cooperative has had the highest percentage of "seasonal consumers" in Michigan, about 60 percent. The highest peak demand for electricity on the Presque Isle system each year is the night before deer hunting season opens.

■ The Presque Isle Co-op office was moved from Posen to Onaway in 1942, occupying the former offices of Onaway Power and Light Company, which the cooperative purchased in 1941. A new office building was built in 1956 on Highway M-68, just east of Onaway. The building was recently remodeled and facilitates a staff of 65, including line personnel.

■ Presque Isle Electric Cooperative has the distinction of being the first co-op in Michigan to initiate electric service to members when it energized 70 miles of line December 23, 1937, approximately two months before the Tri-County Electric Cooperative began service.

■ Former Presque Isle Electric managers other than those mentioned in the preceding article are: Clayton Smith, Barkley Travis and Gary Cavitt.

cially and to keep rates as low as possible," said Pauley.

He and his successor, Mike O'Meara, put emphasis in the 1970s and '80s on improving service quality. Mel Basel, who served on the board from 1965 to 1995, said the board agreed and system improvements were made. "We're not a small utility anymore," said Basel, looking at statistics showing 28,000 member-consumers and $19 million of revenue in 1995.

General Manager Martin Thomson, who took the helm in 1993 after serving on the board for 16 years, believes customer service is paramount. That was a prime reason for the cooperative to break tradition and enter the natural gas business in 1994. "We knew that many rural families needed and wanted natural gas service and that it would reduce their overall energy costs," said Thomson. "And it helps spread the co-op's overhead costs as well as add to our revenue stream."

The board and management see the move as an economic boost to the cooperative's service area, helping attract business and industry and, thus, generating more jobs. The board, with the membership's approval, changed the co-op's bylaws to allow the diversification and to adopt a new name: Presque Isle Electric & Gas.

As of August, 1996, the cooperative was serving 1,300 customers with natural gas. "Even though it will take four or five years for the gas business to show a profit, we have become a more efficient utility and a more service-minded business," added Thomson.

## TELLING IT LIKE IT WAS:

"When I came to the co-op in 1943, we served 2,500 meters, and when I left in 1981, we were serving 25,000. No one anticipated the kind of growth that this co-op and many others have had, especially when you consider the big reduction in number of farms over the years."— *Harry Pauley, former manager of Presque Isle Electric*

"I don't need to tell you that these seven green directors (members of the original board) knew very little about setting up an electric co-op and much less on how to run one. But one thing they did know was the need for electricity and they were determined that this task would be accomplished...I can't think of anything that has meant more to the members of our cooperative than this electric service."— *Edgar Rambadt, incorporator of the co-op and treasurer for 28 years, giving his last report to the co-op membership meeting December 7, 1965, upon his retirement from the board.*

"The White House should tell labor and management to keep wage demands and prices within certain guidelines. Government can loosen the tight money policy which makes it more difficult for small business to compete with the giants...it is discouraging that despite cutbacks in federal programs, high interest rates and tight money, prices continue to climb."— *U.S. Senator Philip Hart, speaking at the Presque Isle Co-op 1969 annual meeting in Posen.*

"On behalf of the Rural Electrification Administration, I hereby dedicate this first pole in Michigan and turn it over to the community as a part in the great project that will mean so much in the fulfillment of a larger and happier life for the home and for the community."— *U.S. Congressman John Luecke at the dedication ceremony September 22, 1937, in Posen.*

"It seems to have been the thought of Congress in making appropriations for Extension work to foster rural cooperatives...A lot of our people had no way of getting electricity — or if they could get it, it was at a cost that was prohibitive. So, REA is really the first cooperative venture that I've ever been able to get steamed up about."— *Presque Isle County Agent Jack Brown, one of the co-op's founding fathers, speaking in 1939.*

151

**At left:** Barney Kline, right, longtime Presque Isle board member, was a key figure in forming Northern Michigan Electric Co-op for power supply. On the left is Clayton Smith, Presque Isle manager in the 1950s.

**At left:** Otto Grambau, who served as Presque Isle board chairman for several years and also was a leader on the Northern Michigan Co-op board. **At right:** Mel Basel, longtime board member and president of Presque Isle Electric.

**Left:** Young and old came to this ceremony in Posen for setting the co-op's first pole Sept. 22, 1937. An historical marker was placed there in 1985.

**At right:** Four former Presque Isle Co-op managers are in this photo with U.S. Rep. Phil Ruppe. Standing left to right: Harry Pauley, Mike O 'Meara, Ruppe, Clayton Smith and former line superintendent Nelson Free. Seated is William Reutter.

# SOUTHEASTERN MICHIGAN RURAL ELECTRIC COOPERATIVE

In 1936, farmers in Lenawee County heard about the Rural Electrification Administration program getting started in Ohio, and they took action to establish a cooperative and borrow funds from REA. But they encountered roadblocks from the State of Michigan as they attempted to formally organize and were forced to wait until 1937 when a new Governor, Frank Murphy, took office.

Murphy's Attorney General Raymond Starr issued a ruling in March that directed the Michigan Corporation and Securities Commission to accept the incorporation papers of rural electric cooperatives.

It was April 13, 1937, when the group of farmers met in the Courthouse at Adrian to make plans for the state charter and take the necessary steps to qualify for an REA loan. They elected Lee Bettis president of the board, and Henry Silberhorn treasurer. Meeting again two days later, the board signed incorporation papers and expressed appreciation to the County Extension Agent and Board of Supervisors for their assistance. Each board member agreed to pay $2.25 to defray expenses of filing incorporation documents.

> **Incorporated April 15, 1937**
>
> **Original Incorporators:**
> Lee Bettis, Riga
> Elmer Green, Raisin
> Henry Silberhorn, Riga
> C.C. Nye, Hudson
> L.F. Stautz, Manchester
> W.S. Kauffman, Blissfield
> W.W. Sell, Blissfield
> William Thompson, Riga

First known as the Lenawee County Electric Membership Association, the name was changed to Southeastern Michigan Rural Electric Cooperative. Clarence Winder of REA helped the co-op in getting its first loan. He came to Michigan in 1937 and worked with the Public Utilities Commission to facilitate the new rural electrification program.

In May of 1937, the cooperative's first loan was approved in the amount of $250,000 to build 120 miles of line and a generating plant.

The board set the membership fee at $3 per connection and outlined plans for obtaining sign-ups and easements. Roy White was hired as consulting engineer.

Lee Bettis resigned as board chairman to become the co-op's project superintendent. William Thompson was elected as the new chairman and C.C. Nye, vice chairman. After long discussions with REA, the board approved construction contracts and work commenced in the summer. Right-of-way problems and complaints regarding tree clearing caused delays. Board meetings in September, 1937, addressed ways of "speeding up" the right-of-way and staking work. More people were employed to get easements on the basis of receiving $1 for each, with half of the payment deferred "until the poles are erected."

The next problem was power supply. Plans proceeded for the co-op to build its own plant, and REA approved funds for two diesel generators. The cooperative's growth, which included serving a portion of Fulton County in Ohio, exceeded the plant's capacity in a few years and arrangements for power purchases were made with Consumers Power Company.

The co-op's first section of lines served less than 500 member-consumers. After World War II, construction resumed by 1960 and, the cooperative was sending power to 2,000 farms, homes and businesses.

From the start, there had been disputes with Consumers Power over service areas and the company's "spite lines" — lines that the company built parallel to the cooperative's in order to connect customers the co-op had planned to serve. Territorial disputes continued and, in the 1960s, Southeastern lost a number of members who were persuaded by Consumers Power to switch from the co-op to Consumers.

Southeastern and other cooperatives appealed to the Michigan Public Utilities Commission and, in 1966, the Commission issued an order establishing rules to stop duplication of "single-phase" lines and to govern the extension of single-phase distribution lines of the co-ops and power companies.

That wasn't the end of the cooperative's troubles with the investor-owned utilities. In 1968, the co-op's decision to build a transmission line and buy power from Detroit Edison was contested by Consumers Power in a complaint filed with the state Public Utilities Commission. The matter came to a head in 1969 when the Southeastern board of directors deferred action on the Detroit Edison agreement, discharged the co-op manager, Ray Nash, and all board members resigned.

REA sent one of its officials to manage the cooperative on an interim basis and members elected a new board of directors. The board, chaired by Richard Stutesman, hired a new manager, James Heifner. Also elected to the board in 1969 was Roger Wolf, who continued to serve on the board as vice-president in 1996.

With Stutesman's leadership, the new board reviewed the co-op's options and decided to construct a transmission line and contract with Detroit Edison for wholesale power. Wolf remembers the late night board meetings — every week for months — to get the cooperative "back on track" and he credits Stutesman for saving the cooperative when it was in danger of a sellout.

By 1970, the cooperative was a $1.5 million business with annual revenue of over $500,000. Power sales were climbing as people increased their use of electricity and more families moved to rural areas. Twenty years later, the co-op passed the mark of 4,000 member-consumers. In 1996, the co-op provided electricity to 4,500 homes and businesses, including 1,000 in Ohio.

---

**First Board of Directors:** same as the original incorporators

**Early Co-op Project Superintendent/Managers:** Lee Bettis

**Other Early Leaders:** Henry Raymond and Leo Driscoll

**First Lines Energized:** Spring, 1938

**First Annual Membership Meeting:** May 13, 1937

**First Employees:** Dorothy C. Riner, Lee Bettis

**First Office:** 2nd floor of Masonic Temple, Adrian.

In 1964, the board agreed to join with the Ohio electric co-ops in contracting for power from the new Buckeye Electric Power Cooperative generating plant. Southeastern's power allotment from this plant serves the needs of its members in Ohio.

In 1986 General Manager Donald Grimes initiated negotiations that resulted in a new power supply agreement with the Lansing Board of Water and Light. The contract provides the bulk of the co-op's power needs at significant savings over rates paid to Detroit Edison.

In the 1990s, the cooperative has seen a turnaround in its competitive position with other utilities. Board members Roger Wolf and Norman Bless, chairman of the board in 1996, stated that the co-op's continuity of service tops investor-owned utilities and the rates are at the same level or even better in some cases.

"It's a new ball game now," said Wolf. "We have people on Consumers Power lines who want our service."

In 1996, the cooperative changed its name to Southeastern Energy Cooperative. The Southeastern board discussed the possibility of a merger with a co-op in northwest Ohio, but the talks ended with no agreement. In 1997, the board conferred with Fruit Belt Electric Cooperative of Cassopolis, and a merger was approved in early 1998. The new entity is known as Midwest Energy Cooperative.

General Manager of Southeastern Michigan Co-op from 1994 through 1997 was Les Teel, former operations manager at Thumb Electric Co-op. He succeeded Don Grimes who retired in 1994 after 17 years with the co-op. Grimes was active in the Michigan Electric Cooperative Association, serving as its chairman two years. Other former managers included Carl Hoffman, Joseph Lower and John Winn.

■ Southeastern Michigan was one of the first electric cooperatives to be chartered under Michigan law. It was necessary to become a legally incorporated body to be eligible for REA loans. Co-ops were held up by in-state political obstacles in 1936 when the REA Act was passed by Congress. When newly-elected Governor Frank Murphy took office in January, 1937, the cooperatives were given the green light.

■ Southeastern Michigan was the second smallest electric co-op in Michigan, but close to the average size of co-ops in Indiana and other Midwestern states. Michigan electric cooperatives range from 3,900 members (Ontonagon) to 50,000 (Top O' Michigan).

■ Carl Hoffman, former manager, and Joseph Glenn, former board member, were among the 16 original incorporators of the Michigan Electric Cooperative Association in 1978. Southeastern also is a member of the Ohio Association of Electric Cooperatives.

■ A 1963 editorial in the *Adrian Daily Telegram* attacked REA and electric co-ops, alleging that 97 percent of the co-ops' business was in competition with investor-owned utilities and that the co-ops do not pay taxes. Both charges are false. Co-ops pioneered service in the areas left dark by the power companies, and co-ops pay all taxes except federal income tax. Power companies' propaganda in the 1960s prompted such editorials.

■ Farmers who worked as canvassers to get sign-ups when the co-op was being organized in 1937 were paid $5 per day and 5 cents per mile, up to a maximum of 40 miles. The first board members received $3 per meeting.

## TELLING IT LIKE IT WAS:

"We could hardly wait for the electricity to get turned on...Our farm was one of the first to be connected. It's the cheapest hired man I ever had, and it meant a lot less work in our dairy operation. The co-op has done well considering that Consumers Power got the cream and we got the leftovers."— *Clyde Knisel, former Southeastern board member and longtime farmer south of Adrian.*

"We have new challenges today, but the board and staff have become more responsive to the members' needs and wants and I believe we will be more competitive both in quality of service and rates. I am proud of what this cooperative has accomplished the past several years."— *Norm Bless, President of the Southeastern board of directors and retired Extension Service leader.*

"This cooperative may be small by some standards but it has a good performance record. Our crews respond quickly to service problems, and the co-op now is number one in quality of service. I'm very proud of that."— *Roger Wolf, Southeastern board member since 1969.*

"Although our co-op is isolated from other electric co-ops in Michigan, we have worked together in many ways, including legislative and regulatory issues. Through our statewide association (MECA), we have gained strength and achieved many goals."— *Donald Grimes, former manager of Southeastern Michigan and officer of MECA.*

**At right:** Southeastern's generating plant, new in 1938, became obsolete when power supply contracts with Detroit Edison and later with Consumers Power and the City of Lansing were negotiated.

**Below left:** The old and the new. Building line in the early days took more time and more muscle without boom trucks.

**Below right:** With the use of new hydraulic operated booms for digging and setting poles crews were able to build lines much faster and get power to waiting customers.

**At left:** Southeastern Michigan Electric board of directors in 1979. Left to right: Donald Powell, Gene Winzeler, Harold Willett, Richard Stutesman (president), Norman Bless, Roger Wolf, Roger Andries, Warren Severence, and Joe Glenn.

**At right:** The Lifesaving Award was presented in 1967 by Employees Insurance representative Robert Possanza (second from left) to Southeastern lineman Marvin Nash. Robert Riley, line superintendent (far right) and manager Ray Nash (far left) look on.

# THUMB ELECTRIC COOPERATIVE

Just months after President Franklin Roosevelt issued his Executive Order in May, 1935, creating the Rural Electrification Administration, a group of farmers got together in the Wadsworth schoolhouse in Huron County to talk about how they could tap this "New Deal" program to get electricity in the Thumb area. The meeting was called by E.C. Stieg, who became one of the cooperative's incorporators.

The group of 25 to 30 people elected Frank Wilson of Ubly as chairman, and he wasted no time in pursuing the possibility of a cooperative project financed by REA. He said he made a dozen or more trips to Lansing and Washington before the co-op became a reality.

"It was a real battle," he told a reporter interviewing him in 1982. He encountered what several other electric co-op leaders did in 1936: the State of Michigan wouldn't grant legal status to the co-op groups.

"We had to wait for Frank Murphy to become Governor, and as soon as he was elected (November, 1936), I went to see him," Wilson said. Murphy was from Harbor Beach and supported the REA electrification program.

More than 600 farmers had gathered in Bad Axe on January 31, 1936, to start organizational action.

> **Incorporated April 13, 1937**
>
> **Original Incorporators:**
> Frank Wilson, Ubly
> Elmer C. Stieg, Bad Axe
> Ruth Brandmair, Caro
> Martin Fisher, Ubly
> Guy Petiprin, Unionville
> Joseph Romain. Caro
> Bob Spencer, Cass City
> Albert Grifka, Tyre

Wilson was elected president; Stieg, vice president, and Charles Gates, secretary. Township chairmen agreed to coordinate the initial canvassing.

The canvassing showed wide support of the proposed electric cooperative. By March of 1937, when Governor Murphy's Attorney General Raymond Starr issued his ruling for accepting the cooperatives' charters, some 5,500 farmers in Huron, Sanilac and Tuscola counties had signed up to be members of the co-op. Approval of Thumb's incorporation papers came on April 13.

Two weeks later came word from REA that Thumb's application for a $2,000,000 loan was approved.

With 5,500 signers and a $2 million loan, the Thumb Electric Cooperative was the nation's largest REA project. When it was energized in June of 1938, it was the largest REA-financed system in operation.

The loan included $300,000 for a diesel-fired generating plant just north of Ubly. Three Fairbanks-Morse units, totaling 2,000 kilowatts were installed to provide power to the members over 1,500 miles of line. A fourth unit was added in 1947.

According to Thumb Electric's records, the first pole for the co-op was set in front of the power plant on September 10, 1937. That's 12 days earlier than the pole-setting event at Posen, which was recognized by the State Historical Society as the first pole erected in a REA-financed project (Presque Isle Electric Co-op).

Frank Wilson worked as the cooperative's first superintendent and Harry Grayson, who had engineering experience, was named associate supervisor and later the manager. Together with dozens of helpers, they got the right-of-way easements and construction got underway to bring electricity to the first 2,000 families.

The biggest public event in the history of Ubly was held June 18, 1938, when Governor Frank Murphy and REA Administrator John Carmody came for the dedication ceremonies and energizing of the cooperative's first lines. The all-day program, starting with a band concert and baseball game, attracted 10,000 people from  throughout the Thumb area.

At 1 p.m., bands from Cass City, Marlette, Bad Axe and Caro led a parade from the baseball park in Ubly to the co-op's generating plant north of town to dedicate the plant and turn on the power. Ruth and Wanda Wilson, daughters of Frank Wilson, turned the control wheel to start the generators, and Governor Murphy threw the switch energizing the lines.

"Today, after more than a year of trials, difficulties and problems — and in some cases, skilled opposition — the REA development in Michigan is an undeniable success," said Governor Murphy. "We have arrived at a milestone in the progress of rural electrification, and it is inspiring to observe how thoroughly you have grasped the significance of that milestone by celebrating in this impressive manner the completion of your splendid generating plant and the energizing of  your lines."

Concluding his remarks, he said: "The labors of countless men and women will always be lightened because of this development, and untold happiness and enjoyment will be the lot of those to whom this blessing is being brought."

REA Administrator Carmody praised the board of directors and the other community leaders who gave freely of their time to make the cooperative a reality. Also on the program were Ernest Anthony, dean of agriculture at Michigan State College, and Joseph Donnelly, Public Utilities Commissioner.

As more members were added to the system and use of electricity increased, additional generation was needed and a new plant with two supercharged diesel engines was built near Caro in 1949, almost doubling the generating capacity. Two more diesel generators were added at Caro, and two were added at the Ubly plant, one a dual-fuel unit installed in 1992.

Under the management of Orville Hurford in the 1950s and 1960s, many major additions and improvements were made to the Thumb Electric system. In 1953, 40 miles of transmission line and four substations were added, and more transmission lines were built in subsequent years. By 1995, the co-op had 146 miles of transmission line and 1,900 miles of distribution line in service. Hurford managed the co-op for 34 years, retiring in 1975.

"We have a sound, reliable system with a total plant value of $35 million and, most importantly, it is functioning to provide the best quality of service that a utility can give today," said Michael Krause, general manager of the cooperative. He also points out that the co-op now has lower rates for most classes of customers than Detroit Edison.

An event that Krause and all the linemen hope will never recur is the ice storm of 1968 when much of the system was hit by freezing rain and high winds, which broke crossarms, poles and conductors. Over 100 linemen from contractors and other co-ops were brought in to restore service. The severe damage caused a deficit in the co-op's year-end financial status. Another big storm in 1976 also did widespread damage.

The cooperative built a new headquarters facility in 1956 across the street from its original location. Of the co-op's 31 employees, 11 are linemen

In 1956, the co-op entered into its first contract with Detroit Edison for power to help meet the fast-growing demands. In the 1960s and later, Detroit Edison wanted Thumb to abandon its diesel generators altogether and buy all of its power from Edison. The co-op board said no, and the decision has paid off handsomely. The generators are kept in running order.

"Those generators are like pure gold to us," Krause explains, "because by having them always ready, we have an agreement with Detroit Edison that they can be used if needed, upon an hour's notice, and that enables us to save $2,500,000 or more per year in our wholesale power rates from Edison."

The cooperative's kilowatt-hour sales have reached 116,450,000 —about 35 times the number in 1941. Load management programs have been in place at Thumb for several years, helping trim peak demands and, in turn, keeping purchased power costs down. "Members participating in load management still use electricity to run most all appliances, and many use a form of electric home heating in our dual-fuel management program," says Krause. Special rates or credits are given to those participating.

**First Board of Directors:** same as the original incorporators

**Early Co-op Project Superintendent/ Managers:** Frank Wilson, Harry Grayson, George Schroeder

**First Project Attorney:** Alfred H. Sauer

**First Lines Energized:** June 18, 1938

**First Annual Membership Meeting:** February 1, 1938

**First Employees:** Harry Grayson, Francis Hund, Jack Glaza, Fred Maurer, Clayton Bensinger

**First Office:** Temple Building in Ubly

Krause was operations manager at Thumb before being appointed general manager in 1980. John Kutter preceded him as manager. Kutter was one of the original incorporators of the Michigan Electric Cooperative Association (MECA) and was its first treasurer. Krause served as chairman of the MECA board for two years.

## TELLING IT LIKE IT WAS:

"Engineers who have looked at the diesel generators at Ubly remark that their capacity is three times what they will ever be called on to supply....Detroit Edison offered to take over the lines from the co-op before the extravagant plant was built and supply juice at D.E. rates. But no, the co-op directors went the New Deal way and now the customers are paying the shot."— *from the Lapeer County Press in 1938, when only the first three generators were installed, outgrown in a matter of seven years by the co-op's members.*

"Back in the 1940s and 50s, a 35-mile-per-hour wind would cause an outage; in July of 1995, we had an 80-mile-per-hour gale and our lights didn't even blink...We've come a long way in making our system as good or better than the big utilities."— *Walter Cook, longtime Thumb board member and former chairman of the board.*

"I didn't know anything about electricity when I came to work at Thumb in April of 1938, but I learned fast and became a lineman in 1942. Fortunately, I didn't have any serious mishap in the 40 years I worked...it pays to think of electricity as the boss."— *Fred Maurer, retired lineman and line foreman from Thumb Electric Co-op.*

"Many families didn't have the money to get their places wired, so we had a special lending program from REA that helped them and we insisted on wiring jobs that met REA specifications. That helped the co-op and the consumer in the long run as they used more and more electricity."— *Francis Hund, longtime Thumb employee who worked various jobs over 41 years at the co-op.*

"We still have a lot of member interest in the cooperative. A thousand or more usually attend the annual meeting with the noontime meal, prizes and entertainment. But we have discussion, too, about the co-op's services, such as our load management program. At our smaller district meetings, we get into any topics the members want to — their input helps us in making plans and future decisions."— *Michael Krause, general manager of Thumb Electric Cooperative.*

■ Longtime employee Francis Hund told of the time he was trying to get an easement from a landowner who just wouldn't sign —"so I bought the 80 acres myself." Hund was mayor of Ubly for 30 years, and worked many jobs at Thumb over 41 years.

■ Washing machines and irons were the first appliances most farm wives got because of the work they saved. Water systems and indoor toilets were high on the "wanted" list, too, but many families had to wait because of the relatively high cost for the plumbing and adding a bathroom.

■ The first rate schedule of the Thumb cooperative prescribed a minimum of $2 per month (25 kwh) and a bottom rate of 1.5 cents per kwh for use over 200 kwh per month. With an electric water heater and electric range, the rate could go as low as one cent per kwh if monthly use reached 500.

■ In March, 1938, the REA News from Washington, D.C., featured an article on the Thumb co-op and, in part, referred to heavy winter storms hitting the co-op's area: "An indication of the ruggedness of the construction (of the co-op lines) is seen in the fact that despite the storms there have been no "casualties" of REA poles while other utility lines didn't fare so well. REA said the same was true in other parts of the country and credited careful pre-shipment pole inspection as a big factor.

■ Thumb Electric Co-op annual meetings have drawn big crowds, but not always as many as the 5,000 attending the 1939 meeting in front of the Thumb office on Main Street in Ubly, population 600. The event featured horse-team pulling contests, street dancing and speeches. In the 1980s, the co-op introduced district meetings, which are discussion-oriented and usually involve 20 to 30 members.

■ The first co-op directors were key persons in organizing and coordinating work, such as the mapping and right-of-way easements. One of those was Ruth Brandmair who was responsible for Tuscola County. She was the first woman board member of an electric co-op in Michigan.

**At left:** Power plant operators Al Bragg (left) and Floyd Brown (right) with Thumb's engineer, Don Decker, in the Caro plant which was added to the system in the 1940s. **Top right:** Current Thumb manager Mike Krause. **Middle right:** Jack Glaza, who started with the co-op in 1938 as operator of the Ubly generating plant. He retired after 43 years at the plant. **Bottom right:** 1985 photo of Thumb Electric's founding father, Frank Wilson, and his wife, Pearl, celebrating their 64th wedding anniversary.

**Above:** Two longtime employees of the cooperative, Francis Hund (left) and Alfred Lowell.

**Right:** Members of Thumb Electric's first board of directors in 1937. Left to right: Robert Spencer, Martin Fisher (treasurer), Ruth Brandmair (secretary), Frank Wilson (president), Albert Grifka, Guy Petiprin, and Joseph Romain. **Below:** The 1951 board of directors, left to right: Joseph Weltin, Oscar Voelker, Joseph Korolski (secretary), Milton Bedore, Orville Hurford (manager), Oliver Wood, Joseph Romain, Warren Sweet (president), Clarence Murray, Clem Schiestel and Alfred Sauer, attorney.

# TOP O' MICHIGAN ELECTRIC COMPANY

It's legend now, but was a startling surprise in 1937 when a man from the Rural Electrification Administration in Washington, D.C., knocked on the door of Thomas Colter's farm home near Elmira and said he had answers to questions that Colter asked in a letter sent to President Franklin Roosevelt.

Tom Colter wanted to know how farmers "could get the 'lectric" because he'd heard about the REA being started up. The REA representative told Tom he would need to get a map showing all the farms in the area and form a committee to go and see how many farmers were interested.

Colter and LeRoy Hardy, area Grange Master, and Bert Mellencamp, Charlevoix County Agricultural Agent, proceeded to do just that. As Bob Daverman, consulting engineer who did work for Top O' Michigan over the years, tells it: "Tom and a few others worked with the county agent (Mellencamp) and they contacted farmers within a 25-mile radius of Boyne City to get sign-ups. People on the committee worked day and night without any compensation. That's how Top O' Michigan got its start."

After months of surveying, answering questions and talking with REA, the committee met at Mellencamp's office in Boyne City on September 11, 1937, and decided to file incorporation papers with

> Incorporated September 22, 1937
>
> Original Incorporators:
> Thomas Colter, Elmira
> Peter Wieland, Ellsworth
> LeRoy Hardy, Boyne City
> Frank Sluyter, Petoskey
> Calvin J. Bennett, East Jordan
> Christian Jensen, Petoskey
> Martin E. Schaff, Elmira
> Herman Flott, Elmira

the state and form the Top O' Michigan Rural Electric Company. The charter was approved on September 22 and the eight incorporators became the cooperative's first board of directors.

Each of the incorporators signed membership applications, agreeing to buy a minimum amount of electricity each month and pay all other necessary fees and provide easements for construction of power lines. Now all they had to do was convince hundreds of other farmers to do the same.

The campaign for sign-ups was launched in Antrim, Emmet, Charlevoix and Otsego Counties and, as reported by the local newspaper in February of 1938, many farmers came to Boyne City on horseback to sign memberships and give right-of-way easements. For some farmers still recovering from the Depression, payment of the $5 membership fee had to be spread over several months.

Despite the obstacles and uncertainties initially faced by the founders of the co-op, the board moved forward with a loan application to REA and engineering assistance to design the basic system. Approval of the initial amount of $250,000 had been given in November of 1937, and another $700,000 was approved in the spring of 1938, allowing construction to start in June with the first pole set between Boyne City and Boyne Falls near the Boyne River Dam.

It first looked like the cooperative would have to build its own power plant; in fact, some REA loan funds were earmarked for diesel generators to be installed on property in Boyne City where the co-op's first office was located. However, arrangements were worked out with Michigan Public Service Company to deliver power to the cooperative at four substations. The company was later sold to Consumers Power.

The "miracle of REA electricity" came to 51 families in Charlevoix County in October, 1938. The first lines were energized on October 15 and, on October 18, a gala celebration was held in Boyne City at the city park with Michigan Governor Frank Murphy as the main speaker. George J. Long, Deputy Administrator of REA, threw the switch at the substation.

"Michigan has won the fight for electricity for the farmers," said Murphy. He reviewed how his administration allowed the electric co-ops to formally organize after being blocked by the previous Fitzgerald administration in 1935 and 1936. "Four out of every five farms will soon have the blessings of the electric washing machine, refrigeration, the radio and all the modern aids to lighten the work of the farm wife as well as the electricity on the farm itself."

As described in a Top O' Michigan publication, "There was truly a sense of pride and accomplishment along with a dedication to the future of the cooperative" at the October 18 ceremonies. The coming of electricity was enthusiastically embraced by the people. It was a day long awaited by the gritty co-op leaders who had put almost two years of their time and effort into "getting the 'lectric."

Elected chairman of the first board was Dr. Christian Jensen of Petoskey who served on the board until his death in 1969. Treasurer was Martin Schaff of Elmira. He had moved to Boyne City temporarily to work on the co-op project, helping obtain sign-ups and easements. He became an electrician and wired many farms. He was killed in a car-train accident in 1952 while still serving on the board.

Walter Wiegandt of Johannesburg was elected to the board in 1939 and served continuously until 1978, longest of any Top O' director. He helped get easements and, in a 1987 interview, he said many of the older farmers were skeptical and reluctant to give an easement. "I had to use quite a sales pitch to convince them it was the coming thing for rural people," said Wiegandt. He knew most every farmer in the area from survey work he did for the Soil Conservation Service and his job as rural mail carrier.

That's what it took for electric cooperatives to become a reality: leadership and neighbors working together willing to give the new REA idea a try. And, once it got into operation and people started using the electricity, there was no stopping it.

A full-time manager, Harold Lees, was hired in 1940. The first project superintendents or managers were board members: first Tom Colter, followed by LeRoy Hardy. When Lees took the helm, the co-op had 662 miles of line serving 1,628 members. Eric Rasch had been hired in 1939 to do line work.

By 1942, the co-op was serving 2,400 members with average monthly use of 60 kilowatt hours and an average bill of $4.50. Consumers numbered only an average of 2.87 per mile of line.

A new headquarters building was occupied in May of 1942 on the property leased from the city at 319 N. Lake Street, Boyne City. Construction of lines was at a virtual halt due to the war.

During the war, the cooperative sent its newsletter to hundreds of young men from the area who were serving in the Armed Forces, and the co-op heard back from many of them. Several commented how they looked forward to returning to their home or farm with electricity. But Top O' Michigan, like all other rural electric co-ops, couldn't extend lines to farms except for short distances, subject to approval of the War Production Board. This was true for the duration of the war because copper and other materials were needed for the military.

But, as one Top O' Michigan farmer wrote to Manager Harold Lees: "We find more use for electricity every day. Electricity on the farm has certainly helped the farmers in helping to win this awful war."

Pointing to new food production records in the United States — enough to feed all of the U.S., its troops and part of our allies — Lees said in the co-op's newsletter that REA power on nearly 1,000,000 farms across the nation was a big factor in meeting the wartime production goals. "Food is as necessary as bullets," he added.

The Top O' Michigan board recognized Lees in 1945 for "his untiring efforts for the cooperative under very trying and adverse conditions during the past four years." He and his staff did what they could to keep outages at a minimum, but material shortages prohibited system improvements.

In a manager's report in 1946, Lees asked members to "please explain to your neighbors why it is taking so long to give them service." Materials, including poles, were still in short supply, and it was another year before construction resumed at full speed. The co-op was receiving almost 100 applications per month for service in 1946.

The cooperative had 1,000 miles of line serving 3,600 members in the summer of 1946 and, before it could serve many more, the problem of a "critical power shortage" needed an answer. Lees requested "practical conservation" by the members, saying it was urgent at peak periods because the supplier, Michigan Public Service, could not meet the increasing demands. For a time, the shortage forced outages on the co-op's system.

The post-war growth and the power shortage in northern Michigan brought Top O' Michigan and two other cooperatives together to collectively solve the supply problem. In 1948, they started on plans to form their own power supply co-op, and in 1949 they formally organized the Northern Michigan Electric Cooperative. It was known as a "G & T" co-op because it was responsible to generate and transmit electricity over high voltage lines to the three distribution co-ops.

The Northern Michigan "G & T" started operating in 1950 and built a coal-fired generating plant near Boyne City in 1952. Through a mix of power supply sources, including large power purchases from Consumers Power and Detroit Edison, the G & T co-op met the needs of Top O' Michigan and its two co-op partners.

A merger of Northern Michigan and another G & T, headquartered in Big Rapids, in 1982 created the Wolverine Power Supply Cooperative which has seven distribution co-op members, including Top O' Michigan.

By 1960, Top O' Michigan was serving 13,000 members and had 43 employees. It had erased deficits of earlier years and now recorded margins of $50,000 or more each year. Even more rapid growth and bigger margins were ahead as people built homes and cabins in the countryside, and commercial development — including ski resorts, golf courses and oil exploration — boomed.

Harlan Ruback was manager of Top O' Michigan then, and he and the board saw the use of electricity expand like never before. "All-electric living," with electric home heating at special rates, was in vogue. By 1971, the co-op had grown to 20,000 members, the largest rural electric cooperative in the state.

Roger Westenbroek was promoted to manager and he guided the co-op through the challenging decade of the '70s. The oil embargo of 1973, coupled with inflation, high interest rates, legislative battles, labor problems and the specter of nuclear power, brought co-op managers and boards together to try and find palatable solutions.

Westenbroek recognized the need for the Michigan cooperatives to unite and he led efforts to create a new statewide organization, one that would have a full-time staff to conduct legislative work and help deal with the avalanche of regulatory issues and other problems common to all of the co-ops. In July, 1978, Top O' Michigan and seven other co-ops signed incorporation papers giving birth to the Michigan Electric Cooperative Association (MECA).

MECA began operations in January, 1979, and is governed by a board comprised of two representatives from each of the member cooperatives. Westenbroek's successor at Top O' Michigan, Tom Hanna, served as president of MECA in 1982.

**First Board of Directors:** the original incorporators

**Early Co-op Project Superintendent/ Managers:** Thomas Colter, LeRoy Hardy, Harold Lees

**Other Early Leaders:** Walter Wiegandt, Johannesburg; Bert Mellencamp, Charlevoix County Agent; Arthur Glidden, Otsego County Agent

**First Project Attorney:** Leon W. Miller

**First Lines Energized:** October 15, 1938

**First Annual Membership Meeting:** October 1, 1938

**First Employees:** Eric Rasch, Henry Lamb, Marion Kindy

**First Office:** small building on north Lake Street, Boyne City

Top O' Michigan also actively supported the National Rural Electric Cooperative Association (NRECA) and played a role in creating the National Rural Utilities Cooperative Finance Corporation (CFC) in the late 1960s. Both Ruback and Westenbroek served on CFC committees.

Two Top O' Michigan directors have represented Michigan on the NRECA board: Christian Jensen in the 1950s and William Parsons in the 1970s. Both had been chairmen of the Top O' Michigan board.

Taking the reins as general manager in 1996 following Hanna's retirement was Edgar Doss who had been an executive with Consumers Power Company for 30 years. The co-op's membership approached 50,000 in 1996 — dramatic growth from 1937, and a new era for the state's largest electric cooperative.

## TELLING IT LIKE IT WAS:

"Top O' Michigan has brought progress and prosperity not only to the farmer but to the businessman on main street in every city and village in the area...for every dollar the co-op invests in facilities, about $4.50 is spent by consumers on appliances, electric equipment and wiring."— *Clinton Blanchard, president of Top O' Michigan board of directors, 1960.*

"My father put his heart and soul into getting the co-op started, and sometimes it could be frustrating trying to get sign-ups and easements because some folks were quite skeptical...but he was optimistic and dedicated, and very happy when the actual construction started."— *Mary Bailey, Mancelona, daughter of Top O'Michigan pioneer and first treasurer, Martin Schaff.*

"Through our state and national organizations, we have fared well over the years in the face of considerable opposition, especially over the REA financing program. We had no choice but to be in politics and fight for our cooperatives."— *Bill Parsons, past president of Top O'Michigan and member of NRECA board for eight years.*

"The 1960s were big growth years for electric co-ops...kilowatt-hour sales were increasing 10 to 12 percent a year. But we had problems with one or two utilities taking co-op customers and that brought us under the Public Service Commission which I believe was necessary to stop the pirating."— *Roger Westenbroek, former manager and assistant manager of Top O'Michigan.*

## SILENT WITNESS

This is an excerpt from a letter sent to *Michigan Country Lines* from a member of Top O' Michigan Electric in March, 1995:

*"My concern is that those in the U.S. Government who are beleaguering REA may destroy what was to the farm, the greatest all-around help ever used. I recently came across our (co-op) membership certificate. It brought back so many memories of the washboard, the dasher churn and the old kerosene lamps. I'm going to frame it and may it be a silent witness to the blessings rural electricity brought to our Echo Township community back in 1938."--Mrs. Doyle Wilson, Central Lake Michigan*

■ Because of forested areas and rougher terrain, construction costs were somewhat higher in northern Michigan than for co-ops in the south and central parts of the state. Much of the right-of-way clearing work was by hand. "Most everything we did was hard work in those days," said Eric Rasch, one of the first line workers at Top O' Michigan.

■ In December of 1946, the cooperative recognized a local union of line employees as the "lawful bargaining agent for such employees." A contract had been in force for two years with the co-op's line workers. In 1978, the cooperative experienced a traumatic strike by employees represented by the IBEW. The five-month long strike involved unionization of the co-op's office employees.

■ The average Top O' Michigan member's bill in 1946 was $4.69 for 95 kilowatt hours. It was difficult to get appliances during the war. The co-op reported a "trickle of appliances received for our merchandising operation" in 1946. The cooperative sold a full line of electric appliances until 1959. Wil Roisen, longtime employee who was in charge of merchandising, said the co-op often had truckload appliance sales to help build electric use. In the late 1960s, his job was to promote electric heating. The co-op then had a special rate of 1.9 cents per kilowatt hour for electric heating.

■ Two women on the Top O' Michigan board of directors in the 1980s were well-known in the area: Emma Reinbold and Martha Drake, the latter for her anti-nuclear and energy conservation views. Reinbold was an incorporator of the Michigan Electric Cooperative Association and served 12 years on the MECA board. "Both ladies were sincere, dedicated directors," said Tom Hanna, former manager of Top O' Michigan.

■ Biggest change in the co-op office was the transition to computers, said Jackie Bates. She should know — she worked in the Top O' Michigan office for 46 years, retiring in 1993 after working the last several years as a dispatcher. The dispatch system has been improved, too, expediting repair work.

■ The new office building at the east edge of Boyne City was built in 1978.

■ Top O' Michigan provides electric service to the residents of Beaver Island via a cable installed by Northern Michigan G & T co-op (now Wolverine Power Supply Co-op). Lines are maintained by TOM personnel. It is one of more than 40 islands served electricity by Michigan co-ops.

**Above left:** Top O' Michigan employees in 1950 photo, left to right (back row): Marc Lund, Marion Kindy, Harlan Ruback, Joan Bates, Jackie Bates, Marie Schmittdiel, and Ted Erfourth. Front row: Eleanor Mills, Yvonne Hocquard, Mary Pratt, and Colleen Ouderkirk. **At right:** The cooperative's 10,000th meter was installed in 1954 at the Ted Kucharek farm. Manager Harold Lees is on the left, Jim Pearson on the right, with the Kucharek family. **Below left:** Four of the co-op's linemen in 1954, left to right: Tag Mapes, Orvis Lyons, John Kirby and Jim Colley.

**Above:** Martin Schaff, Top O' Michigan's first treasurer, killed in an auto-train accident in 1952. **Below:** Former manager, Roger Westenbroek.

**Below:** Top O' Michigan board of directors 1957, left to right: Manager Harold Lees, assistant manager Harlan Ruback, Walter Wiegandt, Herbert Ruggles, Ralph Ball, William Korthase, Judge Leon Miller, Christian Jensen, Ray Deibert, William Parsons, Peter Wieland, and Clinton Blanchard, president.

# TRI-COUNTY ELECTRIC COOPERATIVE

In the summer of 1936, a group of farmers from Ingham and Eaton counties got together and applied to the Rural Electrification Administration for a loan, but it wasn't processed.

On REA records, the application was among the first 25 received from around the nation. It didn't get approved because this new breed of utility — an electric cooperative — wasn't being recognized by the State of Michigan as a legal corporation. But the farmers' efforts were renewed after the election in 1936 of Governor Frank Murphy who pledged to get the REA program off the ground in Michigan.

Murphy was from the Thumb area and knew of the need for aggressive rural electrification efforts. His Attorney General, Raymond Starr, issued a ruling in March of 1937 enabling the farmers to formally organize and incorporate their electric co-ops.

> **Incorporated March 26, 1937**
>
> **Original Incorporators:**
> William Clegg, Eaton Rapids
> Jasper Terry, Onondaga
> D.L. Cady, Mason
> Lawton Heeney, Stockbridge
> James E. Houston, Eaton Rapids

The Tri-County group was one of the first to move ahead. Under the leadership of William Clegg of Eaton Rapids, the first official meeting was held March 29, 1937, in Lansing where it opened a small office at 112 Allegan Street. The Articles of Incorporation had been sent to the state and the five incorporators now drafted by-laws, set the membership fee ($2.50) and applied for a $400,000 loan from REA.

Some canvassing had been done and the board planned to initially serve close to 2,000 members — mostly farms — over 350 miles of line in parts of eight counties. The board added Wilfred Gierman and Donald Way, and elected Clegg as chairman and James Houston as vice chairman.

Clegg and Houston looked into a possible power source at the Miller Brothers ice cream plant at Eaton Rapids. They were willing to sell power from their hydro facility and agreed to adding diesel generators so there would be adequate capacity to serve Tri-County's needs. Other sources, including the city of Portland, the city of Lansing and Consumers Power, were investigated and the board decided to borrow funds for the diesels at Eaton Rapids.

Dolph Wolf was named project superintendent in July, 1937, and a stenographer/bookkeeper, Dorothy Sweet, employed for the office. Memberships were coming in and the first contract was being let to Fry and Kein for the first section of distribution line. A line was built from the Miller Brothers plant to Potterville and the Portland area with instructions to energize each section "just as fast as they are completed."

However, the diesel generators were not installed until mid-1938, and only a few farmers received electricity from the Miller hydro before the installation of the diesels. Lines were energized to the first large group of Tri-County members later in 1938. Two other small hydros at Farwell and Rustford also supplied power the first year.

Power supply for the entire project was still uncertain as talks with the city of Lansing and Consumers Power continued. But discussion with Consumers came to an abrupt halt when the power company offered to buy the co-op's lines. At the February 14, 1938, Tri-County board meeting, the directors unanimously passed the following resolution:

"We condemn the activities of the Michigan State Farm Bureau and the Michigan State Grange in opposing legislation favorable to cooperative rural electrification projects and in advocating legislation that would be detrimental to the cooperatives. We particularly condemn their attempt to make agreements for our cooperative with Consumers Power against the interests of our members.

"This board is very familiar with the spite line activities of Consumers Power and we are ready to furnish evidence at any time to prove that this policy (spite lines) has been carried out by Consumers Power in the past. During the past few days, we find Consumers Power employees canvassing our patrons, reading their meters...and we refuse to let such coercion and conduct dissuade us from our efforts to bring the benefits of electricity to us and our neighboring farmers."

That wasn't the end of the cooperative's problems with Consumers Power. Pirating of co-op members and skirmishes over new customers were frequent into the 1960s and 1970s. New Michigan Public Service Commission rules stopped most of the fighting. That meant state regulation of the co-ops effective in 1966.

**First Board of Directors:** same as incorporators; Cady resigned in July of 1937.

**Early Co-op Project Superintendent/Managers:** Lynd Walkling, Dolph Wolf

**Other Early Leaders:** Wilfred Gierman, Reed Cardey, Donald Way and Herbert Woodruff

**First Project Attorneys:** Charles F. Cummins and Harold E. Storz

**First Lines Energized:** February 21, 1938

**First Annual Membership Meeting:** January 7, 1938

**First Employees:** Dolph Wolf, Dorothy Sweet, Clara Noren Chorley, Herb Densmore, Nick Zimmerman, Bert Short

**First Office:** 112 E. Allegan, Lansing; moved to Portland in summer of 1938

An engineer at the Commission, Clarence Winder, was credited for helping Tri-County and other cooperatives accelerate their construction programs and all the other planning and coordination  involved in getting a new electric utility into operation. He knew rural electrification well, being on loan to the Commission from REA.

A temporary rate schedule was adopted in February of 1938 and modified later. It prescribed a minimum of $20 per month, the next 25 kilowatt hours at six cents per kwh, the next 50 at two cents and all use over 100 kwh at one and half cents per kwh. Separate rates for seasonals and schools and churches were also established.

In November of 1938, the board let bids for a generating plant to be located at Vestaburg in Montcalm County to serve the load of hundreds more farmers signing up for service. Convertible gas diesel engines were installed in this plant which began operation in 1939. In 1941, another diesel generating plant was built at Portland along with new offices for the cooperative. It was dedicated in the name of Clarence Winder, the REA engineer so helpful to Michigan cooperatives.

Lines were built into Mecosta, Clare, and Isabella counties and, by 1941, the co-op was serving 4,800 members in 12 counties. The board then included: Herbert Woodruff, chairman; Lee Post, vice chairman; A.R. Snyder, secretary-treasurer; William Wieber; Harry York; James Mobbs, and Harold Main.

Dolph Wolf, co-op manager, had considerable experience with electric and telephone systems, having built plants at Sunfield and Sheridan in Michigan and telephone companies in Wisconsin and Oklahoma. He worked for electric supply companies and for the State of Michigan. He was a "mover and shaker," so it was no surprise when he and nine other electric co-op leaders met in Washington, D.C., in early 1942 and founded the National Rural Electric Cooperative Association (NRECA). He knew of the need for unity to get legislation the cooperatives needed and to get insurance protection at reasonable cost.

The NRECA started with the hiring of Clyde Ellis and a handful of others in 1942. It became one of the most effective rural-based lobbying organizations in the nation and developed management and employee training as well as insurance and retirement programs. In 1996, it employed some 500 persons.

Wolf died in 1954 and Vernor Smith, assistant manager, was named to succeed him. Known as "Smitty," he managed the co-op for almost 30 years, retiring in 1983. When he took the helm, Tri-County served 7,000 members and average use was 350 kilowatt hours a month. In 1983, the co-op was serving 16,000 members and average use topped 500 kilowatt hours a month.

Smith was active as one of two electric co-op representatives on the Michigan Committee on Rural Electrification for 20 years. The committee worked closely with Michigan State University and the Extension Service to advance the knowledge and use of electricity in rural areas, with emphasis on agricultural uses.

When Smith retired in 1983, the board hired Robert Matheny, who had been with Lee County Electric Cooperative in Florida, as general manager. He has seen the co-op grow to more than 20,000 members with annual revenue exceeding $20 million.

One important development in the growth of Tri-County Electric and six other electric co-ops in the Lower Peninsula of Michigan was the establishment of their own power supply cooperative. In the late 1940s, when the cooperatives were experiencing rapid growth, they saw that they could no longer rely on the power companies to meet the rising demands. Forming their own generating and transmission co-op (G & T) was clearly the most economical answer and, with transmission tie lines, it would improve service dependability, too.

Tri-County and two other cooperatives organized the Wolverine Electric Cooperative in 1949 to supply all their electric energy needs. Two representatives from each co-op comprised the governing board of Wolverine. Another group of three cooperatives further north formed the Northern Michigan Electric Co-op to supply all their power. Following a study in 1981 and at REA's urging, the two G & T co-ops merged in 1982 and became the Wolverine Power Supply Cooperative.

William Chapin, who served on Tri-County's board for 28 years until his death in 1996, chaired the study committee that steered the Wolverine-Northern Michigan merger and became the first president of the new Wolverine Co-op. Chapin commented about the merger: "Many factors made it a natural thing to do. I don't think anyone would argue with its success."

Neither would anyone who knows the Tri-County Electric Cooperative today argue with its success. The co-op has added services such as Rural TV for satellite reception and was the first in Michigan to institute what the co-op calls the "People Fund." The fund is separate from the cooperative, but its revenue comes from Tri-County members who "round up" their monthly electric bill payments to the next even dollar (for example, $41.55 would be rounded up to $42).

The "People Fund" makes contributions to community organizations and families with urgent needs.

From 1993 to January, 1997, the fund had made donations totaling $377,350 to organizations and families. A board of directors, separate from the co-op, makes all decisions on contributions.

One recipient said this in a letter to the People Fund board: "Thanks so much...this shows that together we can help each other...What a wonderful program."

■ A big celebration was held in Portland on August 9, 1941, when the new Tri-County Electric offices and generating plant were dedicated. Board Chairman Herbert Woodruff told of the co-op's progress and introduced U.S. Senator Prentiss Brown, who gave the dedicatory address. This was followed by a barbecue, band concert and dancing. The REA movie, *Power and the Land,* was featured at the local theater and over a thousand people toured the cooperative's facilities.

■ Seven district meetings are conducted each year for Tri-County members. Attendance ranges from 30 to 150 members. One board member is elected from each geographic district. Terms are three years. As Board Chairman Carl Morton points out, the smaller district meetings give members the opportunity to ask questions and get specific information they want.

■ In 1954, Tri-County records show that average density of member-consumers on the co-op lines was 3.9 per mile of line. In 1996, it was 7.2 per mile with the building of new rural residences and businesses — impressive considering the sharp decline in number of farms the past 40 years.

■ There are many miles of the cooperative's first REA-designed single-phase power lines still in service, according to Herman Fedewa, retired Tri-County Line Superintendent who started with the co-op in 1945. The cooperative's annual pole-testing program detects the bad ones and they are replaced. The unique REA design and construction methods of the 1930s cut costs substantially, making rural electrification feasible even in sparsely-populated areas.

■ From a half dozen employees in 1939 to 53 in 1996, the Tri-County Cooperative has grown in member services as well as adding a subsidiary, Tri-Co Services in 1990 to provide DIRECTV via satellite. Bob Matheny, Tri-County manager, is on the board of the National Rural Telecommunications Cooperative, distributor of the DIRECTV programming.

■ Tri-County no longer requires its members to read their own meters and calculate their bills, which has been the practice of member-owned cooperatives since they started in the 1930s. "We get more accurate and timely readings which also reduces high bill complaints," says Joyce Rogers, Tri-County accounting clerk.

## TELLING IT LIKE IT WAS:

"This is an important message. Please read every word." This was the opening statement from Manager Dolph Wolf to members in announcing a rate increase in 1947 to get the co-op out of the red. He said the co-op's rates were "rock-bottom."

"I thought a string of two or three kerosene lanterns was the best lighting I'd ever have in the barn. When we first got the electricity, we left all the lights on for 24 hours straight. It was wonderful."— *Willard Haenke, board member of Tri-County for 36 years and former Wolverine director, deceased.*

"My dad and I helped haul poles with our tractor for the first lines Tri-County built. We needed electricity badly so we could pump water and run silo unloaders and do a lot of things that saved time and labor. Now, we've got four meters and using electricity for just about everything."—*Jim Clarke, Onondaga, Tri-County board member for 23 years, several as board chairman.*

"We had to have our own generating cooperative (Wolverine) for two reasons: we couldn't get assurance of enough power from the other utilities and we needed to tie our systems together for economy and dependability. We've done a lot in the past 25 years to improve our service and I think we rank above Consumers Power now for quality of service."— *William Chapin, Blanchard, 28 years on the Tri-County board and former chairman of the Wolverine board, deceased.*

"We've seen tremendous changes in 30 years, and I think one of the most important has been the improvements in communications — bringing the co-op and the members closer together and speeding up repairs when there's an outage."— *Roy Kissane, Tri-County office employee since 1965.*

"Miss Dig is one of the best things the utilities have ever done to protect our lines and coordinate work. I feel good about having been on the committee that started it. We need more cooperation like this."—*Herm Fedewa, Portland, retired from Tri-County after 39 years including 20 as Line Superintendent.*

"One of the most humorous requests I remember receiving at the co-op was the phone call from a woman who wanted to know if Tri-County would replace filaments in light bulbs — and she wasn't kidding."—*from an interview with the late Vernor Smith, longtime Tri-County manager.*

**At right:** Herm Fedewa, who retired as line superintendent after 40 years with the co-op. **Below left:** Jim Clarke, who served more than 20 years on the Tri-County board of directors receiving the Distinguished Service Award from Michigan State University representative in 1974. **Below right:** Congressman Bob Carr brought U.S. Rep. Kika de la Garza of Texas, chairman of the House Agriculture Committee, to speak at Tri-County's dedication of headquarters addition in 1988. Here the Texan signs autographs for Tri-County people.

**At left:** Julius Platte, operations supervisor, and Phil Conklin, Tri-County board member, with visitors from Ghana, Africa, at Conklin's farm in 1996.

**Below:** The Tri-County board of directors in 1956, left to right: Homer Downing, John Ondrus, co-op attorney Harold Storz, manager Vernon Smith, I.E. Royer, Harold Main, Leonard Balgoyen, Willard Haenke, and Howard Pung.

# WESTERN MICHIGAN ELECTRIC COOPERATIVE

Farmers from Mason County were part of a group that met in Oceana County in January, 1938, to make plans for applying to REA for rural electrification funds. Possibly for funding reasons, farmers from the two counties went separate ways and groundwork moved forward for an electric cooperative in each county.

The Mason County group, led by Louis Rohrmoser, George Allard and Floyd Wood, met on June 8, 1938, to adopt bylaws and to apply to the state for a charter. Incorporation papers were prepared by Rupert Stephens, Manistee attorney who later became a Circuit Court judge. The state approved the charter on June 16, 1938.

The board of directors elected Rohrmoser as chairman, Allard as vice chairman and Wood, secretary. Each of the seven board members paid their $5 membership fee, agreeing to buy electricity from the co-op and pay a monthly minimum when service was turned on.

Meetings were frequent as members of the board and other farmers anxious to have electricity solicited more sign-ups to assure feasibility of the project. The canvassing continued into 1939. The first REA loan came through in early November, 1938, in the amount of $334,000 to build the first section of lines. More right-of-way easements were needed and Leroy Young left the board to work full-time getting easements and more sign-ups. He was paid $4 a day and four cents per mile.

> **Incorporated June 16, 1938**
>
> **Original Incorporators:**
> Louis Rohrmoser, Scottville
> Floyd Wood, Scottville
> Herman Beyer, Freesoil
> John Wilson, Custer
> George Allard, Ludington
> David K. Smith, Freesoil
> Leroy Young, Scottville

Laird Construction of Battle Creek built the first lines energized by the cooperative. Records do not show the precise date of the energization, but it was in May, 1939, when 163 miles of line were put into service and the "REA lights" came on in rural Mason County.

The first power supply for the cooperative came from Michigan Public Service Company. Only a year and a half later, disputes with the company about purchased power costs led to a decision to construct a generating plant for the co-op. After several meetings with REA engineers and with Oceana Electric Cooperative, it was agreed that a diesel plant would be built by Western Michigan at Scottville and power would be supplied to Oceana as well as Western Michigan.

Ground breaking for the plant was held in early 1941 and the first power was generated in June, 1941. The first units installed could generate a total of 3,000 kilowatts. Additional capacity was added in 1960, bringing the maximum output to 5,000 KW.

The availability of power in adequate amounts and at reasonable rates became a serious problem for several cooperatives in Michigan in the late 1940s. O & A Electric Co-op, Newaygo, and Tri-County Electric Co-op, Portland, took initial steps to form a generation and transmission cooperative (G & T) and Oceana joined in that effort. The three formed Wolverine Electric Cooperative in 1949 with offices in Big Rapids.

An advantage of forming the G & T co-op, in addition to assuring power supply was to tie the existing plants together with transmission lines, saving on fuel and operating costs while also significantly improving service reliability.

During the 1950s, Western Michigan's plant provided all the power the co-op needed. But when growth in members and kilowatt-hour sales accelerated in the early 1960s, the co-op's board and manager Ivan Morse consulted with REA and concluded that it would be wise to join Wolverine, rather than add another generator.

Dan Hesslin, who was the cooperative's attorney starting in 1957, accompanied the board to a meeting with Wolverine in 1963. "It was a big decision and the economics of joining Wolverine were persuasive," said Hesslin. The proposal to join Wolverine Electric Co-op was put to a vote of the membership in February of 1963. The vote was in the affirmative and Western Michigan became the fourth member of Wolverine.

Hesslin also represented the Wolverine G & T co-op for several years and worked on power supply contracts and prospective generating projects that Wolverine explored in the 1970s and 80s. At the 1996 annual meeting of the Michigan Electric Cooperative Association, he was given a Special Recognition Award for his many years of counsel and contributions to cooperative electrification in the state.

As former Western Michigan Manager Jack Stickney said, "Dan Hesslin has attended countless meetings in Washington and around the country, in addition to probably hundreds here in Michigan, and has become one of the top legal experts in electric cooperatives." He has served as Western's legal counsel for 40 years.

Western Michigan's longest serving board member and president of the board for 24 years was Leo LaPointe from Branch. An active leader on the board for 33 years, LaPointe represented Western Michigan on the Wolverine G & T board and served as president of Wolverine for several years.

Another prominent board member was Elwyn Olmstead, who served as secre-

**First Board of Directors:** same as incorporators

**Early Co-op Project Superintendent/ Managers:** Frank Comstock

**Other Early Leaders:** George Tyndall, Harry Cory, Fred Reek

**First Project Attorney:** Rupert Stephens, Manistee

**First Lines Energized:** May, 1939

**First Annual Membership Meeting:** 1938

**First Employees:** Frank Comstock, Marguerite Lorenz, Russell Allen, Charles Cole, Howard Dodson.

**First Office:** 101-2 Broadway, Scottville

tary-treasurer for 15 years. In 1965, he was elected by the state's co-ops to represent them on the National Rural Electric Cooperative Association board. Later, he was asked to consider appointment as REA Administrator. (See sidebar in Chapter 8).

One of the most significant changes in the Western Michigan Co-op over the years, starting in the 1950s, was the rapid growth of lake homes and cabins — seasonal consumers who became members of the co-op. Coupled with the fact that many farmers were leaving the land, the co-op found itself with more seasonal members than farms. In 1995, the seasonals were 60 percent of the total membership.

Stickney, who started with the co-op in 1967 and served as manager from 1984 to 1995, explains that the revenue per mile of line is considerably less from the seasonal accounts than farms and, due to their lower seasonal use, a separate rate was designed and put into effect for the seasonals several years ago.

Another change for the cooperative has been adapting to the rules and regulations of the state Public Service Commission. "It has meant a great deal of extra time and expense for a small co-op like Western Michigan to comply with every rule of the MPSC and sometimes have business decisions we make disputed or rejected by the Commission," said Stickney. "I really don't think regulation has been in the best interest of our consumers."

Manager of the co-op prior to Stickney was Frank Anderson, who began work with the cooperative in 1945 as a generator operator. He became an accountant and office manager before being named manager in 1965. He was on the board of the Rural Electric Supply Cooperative (RESCO) and the Michigan Electric Cooperative Association. He and former director John Tyndall were incorporators of MECA.

Named general manager of the cooperative in the summer of 1996 was Stephen T. Rhodes who previously worked for electric co-ops in Arizona and his home state of Ohio. The cooperative has 21 employees and serves over 12,000 members. Chairman of the board of directors in 1996 was Phillip Eikenberry of Scottville.

"We take pride in the many improvements over the years and the fact that the cooperative today has an outstanding quality of service record," said Eikenberry.

■ The plaque on Western Michigan's old generating plant building states: "To advance the position of agriculture, to enrich the life of the community, to free men and women from the heavy drudgery of the farm and home, this generating plant was erected in cooperation with the federal government by farmers of the neighborhood to whom it supplies the limitless service of electricity." (August 23, 1941)

■ Rent and utilities for the entire year of 1939 cost the cooperative $294. The small office was located on Broadway in Scottville. In 1941, the co-op moved to the building housing the generating plant just west of Scottville.

■ One of the original Western Michigan board members, John Wilson, left the board to be an employee of the cooperative in 1955. He was the "voice of the electric co-op" for years with a radio program every Saturday afternoon from Ludington. He talked about the co-op's annual meeting, why outages occurred, how the co-op generated power, electric home heating and dozens more topics.

■ August 23, 1941, was proclaimed "REA Day" by Scottville Mayor Glenn Wallace and the town hosted special activities for co-op members. Forty-seven years later, Mayor Glenna Wallace Anderson, daughter of the former mayor, proclaimed June 16, 1988, "REA Day" commemorating 50 years of operation by the Western Michigan Electric Cooperative. She said she remembered being with her father and seeing the huge crowd gathered for the 1941 event.

■ Having just started with a few hundred customers in 1938, it wasn't easy for the small co-op and many others across the U.S. to make it through World War II because of the construction halt, hence hardly any growth. Western Michigan experienced deficits that caused concern at REA, but the growth years after the war more than made up for the lean years.

■ Marguerite Lorenz, the co-op's first bookkeeper, had to wait four months for her first paycheck because of lack of start-up funds. Her monthly salary was $59.40 in 1939.

# TELLING IT LIKE IT WAS:

"Line work was all manpower back in the 1940s and we had some tough territory to go through in building the lines...we carried the poles, dug the holes and set the poles all by the muscle of the workers."— *Howard Dodson, one of Western Michigan's first employees who served as line superintendent for years.*

"Trimming trees was one of the worst jobs for a lineman before we had bucket trucks. There was only one way to do it and that was to climb 'em. I probably climbed as many trees as poles."— *Byron Bayle, former lineman and line superintendent for the co-op.*

"Electric cooperatives have done great things for this country. Not just for farmers but for everyone because we have an abundant supply of the best food produced in the world, and electricity has a lot to do with that."—*Elwyn Olmstead, former Western Michigan board member (1954-1977) who represented Michigan on the national board for six years and is a recipient of the MECA Special Recognition Award.*

"Electric co-op board members tend to stay on the board for several years, which I think is good because it takes at least three or four years to learn the basics and become knowledgeable about this business, and it is getting more complex every year."— *Dan Hesslin, attorney for Western Michigan since 1957.*

"I consider REA a very beneficial, self-liquidating government program, especially considering the many outright grants in other programs. Electric co-ops have repaid over $3 billion to the Treasury on their loans, plus more than a billion in interest."— *John Wilson, charter board member and the "voice of Western Michigan" for 18 years, in commentary he gave in 1965.*

"Working for the co-op was like being part of a family...we had good times along with the hard work. But to get better wages, the linemen joined the union. Sometimes negotiations would be stalled arguing over a half-cent per hour."— *Everett Lebrun, retired lineman who worked 23 years for the cooperative.*

**Above:** Longtime co-op attorney, Dan Hesslin. **Below:** Retired manager Jack Stickney.

**Above:** Western Michigan lineworkers in the mid-1950s, left to right: Bernie Marcinkovich, Everett LeBrun, Al Loty, Waite All, John Dereske, Phil Sterling, and Dan Miller.

**Below:** Retired employees Howard Dodson, Byron Bayle and Everett LeBrun.

**Above:** The co-op's board of directors in the early 1960s. Leo LaPointe, board president for 24 years and a leader of Wolverine Electric Co-op (on the right). Others (left to right): Myrvle Miller, Clyde Waite, John Tyndall, Holly Wilson and Maurice Butler. Board member Elwyn Olmstead is not pictured (see item in Chapter 8 about Olmstead). **Below left:** Western Michigan board of directors in 1985, left to right: Don Harmon, Rob Hasenbank, Clare Reeds, Phil Eikenberry, Harold Cotton, Bob Thurow and Paul Hansen. **Below right:** Former employee John Wilson–radio voice of the co-op for several years–with a big catch.

# EPILOGUE

What's ahead for Michigan's electric cooperatives? Will they survive in the increasingly competitive and fast-changing utility world?

It is important first to remember that when the cooperatives started, they brought electric service to the most remote and least-populated rural areas. Parts of their service areas have experienced growth as towns and cities sprawled into the countryside. Co-op leaders feel strongly that the co-ops must keep the growth areas if they are to continue to serve the less-populated areas at reasonable rates.

"We are threatened by some of the proposals for open competition, especially the commercial and industrial loads we serve," says Bob Hance, general manager of Great Lakes Energy Cooperative, Newaygo. "But we have coped with changes and we are determined not to lose this battle."

Michigan's co-ops have relatively few industrial loads—in most cases, those loads comprise less than 10 percent of the cooperative's total power sales.

The cooperatives have accepted and adapted to change over the years. They applied new technology in their electric facilities, acquired new modern equipment including computerized billing systems, and adopted management practices that improved efficiency and productivity. "We haven't stood idly by while other utilities made changes," says Mike Krause, general manager of Thumb Electric Cooperative, Ubly.

**Bob Hance**

Size may be a handicap in respect to the limited resources a cooperative can draw upon as compared with a large utility like Detroit Edison or Consumers Power. "But we more than make up for it in giving top notch customer service with locally-based crews, and we have very competitive rates," says Krause of Thumb's operation.

Other co-op managers agree. "Over the past nine or 10 years, we have become more aggressive in serving new commercial and industrial loads because we believe that we have the best value package to offer new customers," says Hance.

**Mike Krause**

The "package" includes competitive rates, reliable service and a close working relationship with customers. The results: his co-op now serves three large-size loads, including the Donnelly Corporation on the outskirts of Newaygo, and several smaller businesses.

"We took a leadership role in the community (Newaygo), participating in many activities and, as a result of our collaborative efforts, we have created 500 new jobs in new industries and businesses," says Hance.

His philosophy is that the cooperatives today need "to do more steering" and be in charge of their own destiny. He wants less regulation by the state MPSC, fewer restrictions from the federal banker (the Rural Utilities Service) and more options for power supply. He sees more flexibility as key to the electric cooperatives' future.

Bruce King, general manager of Cherryland Electric Cooperative, Grawn, has a similar vision. "We have to question virtually everything we do and make changes necessary to continue to merit the customers' business," says King, who came to Cherryland in 1993 from an investor-owned utility in Maine.

"I like the consumer ownership aspect of a cooperative utility, and I believe that we can more quickly adapt to changes than the large utilities with their layers of management and corporate structure," says King. "One of our strengths is our smaller size along with the local ownership and decision-making."

**Bruce King**

Ed Doss, general manager of Top O' Michigan at Boyne City, agrees.

"The cooperatives have a built-in edge because they are customer-owned and therefore, customer-focused," says Doss, who came to the Top O' Michigan co-op after 30 years of employment with Consumers Power. However, Doss believes that mergers of cooperatives is a necessity if they are to survive in what some call the "brave new utility world." Even Top O' Michigan with 50,000 customers — largest cooperatively-owned utility in the state — will need to become larger, he says.

Ed Doss

"We are becoming more competitive, and we will continue to make changes to serve the customer better — probably more in the next five years than the cooperative has made in the past 50 years," says Doss.

The Top O' Michigan chief executive advocates diversification of services to customers. In his first year at the helm, he has led the co-op into the propane gas business and mapped plans for a customer credit card and a leasing business.

Another manager who sees change as a necessity for survival is Martin Thomson, of Presque Isle Electric & Gas Co-op, Onaway. He led the way in the co-op's decision to provide natural gas service to the general area where the co-op serves electricity. "We believe it was a sound business decision, one that will result in a lowering of overall energy costs for many families in our area," says Thomson.

Electric co-ops in the gas business? Yes, at least three others in the state have taken the step to provide propane gas service. Great Lakes Energy Cooperative was the first. Hance says it was a logical move to serve the members' total energy needs, and is part of the "one-stop shopping" marketing strategy prevalent today.

Top O' Michigan, Thumb, Midwest Energy and Tri-County also entered the propane business.

Martin Thomson

Other dimensions of change in the electric utility industry today are cause for serious concern by electric cooperative leaders. "There is no doubt that our industry is undergoing unprecedented change — change that will dramatically impact the cooperatives," says Michael Peters, general manager of the Michigan Electric Cooperative Association.

The 1992 Federal Energy Policy Act mandated open access to transmission lines, vastly expanding the market for wholesale power and inviting more non-utility generators into the market. Another effect was to trigger "retail wheeling" — that is, direct access by customers to another source of power which would be delivered over the local utility's lines. This option has been pushed vigorously by large industrial users who threaten self-generation if they do not get "retail wheeling" of power from their local utility.

This has stirred deep and widespread controversy among utilities, regulators, industries and legislators, including those in Michigan. In 1994, the Michigan Public Service Commission (MPSC) ordered an experimental retail wheeling program for the state's two largest electric utilities. A task force was formed involving the various stakeholders in an effort to develop recommendations that would be workable in implementing not only retail wheeling but deregulation and restructuring of the electric utilities.

Governor John Engler took an active role in January, 1996, with the release of a utility restructuring and deregulation plan authored by the Michigan Jobs Commission. In late 1996, the Public Service Commission released a report recommending sweeping changes in the industry and how customers would buy electricity.

In early 1997, discussions were continuing on the Commission's proposals. The cooperatives, with much at stake, have played an active role throughout this process and, says Peters, will continue to emphasize that any new restructuring or deregulation policy must not be detrimental to the rural residential electric customers throughout the state.

"We are working with state legislators to gain their understanding and support for the tens of thousands of rural families and businesses in the state who would be affected by any new public policy in the regulation and operation of electric utilities," the MECA manager adds.

Peters believes the cooperatives will continue to experience growth into the foreseeable future, assuming regulators and lawmakers treat the cooperatives fairly. He sees the possibility of the co-ops acquiring some of the rural service areas of the larger urban-based utilities.

"Quite frankly, Consumers Power and Detroit Edison concentrate their attention and efforts on their urban service areas and are not as efficient in the rural service areas," says Peters. "This could prove to be a real opportunity for the cooperatives in the not-too-distant future as the investor-owned utilities make moves to streamline and improve their profitability."

Mike Peters

That may be, but cooperatives are confronted with new forces that demand innovative, skilled management, according to one veteran utility regulator. "The cooperatives, like all utilities, must look at the big picture, which is changing rapidly," says John Abramson, head of the MPSC Electric Division. "They will need to be competitive with large companies to survive."

He points out that companies other than utilities will enter the fray—some already have—providing more choices for power supply. Abramson predicts more mergers, creating mega utilities and believes that co-ops need to look hard at mergers, too. The recent merger of O & A and Oceana co-ops was a good move, he says.

Abramson sees a bright future for the cooperatives if they take steps to become more efficient. "The co-ops tend to be more customer-focused than the large utilities and that is one advantage they have to succeed in this increasingly competitive environment."

Southeastern Energy Cooperative, one of the two smallest co-ops in the state, has merged with Fruit Belt Electric Cooperative, which serves 25,000 member-consumers in southwestern Michigan. Members of both co-ops approved the merger after a study projected savings of almost $6 million over the next 10 years.

"With proposed deregulation and a more competitive utility market on the way, smaller cooperatives could be at risk unless we join together and become stronger and more efficient," said Fruit Belt manager Jon Bellgowan. Southeastern manager Les Teel added, "By combining the resources of two service-oriented companies, we will be able to do more for the customer than either of us could do on our own."

Bellgowan is optimistic about his co-op's destiny, but he contends that over the next few years "it will be a heads-on battle to prove the value and superior service of our cooperatives."

He doesn't see large-scale restructuring as a benefit to consumers. "What's important is for the cooperative to meet the customers' expectations, and that means working every day in everything we do with the customer foremost in mind."

Jon Bellgowan

One demonstration of this customer focus at Fruit Belt is the cooperative's action in early 1997 establishing 24-hour phone service seven days a week to accommodate "any business that members have with the co-op, including taking orders for new hook-ups and questions about bills, as well as outage calls."

Another possible change seen by some co-op leaders is in the structure and mission of the generation and transmission (G & T) cooperatives. Originally created to open up the wholesale power market for the co-ops by building and operating plants of their own, the G & Ts "will likely become power brokers and transmission operators for the distribution cooperatives," says Peters.

He doesn't expect the co-ops to buy into future generation on a large scale. Rather, they will benefit from dispersed generation technology which he says will include smaller plants located near the larger loads and growth areas.

Tom Stevenson, general manager of Wolverine Power Supply Cooperative, the only G & T co-op in Michigan, believes that Wolverine will continue to represent the seven distribution co-ops in power purchasing, but with more options. The G & T closed down its major generating facility — the coal-fired plant at Advance — in March, 1997, and purchases nearly all its power from Detroit Edison, Consumers Power and some out-of-state utilities.

"In the new open market power-brokering situation, we can buy power anywhere it is physically possible to transport it to our system," says Stevenson. Wolverine has been buying significant quantities from utilities in Kentucky and Illinois.

But adequate transmission capacity to import more power is seen as a road-block. Michigan's geography limits transmission line construction and, therefore the path of incoming power, to the south. Planning work has been in progress to build more transmission lines through southwest Michigan.

Stevenson, who has managed two other utilities — a G & T co-op in Oklahoma and a power and water supply utility in Alaska — sees a good future for the cooperatives "if they continue to work together as they have in the past and apply the management skills needed in today's competitive utility world."

Tom
Stevenson

Stevenson was elected to the board of directors of the National Rural Utilities Cooperative Finance Corporation (CFC) in 1996, only the second Michigan person elected to the CFC board in 25 years. "CFC is an effective, growing organization that is the main source of capital for many cooperatives today and will be for even more in the future," says Stevenson.

Three Michigan cooperatives have paid off their REA/RUS loans and refinanced through CFC. In 1997, Wolverine negotiated with the Rural Utilities Service to pay off its loans.

As Stevenson sees it, separation from the government lending agency gives the G & T more options and the freedom to innovate.

That freedom to be more flexible and innovative may well be the panacea for the cooperatives "in the brave new utility world." But just as important, if not more so, in the eyes of Mike Peters, Tom Stevenson and others, is the need for unity among the cooperatives.

"Despite all the changes, one thing remains constant: only by working together can our electric cooperatives continue to succeed," says Peters. "Without a doubt, the electric cooperatives of Michigan have a bright future. We will continue to provide first-rate service to the member-customers in rural Michigan and we will meet the competitive challenges of the future."

From the national perspective, Glenn English, CEO of the National Rural Electric Cooperative Association, told electric cooperators that the nation's co-ops are especially well-positioned to meet the challenges posed by deregulation and competition:

"We have almost 50 percent of the wires and poles in the nation. They stretch over 73 percent of the land mass. We are already in the telecommunications business. We have some of the cleanest power plants in the country, $60 billion in assets and we are directly connected to 30 million people (co-op members) in 46 states. And while we are national in scope, we are owned by the people we serve. That is the best of all possible worlds and one in which we should be able to embrace competition.

"As we move into a more competitive world, we must rededicate ourselves to the ingenuity, courage and determination that got us start-   Glenn English
ed.

"Electric cooperatives must seize the opportunity to make history during the transformation of the electric utility industry much as they did 60 years ago when they began to tough job of electrifying rural America"

# CONTRIBUTORS

Most sincere thanks to the following people who contributed to this history by granting interviews or providing materials. The author, and the publisher, appreciate your contributions.

**Alger Delta Cooperative**
Raymond Berger, retired board member
Edwin "Bud" Englund, retired employee
Roy Hawkinson, retired manager
Dan Roberts, general manager
Laurie Young, employee
**Cherryland Electric Cooperative**
Philip Cole, board member & retired manager
Bruce King, general manager
Bob Lambert, retired manager
Lyle Johnson, retired lineman
Betty Gordon, board member
Wayne Nordbeck, board member
John Rockershousen, manager of marketing
Betty Reynolds-Maciejewski, board member
Elizabeth Worden, board member
**Cloverland Electric Cooperative**
Bernard Doll, board member
Carl Eagle, board member
Jack Holt, retired manager
Frank Talentino, retired operations manager
Don Wozniak, general manager
Shirley Farnquist, employee
**Fruit Belt Electric Cooperative**
Margaret Conrad, retired employee
Bill McKenzie, retired employee
Paul Juriga, retired lineman
Rolfe Wells, board member
Jon Bellgowan, general manager
Sondra Sue Vomish, board member
**Fruit Belt and Southeastern Co-ops merged to form Midwest Energy Cooperative*
**O & A Electric Cooperative***
Wayne Bumstead, lineman
Pat Forbes, office manager
Bob Hance, general manager
Bill Vissers, retired board member
Constance Dukes, board member
Matt Berry, employee
**Oceana Electric Cooperative***
Clarence Babbitt, retired board member
Ray Kokx, son of former board member
Bob Fredericksen, retired manager
Richard Walsworth, board member
Cindy Hodges, employee
*O & A and Oceana merged to become Great Lakes Energy Cooperative Jan. 1, 1997*
**Ontonagon REA**
Carlo Heikkinen, board member
Cy Clark, retired manager
Jim Morgan, retired manager
Clarence Marttila, lineman

Tom Haarala, manager
**Presque Isle Electric & Gas Co-op**
Mel Basel, retired board member
Harry Pauley, retired manager
Mike O'Meara, retired manager
Martin Thomson, general manager
Alan Joppich, employee
Sally Knopf, board member
**Southeastern Energy Cooperative**
Norman Bless, board member
Clyde Knisel, retired board member
Roger Wolf, board member
Don Grimes, retired manager
Bob Willet, employee
**Fruit Belt and Southeastern Co-ops merged to form Midwest Energy Cooperative*
**Thumb Electric Cooperative**
Walter Cook, board member
Jack Glaza, retired employee
Francis Hund, retired employee
Alfred Lowell, retired employee
Fred Maurer, retired lineman
Mike Krause, general manager
Michelle Braun, employee
Beth McDonald, board member
**Top O' Michigan Electric Company**
Jackie Bates, retired employee
Marion Kindy, retired employee
Eric Rasch, retired lineman
Wil Roisen, retired employee
Tom Hanna, retired manager
Roger Westenbroek, retired manager
William Parsons, retired board member
Emma Reinbold, retired board member
Mary Bailey, daughter of former board member Martin Schaff
Dave Guzniczak, employee
Ed Doss, general manager
**Tri-County Electric Cooperative**
William & Jean Chapin, former board member and wife
Jim and Dorothy Clarke, retired board member and wife
Herman Fedewa, retired line superintendent
Roy Kissane, employee
Shirley Smith, wife of former manager Vernor Smith
Joyce Rogers, employee
Jayne Graham, employee
Bob Matheny, general manager
Mary Hatinger, Edmore, MI
**Western Michigan Electric Co-op**
Dan Hesslin, attorney
Howard Dodson, retired line superintendent
Byron Bale, retired line superintendent
Everett LeBrun, retired lineman
Elwyn Olmstead, retired board member
Jack Stickney, retired manager
Judy Forman, office manager

**Wolverine Power Supply Co-op**
Craig Borr, assistant general manager, member relations
Walter Garcia, chief financial officer & deputy general manager
Tom Stevenson, general manager
Bill Arnold, retired employee
Ray Towne, retired general manager
Deb Brode, employee

**Others**:
Bob Badner, retired from REA (RUS, USDA); Bob Daverman, retired from Daverman Engineering; John Abramson, Michigan Public Service Commission; Roger Fischer, Mich. Public Service Commission; Bryce Thomson, former Miller Dairy Farms president; Dorothy Wideman, Mich. Public Service Commission; Fred Brandenberg, retired, and John Holt, Detroit Edison Co.; Al Ernst, attorney, Dykema Gossett; Michael Buda, Michigan Electric Cooperative Assn.; Bob Palmbos, Michigan Electric Cooperative Assn.; Gail Knudtson, Michigan Electric Cooperative Assn.; Michael Peters, Mich. Electric Cooperative Assn.; Robert Partridge, retired manager, National Rural Electric Cooperative Assn.; Kathryn Momot, employee, National Rural Electric Cooperative Assn.; Dr. Truman Surbrook, Michigan State University; Les Anderson, retired, Mich. Tax Commission; Mrs. John Keen, Big Rapids; Mrs. Loyal Churchill, Hart

# Bibliography

**Chapter 1 — Roots of REA**
1. Interview with Mr. and Mrs. Walter Cook, Harbor Beach, MI
2. *The Next Greatest Thing*, published by the National Rural Electric Co-op Assoc. 1984
3. Report of Michigan Committee on Rural Electrification, 1974
4. Consumers Power Mason-Dansville plaque on State Highway 36
5. Newsletters and Annual Reports of Detroit Edison Company
6. *The Force of Energy*, by Raymond Miller, Mich. State University Press, 1971
7. Reports of Rural Electrification Administration (1936-1940)
8. Associated Press, May 3, 1997

**Chapter 2 — Cooperatives Team with REA**
1.*The Next Greatest Thing*, published by the National Rural Electric Co-op Assoc., 1984
2. *The Eighty-Year Experience of a Grass Roots Citizen*, by Chester A. Graham
3. *Michigan Farm News* (1936)
4. Michigan Rural Electrification News (1935)
5. History of the Commissioners, Michigan Public Service Commission (November, 1995)
6. *Rural Lines USA*, published by Rural Electrification Administration, 1981
7. Interviews with Clarence Babbitt, Jim and Dorothy Clarke, William Parsons, Bernard Doll, Rolfe Wells, Jr., Ray Kokx, Carlo Heikkinen, and Elmer R. Rautio
8. Minutes of Alger-Delta Co-op Electric Assoc. Board of Directors meetings 1938-1939
9. *REA in Michigan* video, Michigan Oral History Association, 1995

**Chapter 3 — Trials and Tribulations**
1. *Presque Isle County Advance* article (July 28, 1955)
2. Minutes of Presque Isle Electric Cooperative Board of Directors Meetings (1937-1938)
3. News articles from Presque Isle and Alpena newspapers (1937-1939)
4. Michigan *Country Lines* magazine
5. Interviews: Cyril Clark, Ray. Berger, Bob Daverman, Wm. Chapin, & Bob Lambert
6. Reports of Rural Electrification Administration (1936, 1937, 1938, 1939, 1940)
7. *The Farmer Takes a Hand*, by Marquis W. Childs (1952)
8. Minutes of Board of Directors Meetings of O & A Electric Cooperative, Southeastern Michigan Electric Cooperative, Fruit Belt Electric Cooperative and Tri-County Electric Cooperative; also newsletters of the above cooperatives
9. *Michigan Farm Electric News* (October, 1938)
10. *Millers Farm News*, 75th Anniversary Edition
11. Interview with Bryce Thomson, Miller Brothers Dairy, Eaton Rapids
12. Oceana Electric Cooperative newsletters and letter of Louise Snyder to Oceana
13. Records of Thumb Electric Co-op and news clippings from Thumb Electric files
14. Letters from Rural Electrification Administration to Thumb Electric (1938)
15. News release from Governor Frank Murphy's office (1938)
16. News articles from *Huron Daily Tribune* (1938)
17. *Rural Electrification News*, published by Rural Electrification Adm. (March, 1938)
18. Records and newsletters of Top O' Michigan Electric Co., Boyne City.
19. *Michigan Governors: Their Life Stories*, by Willah Weddon (1994)

**Chapter 4 — A New Light Is Shining**
1. Reports of the Rural Electrification Administration (1938-1939-1940)
2. *The Next Greatest Thing*, published by the National Rural Electric Co-op Assoc. (1984)
3. Michigan *Country Lines* magazine (May, 1985)
4. Bob Considine column from the *Pontiac*

*Press* (June 16, 1966)
5. Interviews with Bill Vissers, Bob Daverman, Bernard Doll, and Bill Parsons
6. *Rural Lines USA*, published by the Rural Electrification Administration (1981)
7. Top O' Michigan Electric newsletter and office records
8. Records of the National Rural Electric Cooperative Association, Washington, D.C.
9. *The Farmer Takes a Hand*, by Marquis A. Childs (1952)
10. Interview with Robert Partridge, retired general manager of NRECA

## Chapter 5 — Michigan's Co-op Family Grows
1. Top O' Michigan Electric newsletters and office records
2. *The Next Greatest Thing*, published by the National Rural Electric Co-op Assoc. 1984
3. Reports of the Rural Electrification Administration
4. Interviews with Edwin Englund, Harry Pauley, Wayne Nordbeck, Bernard Kline, Bob Daverman, Jim Wood, and Dick Arnold
5. Cherryland Electric Cooperative records
6. Records & annual reports of N. Mich. Electric Co-op and Wolverine Electric Co-op
7. Records of O & A Electric Cooperative
8. News clippings from several Michigan newspapers

## Chapter 6 — The Golden Years
1. Records of Thumb, Top O' Michigan, Southeastern Mich. and Cherryland Electric
2. Interviews with Edwin Englund, Marion Kindy, Wil Roisen, Mike O' Meara, Phil Cole, Walter Cook, Bob Badner, Clyde Knisel, Roger Wolf, Dr. Truman Surbrook, Roger Fischer, and John Abramson
3. Articles from *Lapeer County Press*
4. Reports of the Rural Electrification Administration
5. *The Farmer Takes a Hand*, by Marquis A. Childs (1952)
6. Report of the Mich. Committee on Rural Electrification -*The First 25 Years*- (1970)
7. Articles from records of Top O' Michigan, N. Michigan and Wolverine cooperatives
8. *The Next Greatest Thing*, - National Rural Electric Cooperative Association (1984)
9. Records of the Michigan Electric Cooperative Association
10. Interview with Les Anderson, formerly with the Michigan Tax Commission
11. *The CFC Story*, by Patricia Lloyd Williams, 1995

## Chapter 7 — Turning Points
1. Articles from several Michigan newspapers (1965-1978)
2. *The Next Greatest Thing*, published by the National Rural Electric Co-op Assoc. (1984)
3. Reports of the Rural Electrification Administration
4. Records of Top O' Michigan Electric Co.
5. Interviews with Roger Westenbroek, Ray Towne, Bob Badner, Bob Daverman, Al Ernst, Phil Cole, Craig Borr & Rolfe Wells, Jr.
6. Annual reports of Northern Michigan Electric Cooperative
7. World Book (1973 and 1974)
8. Annual reports of Wolverine Electric Cooperative
9. Records of Wolverine Power Supply Cooperative
10. Records of Michigan Electric Cooperative Association

## Chapter 8 — Moving Forward Together
1. Records of Michigan Electric Cooperative Association
2. Interviews with Bob Palmbos, Mike Buda, Frank Talentino, Al Ernst, Bob Badner, Betty Gordon, Martin Thomson, Shirley Smith, Bernard Doll, and Herm Fedewa.
3. Records of National Rural Electric Cooperative Association
4. Records of Action Committee for Rural Electrification (ACRE)
5. Michigan *Country Lines* magazine
6. Records of Mich. Geothermal Energy Assoc.

## Chapter 9 — People of Commitment
1. Records of Top O' Michigan Electric Co.
2. Interviews: Cyril Clark, Mary Bailey, Emma Reinbold, Constance Dukes, Sally Knopf, Beth McDonald, Betty Gordon, Betty Reynolds-Maciejewski, Elizabeth Worden, Mel Basel, Jackie Bates, Bill Thomas, Jim Clarke, Bill Parsons, Carl Eagle, John Holt, Don Wozniak, Martin Thomson, Rolfe Wells, Jr., Edwin Englund, Clarence Marttila, Lyle Johnson, Paul Juriga, Wayne Bumstead, Margaret Conrad, Bill McKenzie, Sondra Sue Vomish, Bob Matheny, Harry Pauley, Frank Talentino
3. Records of Michigan Electric Cooperative Association
4. *The Next Greatest Thing*, published by National Rural Electric Co-op Assoc. (1984)
5. Michigan *Country Lines* magazine
6. *Rural Electrification* magazine (March, 1997)
6. Records of Western Mich. Electric Co-op

## EPILOGUE
1. Interviews with Bob Hance, Mike Krause, Bruce King, Martin Thomson, Tom Stevenson, Jon Bellgowan, Mike Peters, Ed Doss and John Abramson
2. Records of Michigan Electric Cooperative Association
3. Newsletters of National Rural Electric Cooperative Association

# Index